The Civil Rights Revolution

The Civil Rights Revolution

Events and Leaders, 1955–1968

FREDERIC O. SARGENT

Foreword by Bill Maxwell

McFarland & Company, Inc., Publishers
Jefferson, North Carolina, and London

LIBRARY OF CONGRESS CATALOGUING-IN-PUBLICATION DATA

Sargent, Frederic O.
The civil rights revolution : events and leaders, 1955–1968 /
Frederic O. Sargent ; foreword by Bill Maxwell.
p.   cm.
Includes bibliographical references and index.
ISBN 0-7864-1914-8 (softcover : 50# alkaline paper)

1. African Americans—Civil rights—History—20th century.
2. Civil rights movements—United States—History—20th century.
3. African American leadership—History—20th century.
4. African American civil rights workers—Biography.
5. Civil rights workers—United States—Biography.
6. United States—Race relations.
7. Civil rights—United States.
I. Title.
E185.61.S315   2004   323.1196'073'09045—dc22   2004009591

British Library cataloguing data are available

On the cover, from the top:
Ronald Martin, Robert Patterson, Mark Martin
February 2, 1960, at the F.W. Woolworth lunch counter, Greensboro, NC
(Library of Congress No. RAP020204).
Martin Luther King, Jr., and others,
Civil Rights March, Washington, August 28, 1963
(National Archives and Records Administration, NWDNS-306-SSM-4C[51]15).
Background ©2004 PhotoSpin

Manufactured in the United States of America

*McFarland & Company, Inc., Publishers
Box 611, Jefferson, North Carolina 28640
www.mcfarlandpub.com*

To the leaders and implementers of
the Nonviolent Freedom Revolution

Acknowledgments

The principal sources of these accounts, biographical sketches, quotations and interpretations are the books listed in the bibliography. Additional insights were gleaned in interviews with curators of several civil rights museums.

Most revealing among the sources are the firsthand accounts by participants and observers. Examples are the books by Abernathy, A. Young, Due, Hunter-Gault, Robinson, Bates, Parks and Lewis, and the oral histories produced by Hampton and Fayer.

Basic to the study of this period are the detailed and scholarly accounts of major campaigns and incidents produced by historians who researched archives and conducted scores of interviews. Examples are Branch, Powledge, Oates, Rowan, Ayres, Garrow, Davis, Townsend and Williams.

Books that focus on single agencies, individuals or cultural dimensions also deepen our understanding of the revolution. Examples are books about the FBI, the KKK, the supreme court, the presidents, black culture and religion, women activists and Thurgood Marshall.

Books by the Rev. Martin Luther King, Jr., are a special category. They elucidate the political, psychological, philosophical and ethical aspects of the revolution and its unique tactic: nonviolent action. A number of encyclopedias provide dates, context and valuable analyses of each event in the civil rights movement.

Because the civil rights struggle was a campaign to make fundamental changes in U.S. law, court records provide an essential part of the story. Two sources are particularly valuable in this regard: the *Congressional Quarterly's Guide to the Supreme Court* (1979), and *Civil Rights and the Black American* (1968).

The civil rights revolution was a complex phenomenon. The sources listed in the bibliography contribute facts, insights and interpretations helpful in understanding the historical happenings involved, and in tracing the shift in the U.S. polity, from support of apartheid to a national commitment to fair and equal treatment under the law, enfranchisement and improved social and economic opportunities for all citizens.

"Freedom is never voluntarily given; it must be demanded by the oppressed."
> —Dr. King, *Letter from Birmingham Jail,* 1963

"What we are seeing now is a freedom explosion."
> —Dr. King, Nobel Prize address, December 11, 1964

"The essence of man is found in freedom."
> —Dr. King, *Where Do We Go from Here,* 1967

"Freedom Now!"
> —Mantra of the civil rights movement

Table of Contents

III. Leaders of the Revolution   133

Foreword

by Bill Maxwell

In 1955, I was ten years old, living in Crescent City, Florida, with my paternal grandparents. "Whites only" and "colored only" signs governed all of our lives in this town of 1,200 residents. White children attended one school, and black children attended another.

Even with such inequities, my childhood was idyllic, until 1955, when everything changed. This was the year when my black schoolmates and I apprehended how Jim Crow's intentional cruelty—its legal separation of the races—had robbed us of our full potential as U.S. citizens and as human beings.

Indeed, our lives changed in September 1955, when word spread that fourteen-year-old Emmett Till had been brutally murdered in Mississippi. A Chicagoan, Emmett was visiting his relatives when he allegedly whistled at a white woman. A few days later, the child's mutilated body was pulled from a local river. He had been beaten and shot.

For most African Americans, the civil rights movement, or revolution, began in earnest with Emmett's death, when our ignorance, innocence, and complacency died. Sure, we knew about the Supreme Court's *Brown v. Board of Education* case that was still sending shockwaves through the nation, but Emmett's death was personal. It frightened and galvanized us into action.

During my undergraduate college years, Emmett's death haunted me and influenced me to join the Southern Christian Leadership Conference. On many occasions, I had the honor of marching with Dr. Martin Luther King in several Southern cities, and I had the responsibility of registering thousands of black voters.

When Frederic O. Sargent first asked me to write the Foreword to *The Civil*

Rights Revolution, 1955–1968, I was not greatly interested. After all, I had personally participated in the civil rights movement. What could I learn from yet another book about it? Still, I marveled that Sargent had begun his book with the year 1955, when I came of age as a child of Jim Crow.

Mr. Sargent and I had never met, and we had not spoken to each other before. He knew me through my twice-weekly column for the *St. Petersburg Times.* After a brief telephone conversation, I agreed to write the Foreword because I wanted to read a manuscript that promised new insight into what Mr. Sargent refers to as the "second great American revolution."

Yes, *The Civil Rights Revolution* delivers. It offers new insight into those tumultuous years mainly because of its methodology. Instead of mining one thesis, Mr. Sargent uses myriad first-hand and eyewitness accounts, scholarly studies, press accounts, and official government reports to give the reader the most comprehensive and intimate view of the revolution ever.

I marched across the Edmund Pettus Bridge in Selma, Alabama, and spent many nights in jails throughout Dixie, the land of America's apartheid. I gained a better sense of the profound significance of the victims' courage and accomplishments through Mr. Sargent's dozens of vignettes of violent confrontations and biographical sketches of the revolution's leaders.

The Civil Rights Revolution makes an essential contribution to the literature of an era when the nation was at a crossroads. Would white America embrace the future or stay the course of legal injustice against an entire group of citizens? *The Civil Rights Revolution* shows the reader how those personally involved in the historic events that changed our nation made their choices. Scholars and average readers alike will benefit from this book.

Bill Maxwell

Preface

From 1955 to 1968 hundreds of thousands of Americans of African descent marched, demonstrated, negotiated, sang, prayed, spoke, wrote, and suffered police brutality, job losses and imprisonment in a campaign to end the U.S. system of apartheid in eleven states. The activists were successful. Supreme Court decisions and new federal statutes wiped apartheid laws off the books and fostered implementation of the fourteenth and fifteenth Amendments to the Constitution with their promises of equal treatment under the law and the right to vote. This book presents a wide-angle view of this revolution with its geographic, temporal, philosophic, legal and human dimensions.

The African Americans' demand for freedom was professionally and well reported. The white media—press, TV and radio—told their audiences everything they could learn before their deadlines. Headlines, sound bites, news stories and photos of violent acts gave the public a vivid first impression. Four decades later historians describe and analyze the same confrontations but present more cases and more details. Historians spend years researching archival records, conducting hundreds of interviews and reading autobiographies and books by other historians. They study each event with the benefit of historical perspective and produce a much fuller understanding of the period than the original media reports. Today's historians explain the root cause of the revolution, namely, U.S. apartheid. They describe the legal precondition of the movement; the NAACP's forty years of court cases against segregation that resulted in the Supreme Court reversing its stand on that subject. They reveal the key roles of black women, the black community and the black church in providing the physical, psychological and spiritual support that was indispensible to the movement. They show how the confrontations were civil and nonviolent on one side and brutal and oppressive on the other.

Was it a movement or a revolution? This question is answered by a comparison of media accounts of the '50s and '60s with historians' accounts of the '90s and beyond. The media reports witnessed one incident at a time and called it a "movement." Historians compare conditions under U.S. apartheid in the '40s and '50s with the freedoms delivered by civil rights legislation and court decisions in the '60s and conclude that there was "a fundamental change in political organization"—Webster's definition of a revolution. For African Americans who lived in the eleven apartheid states it was a revolution. In other states where segregation was de facto rather than de jure, it was a movement. Historians agree that this revolution accomplished one of the principal goals of the Civil War: it gave African Americans the basic civil rights enjoyed by others. President Kennedy and Dr. Martin Luther King called it a revolution and the PBS television program "Eyes on the Prize" termed it the "second great American revolution."

This revolution was ignited by the Supreme Court's decision in *Brown v. Board of Education*, 1954–1955, which found school segregation unconstitutional. It was ended by the passage of half a dozen civil rights laws and the assassination of Dr. Martin Luther King, Jr., the movement's incomparable leader.

This story has been told many ways. Here it is presented in fifty-four vignettes of black-white confrontations and sixty biographical sketches of black leaders. The terminology used is drawn from two cultures. The white culture focuses on "civil rights," i.e., the right to vote, equal treatment under the law and the right to seek elected office. The black culture is focused on "Freedom," which includes civil rights plus the concepts of equality, mutual respect and economic opportunities.

This book is intended for students of unvarnished American history and the informed reader who wishes to know what historians are now saying about the civil rights struggle of half a century ago. Readers who wish to learn more about this subject are referred to the bibliography.

Frederic O. Sargent
August 2004

I

Prelude to Revolution

U.S. Apartheid to *Brown v. Board of Education*

The civil rights revolution of 1955–1968 was a pivotal sociopolitical controversy. It marked the end of racism as the determining ideology in domestic policies. It introduced emphasis on civil and economic rights for all minority groups. To understand that revolution it is first necessary to review its major cause, its philosophical rationale and its legal base.

The principal cause of the revolution was the two-class or apartheid sociopolitical system embedded in the laws of former rebel states. School history books call it "Jim Crow" and minimize its severity, duration and location. Historians call it U.S. apartheid and define it as a sociopolitical system established by federal, state and local governments and enforced by racist courts, police and citizen terrorist groups in eleven states.

The Civil War established the fact that secession is not allowed and it freed the enslaved Africans—temporarily—from the end of the war in 1865 to the end of Reconstruction in 1877. In 1877, the U.S. government, tired of trying to establish democracy in the defeated Confederacy, pulled its armies out and left those states to manage their own affairs. The southern leaders welcomed this decision and proceeded to readopt practices and enact statutes to reconstruct a two-class social system. They were encouraged in this effort by the Supreme Court's decision in *Plessey v. Ferguson* in 1896 that approved "separate but equal" facilities for blacks and by the inaction of the administration and Congress to implement the fourteenth and fifteenth Amendments to the Constitution that guaranteed equal treatment under the law

3

and the right to vote. Slavery was replaced with share-cropping, which tied the "freed" blacks to their landlords' plantations in debt, ignorance and poverty.

The first state to adopt the "Jim Crow" or apartheid laws was Tennessee in 1875. By 1900 ten more states—Alabama, North Carolina, South Carolina, Georgia, Florida, Virginia, Mississippi, Louisiana, Texas and Arkansas enacted them. These apartheid laws were statutory confirmations of the segregation practices that were practiced and enforced by the KKK as soon as the U.S. troops withdrew. If the state statutes omitted some detail of the segregation system it was supplied by municipal ordinances or by local practices.

By 1896 a two-class, apartheid system based on Supreme Court decisions and state laws governed every aspect of the African American's life in the southern states. There were separate white and black facilities for drinking fountains, restrooms, theaters, bus and train stations, hospitals, restaurants, hotels, bars and churches. Black children were excluded from libraries, parks, beaches and pools. The separate black schools were ramshackle cabins that were small, overcrowded, underfinanced, unheated and poorly equipped. School books were castoffs from white schools, except in Florida which had separate "white" and "black" textbooks. Blacks were excluded from political practice, book publishing, good jobs and good housing. Whites treated blacks with disdain and contempt. A black person could be arrested for "loitering" at any time and lynched for talking back to a white person. The state apartheid systems were jointly managed by all agencies of the white establishment: the governor, legislature, judiciary, police and sheriffs. The principal enforcer in the system was the quasi-secret Ku Klux Klan (KKK).

The KKK was founded in Pulaski, Tennessee, in 1865. By 1867 there were hundreds of local units in every state from Virginia to Texas. By 1867 when the federal government was no longer interested in trying to guide the rebel states to democracy, the KKK was well established and operating as needed to maintain a segregated society. The announced goals of the KKK were to prevent blacks from voting or participating in government and from sharing any public areas or facilities with whites. (The term "white" did not include Catholics and Jews.)

The tactics of the KKK were various forms of terrorism: night riding, cross burning, drive-by shootings, arson and lynching. Lynching of blacks in the South escalated rapidly after Reconstruction. W.E.B. DuBois estimated that 1,700 blacks were lynched in the U.S. during the decade 1885–1894. From 1882 to 1927 a total of 3,405 blacks were lynched in seventeen southern and border states. The Klan enforced *de jure* segregation in the South and *de facto* segregation in the North. At the peak of its power in the 1920s it was politically strong not only in the South but also in Oregon, Ohio, California, Oklahoma, Kansas, Indiana, New York, Pennsylvania, Connecticut, Maine and Colorado and it climbed to five million members.

Throughout the South, the Klan leaders were members of the Establishment; U.S. congressmen, planters, lawyers, editors, doctors and local and state officials. The Klan members were white males, including sons of wealthy planters and illiterate poor whites. The Klan was closely allied with white Christian churches. Protestant ministers frequently worked as Klan recruiters. The Klan symbol was the Christian cross and the members' favorite marching song was "Onward Christian Soldiers."

While the Klan employed secrecy, its main protection was their close alliance with establishment leaders. If members were identified after a misdeed, they suffered no penalties. Other Klansmen provided false alibis, intimidated witnesses or officials and manipulated juries. Few were indicted and very few were ever convicted.

By the late '20s the Klan declined sharply in membership and in influence. This decline was brought about by (1) legal attacks on the Klan by the NAACP, (2) an increase in criticism from Golden Rule Christians, (3) inept Klan leadership and (4) public revulsion at their terrorist tactics.

The ideology that rationalized apartheid was racism—a belief that the white race was superior and the black race inferior. Racism originated in the sixteenth and seventeenth centuries in Europe. When Europeans enslaved the peoples they conquered they were strongly criticized by theologians, missionaries and the Pope. In response the slave traders adopted the doctrine of racism. A similar pattern occurred in the U.S. The national policy of military campaigns to exterminate the natives and the importation and breeding of Africans for slave labor brought sharp criticism from some Christian denominations. For instance, in 1688 Mennonites in Germantown, Pennsylvania, considered the ethics of slavery and concluded that slavery violated Christian principles. The slave traders, breeders and owners responded to this charge by adopting the concept of racism.

Prior to the Civil War most Christian churches felt obliged to take a position— one way or the other—on slavery. Congregationalists disagreed on the issue but with their practice of local autonomy some congregations were on each side. Catholics, Episcopalians and Lutherans avoided a public debate by shifting their focus from temporal matters to spiritual and metaphysical concerns. The Presbyterian church split into two divisions—northern, anti-slavery, and southern, pro-slavery. In 1864 the southern Presbyterians adopted a resolution that stated, "We hesitate not, to affirm that it is the peculiar mission of the Southern Church to conserve the institution of slavery, to make it a blessing to both master and slave."

Racism was the dominant ideology governing the whites' attitude toward blacks from Reconstruction to 1964. The Supreme Court was racist in its Dred Scott decision in 1856 that declared that blacks were property. The *Plessy v. Ferguson* decision in 1896 approved separate but "equal" facilities for blacks. All U.S. presidents from Reconstruction to 1964—except Harry Truman—acted as racists. They all failed to implement the fourteenth and fifteenth Amendments to the Constitution that "guaranteed" equal treatment under the law and the right to vote. The U.S. Congress was dominated by racist southern senators and representatives. It rejected innumerable petitions for enactment of civil rights legislation.

During a congressional debate in 1906, Senator Benjamin R. Tillman of South Carolina made a speech that expressed the southern position on Negro rights. He gave three reasons to justify repression of Negroes: (1) the bitter memory of Reconstruction, (2) the belief that Negroes were inherently inferior and (3) a belief in the purity of the white race and the sanctity of white womanhood. Hollywood reaffirmed the belief in white supremacy in such movies as *Birth of a Nation* and *Gone with the Wind*.

Apartheid, enforced by the KKK and rationalized by racism, was successful for over seventy-five years, i.e., it kept the Negro in his second-class place. Its success, however, explains why, in the mid-twentieth century, a black revolution became inevitable. The factor that made that revolution possible was the black Christian church and its theology.

Throughout the civil rights struggle the black Christian church was the principal facilitator of the demonstrations and campaigns for freedom. It supplied facilities for disseminating information, attracting and training volunteers, reporting clashes with police, administering first aid, organizing marches, boycotts and sit-ins and for maintaining community support. The black Christian churches that played this role had a religion that was significantly different from that of the white Christian churches. The black church members tended to be pro-justice and more joyous, friendly, political and participatory. The blacks were especially attracted to Moses and the dream of being led out of the wilderness of apartheid to the promised land of freedom. The religion of the black Christian churches embraced five concepts that differentiated them from the white Christian churches; survival, elevation, liberation, community and nonviolence.

Survival was a dominant objective of blacks under slavery and then under apartheid. Slavery had reduced African Americans to the status of domestic animals governed by ruthless cruelty. The slave's obsession was to hold body and soul together for as long as possible. As the black religion evolved from African, Caribbean and domestic sources, and as slavery was replaced by apartheid, this drive for survival remained a central concept in their religion.

Elevation, meaning achieving literacy and education, was a concept that evolved during the apartheid period when many blacks were moving north, obtaining some education and bettering their situation. The black church taught that literacy, denied under apartheid, was a key to improving one's status.

Liberation. The desire to become a free citizen was a strong feeling in the black's religion from 1800 to the 1960s. This yearning was expressed in Sunday sermons, in Negro spirituals and by marching feet.

Community. The black Christian churches held that the community surrounding the church building was as indispensable to an individual's physical and emotional health as was the family. The black community enabled black people to survive apartheid, hold on to their cultural values and pursue their drive for freedom.

Nonviolence. The concept of employing nonviolent action to achieve political ends was used successfully by Mahatma Gandhi in India and by black activists in the U.S. In the white culture this concept was understood in the "peace churches"—the Society of Friends, the Mennonites, the Amish and the Fellowship of Reconciliation. The value system of the black's Christian religion was not violence oriented and so was amenable to the adoption of this concept in the struggle for freedom.

During the twentieth century, Dr. Martin Luther King, Jr., was the most prominent advocate and practitioner of nonviolent action in America. He spoke, wrote and demonstrated, extensively advocating, teaching and practicing this religious/psychological/philosophical/political concept that was central to the conduct of the civil rights revolution. The best way to define and explain this compound concept is to present ten quotations from Dr. King's writings.

1. "Tested in Montgomery during the winter of 1955–56, and toughened throughout the South in the eight ensuing years, nonviolent resistance had become, by 1963, a logical force in the greatest mass action crusade for freedom that has ever occurred in American history"—*Why We Can't Wait.*

2. "The nonviolent approach does not immediately change the heart of the oppressor. It first does something to the hearts and souls of those committed to it. It gives them new self-respect; it calls up resources and strength and courage that they did not know they had. Finally it reaches the opponent and so stirs his conscience that reconciliation becomes a reality"—*Stride Toward Freedom.*

3. "Nonviolence is a powerful and just weapon. It is a weapon unique in history, which cuts without wounding, and ennobles the man who wields it. It is a sword that heals"—*Why We Can't Wait.*

4. "Nonviolence in the truest sense is not a strategy that one uses simply because it is expedient at the moment; nonviolence is ultimately a way of life that men live by because of the sheer morality of its claim"—*Stride Toward Freedom.*

5. "Nonviolence ... does not seek to defeat or humiliate the opponent, but to win his friendship and understanding"—*Stride Toward Freedom.*

6. "Nonviolent resistence is not a method for cowards; it does not resist. If one uses this method because he is afraid or merely because he lacks the instruments of violence, he is not truly nonviolent"—*Stride Toward Freedom.*

7. "The nonviolent resister must often express his protest through noncooperation or boycotts, but he realizes these are not ends in themselves; they are merely means to awaken a sense of moral shame in the opponent. The end is *redemption* and *reconciliation*"—*Stride Toward Freedom.*

8. "The aftermath of nonviolence is the creation of the *beloved community*, while the aftermath of violence is tragic bitterness"—*Stride Toward Freedom.*

9. "We have experimented with the meaning of nonviolence in our struggle for racial justice in the United States, but now the time has come for man to experiment with nonviolence in all areas of human conflict, and that means nonviolence on an international scale"—*The Trumpet of Conscience.*

10. "Nonviolent resistance ... is based on the conviction that the universe is on the side of justice.... The believer in nonviolence has deep faith in the future.... For he knows that in his struggle for justice he has cosmic companionship"—*Stride Toward Freedom.*

Nonviolent direct action was taught to volunteers throughout the revolution. Diane Nash, a leader of the Nashville Student Movement, taught it in five steps. The first step was investigation—conducting research to understand the problem. Step two was education—educating the volunteers about the situation. The third step was negotiation. This consisted of approaching the opposition, explaining your position and seeking a resolution. The fourth step was nonviolent demonstration. The purpose of the demonstration was to focus the attention of the community on the issue and the injustice. Step five was resistance—you withdrew your support from the oppressive and unjust system. This step consisted of what the public saw on TV—boycotts, sit-ins, work stoppages and noncooperation with the system.

The successful use of nonviolent resistence by Dr. King and his followers was recognized domestically and worldwide. In September 1958, Dr. King's book *Stride Toward Freedom* received wide acclaim. On January 3, 1964, *Time* magazine called Dr. King the "Man of the Year." On December 10, 1964, Dr. King was awarded the Nobel Peace Prize in Oslo, Norway. At that ceremony he was hailed as "the first person in the Western World to have shown that a struggle can be waged without violence."

Nonviolent resistance was a success but its operation required a precondition—a Supreme Court affirmation of equal justice under law for all citizens. That affirmation required the Supreme Court to reverse its position in its 1896 decision of *Plessy v. Ferguson*. Reversals are infrequent as they violate the legal principle of *stare decisis* (stand by things decided). The Supreme Court made that break with its past in its *Brown v. Board of Education* decision in 1954 that negated school segregation.

This legal saga began in 1910 when W.E.B. DuBois, the first black to earn a Ph.D. at Harvard, joined philosopher John Dewey, reformer Jane Addams and the National Negro Committee to found the National Association for the Advancement of Colored People (NAACP). The goal of the NAACP was to eliminate the legal basis of apartheid by challenging it in the U.S. court system. The NAACP and its Legal Defense Fund, led by Thurgood Marshall, worked from 1915 to 1955 to turn the Supreme Court from supporting apartheid to supporting democracy. Then they worked from 1955 to 1968 and beyond reversing apartheid laws in eleven states.

One thrust of the NAACP campaign was to terminate the practice of lynchings by the KKK. They succeeded in getting anti-lynching bills approved by the House of Representatives in 1922, 1937 and 1940, but in every case the bills were filibustered to death in the Senate by racist southern senators. They were more successful in defeating segregation one case at a time through court action. From 1915 to 1995 the NAACP challenged legal discrimination in fourteen states—eventually wining the key case of *Brown v. Board of Education*. The following fifteen cases illustrate how the NAACP selected and argued cases and the Supreme Court decided them in the long process of making desegregation the law of the land.

Cases Argued by the NAACP Before the U.S. Supreme Court, 1915–1955

1. 1915, *Guinn v. United States*. The "Grandfather Clause" of the 1910 Oklahoma Constitution prevented Negroes from voting on the grounds that their ancestors did not have the franchise. The Supreme Court, by a vote of 8–0, held that the "Grandfather Clause" was a clear violation of the Fifteenth Amendment.

2. 1923, *Moore v. Dempsey.* In 1919 Negro sharecroppers in Phillips County, Arkansas, began to organize to improve their economic situation. Whites in the area, scared by the though of a union of black sharecroppers, conducted three days of mob violence—resulting in the deaths of more than two hundred men, women and children. An apartheid-style court trial followed. Negroes were excluded from the jury. Negro witnesses were whipped until they agreed to testify against colored defendants. A white mob threatened violence and lynching if the black defendants were not convicted. The court-appointed defense counsel was a white racist. He failed to ask for a change in venue. He called no witnesses and he placed no defendants on the witness stand. The entire trial lasted less than an hour. Within five minutes the jury voted a dozen Negroes guilty of murder in the first degree. The court sentenced the twelve to death and committed sixty-seven others to long prison terms.

The NAACP appealed the case all the way to the Supreme Court and won freedom for all seventy-nine defendants. Mr. Justice Holmes delivered the opinion of the court.

3. 1927, *Nixon v. Herndon.* Texas passed a law in 1923 that stated, "in no event shall a Negro be eligible to participate in a Democratic primary election held in the state of Texas." Justice Oliver Wendell Holmes, speaking for the majority, held the "white primary" law to be invalid as it violated the "equal protection" clause of the Fourteenth Amendment.

4. 1927, *Harmon v. Tyler.* An ordinance in New Orleans provided racially segregated zoning. Louisiana courts upheld the ordinance. The NAACP took the case to the Supreme Court, which invalidated the ordinance on the grounds that it violated the Fourteenth Amendment.

5. 1930, *City of Richmond v. Deans.* A Richmond, Virginia, zoning ordinance based its segregation requirement on the prohibition of interracial marriage rather than on race or color perse. The Supreme Court held that the legal prohibition of intermarriage is itself based on race and, as such, violates the Fourteenth Amendment.

6. 1932, *Powell v. Alabama—Scottsboro No. 1.* Nine Negroes, two of them boys of thirteen and fourteen, went on trial in Scottsboro, Alabama, in 1931. They were charged with raping two white girls on a freight train in which they were riding. Eight of them were found guilty and sentenced to death. The Alabama Supreme Court set aside one of the convictions. The cases of the other seven were heard by the U.S. Supreme Court in 1932. The Supreme Court noted that the legal representation of the seven was so poor as to make a mockery of the concept of justice. The Supreme Court reversed the convictions and held that in capital cases where the defendant is unable to afford counsel, it was the duty of the court to assign competent counsel. Failure to do so would violate the due process clause of the Fourteenth Amendment.

7. 1936, *Brown v. Mississippi.* In 1934, Ed Brown, Henry Shields and Yank Ellington, Negro farm workers in DeKalb County, Mississippi, were convicted of murder solely on the basis of confessions obtained by torture. None of the men who participated in the torture denied beating the defendants. The Supreme Court re-

versed the conviction and granted a new trial. Chief Justice Hughes said that the use of confessions obtained by torture violated the Fourteenth Amendment guarantee of "due process of law."

    8. 1936, *William Gibbs v. Board of Education*, Montgomery County, Maryland. William Gibbs was an acting principal in the county school system. His salary was $612 per year. The average salary of white principals was $1,475 per year. On December 8, 1936, the NAACP filed a suit to end the disparities in the salaries of white and black teachers. This was the first case on teachers' pay and the NAACP and Gibbs won. The Maryland Court of Appeals ordered equalization of salaries within the county. As a result of this case the cumulative pay won for Negro teachers in nine counties was more than $100,000. The NAACP continued to bring suits to end pay discrimination in southern and border states. It won fifty cases that put over $3 million into the pockets of Negro teachers over a fifteen-year period.

    9. 1938, *Missouri, Gaines v. Canada*. Lloyd Gaines, a black student, earned a bachelor of arts degree at Lincoln University, an institution of higher learning maintained by the State of Missouri for Negroes. Gaines decided to study law and so applied for admission at the all-white University of Missouri law school. The University of Lincoln had no law school. He was refused admission on the ground that it was "contrary to the constitution, laws and public policy of the state to admit a Negro as a student in the University of Missouri." He was further advised that Missouri law stated that if a black student wished to take courses not provided at Lincoln University, the state would pay his tuition to a university in an adjacent state. Gaines sued and the case went to the Supreme Court. The court held that the petitioner was entitled to equal protection of the laws, and the State of Missouri was bound to provide him with facilities for legal education within its borders and that the facilities should be equal to those which the state provided for persons of the white race. The judgment of the Supreme Court of Missouri was reversed and the case was remanded for further proceedings not inconsistent with this opinion. This decision acknowledged that the "separate but equal" requirement laid down in *Plessy v. Ferguson*, 1896, was no longer a functional concept.

    10. 1940, *Chambers v. Florida*. Four Negroes were found guilty of murdering a white fish peddler in Pompano Beach, Florida. The confessions used to convict the defendants were obtained after five days of continuous questioning and grilling by the police in the absence of any legal counsel. The court found that the procedure used to obtain the confessions violated the defendants' right of "due process of law" that was guaranteed by the Fourteenth Amendment and these confessions could not be used in court.

    11. 1946, *Morgan v. Virginia*. A bus driver ordered Miss Morgan to go to the back of the bus. She refused. She was arrested and fined $10. Marshall and the Legal Defense Fund took the case to the Supreme Court. In a 7–1 decision, the court held that the Virginia statute requiring segregation in interstate transportation was invalid.

    12. 1950, *Sweatt v. Painter*. Herman M. Sweatt, a Negro postal clerk, applied

for admission to the University of Texas Law School at the opening of the 1946 term. He was denied admission on the basis of Texas racial policy. Since Texas had no separate law for school for Negroes, Sweatt filed a suit. In a unanimous decision the Supreme Court held that the equal protection clause of the Fourteenth Amendment required that the petitioner be admitted to the University of Texas Law School.

13. 1952, *Gray v. University of Tennessee.* In 1951 the University of Tennessee refused admission to the graduate school to several Negro applicants solely on the basis of race. A federal district court ruled that they were to be admitted but the court order was not carried out. The NAACP Legal Defense Fund won an appeal to the Supreme Court. While the case was being heard, the university revised its admissions policy and accepted the Negroes.

14. 1953, *Davis v. Schnell, Alabama.* Alabama adopted an amendment which required would-be voters to "read and write, understand and explain any article of the Constitution to the satisfaction of the registrars." The Alabama Federal Court struck down this amendment and the Supreme Court affirmed the federal court's action.

15. 1954–1955, *Brown v. Board of Education*, Topeka. This case title refers to five similar cases that were consolidated for a single set of hearings. The other four cases were Gebhart v. Belton, Delaware; Briggs v. Elliott, South Carolina; Davis v. County School Board of Prince Edward County, Virginia, and Bolling v. Sharpe in the District of Columbia. While the Supreme Court authored the decision it was Thurgood Marshall and his colleagues in the NAACP Legal Defense Fund who initiated, researched, argued and won the four cases that they had selected in 1950.

In their argument, Marshall and his team cited legal precedents from forty-six cases. They also used a brief entitled "The Effects of Segregation and the Consequences of Desegregating: A Social Science Statement" that they had written in collaboration with thirty-two social scientists, including sociologists, anthropologists, psychologists and psychiatrists who had worked in the area of American race relations. The LDF had help from several sources. The Truman administration filed an amicus brief that helped to sway the Supreme Court. Additional supporting briefs were filed b nineteen organizations such as the American Civil Liberties Union, the American Council of Human Rights and the Congress of Industrial Organizations.

Although their preparation was thorough and they had wide support the prospect of winning was dim. Marshall and the LDF knew the court and realized they would be lucky to get a split decision. And then fate intervened. Chief Justice Vinson, the leading advocate of continuing the status quo, died suddenly of natural causes. To fill the vacancy, President Eisenhower made a recess appointment of Governor Earl Warren of Californina. Warren was not only prodesegregation but he worked assiduously to obtain an unanimous decision.

On May 17, 1954, the Supreme Court of the United States announced its revolutionary decision on the four state segregation cases. Chief Justice Earl Warren delivered the unanimous opinion in three parts. One: With respect to the attitude of the framers of the Constitution toward segregated schools the evidence presented was inconclusive. Two: Segregated public schools, regardless of tangible factors, deprive the Negro children of equal educational opportunities. Three: The court's conclusion did not overturn *Plessy v. Ferguson* as unconstitutional but rather found that its application to public education was invalid. He concluded that in the field of public education "separate but equal" has no place.

Reactions to this decision were immediate and varied. The U.S. Information Agency that was responsible for reporting on America to foreign countries, hailed the decision as "a victory for democratic principles and practicies." Southern newspapers lashed out against the decision. Sixty-nine congressmen from the South and border states responded with a statement which said in part: "The decision of the Supreme Court is a clear abuse of judicial power. The original constitution does not mention education. Neither does the Fourteenth Amendment or any other Amendment."

In Mississippi, the most racist state, the ruling ignited violence. Gangs of whites committed beatings, burnings and lynchings. Two victims, the Rev. George W. Lee and Lamar Smith, were NAACP organizers who were trying to register blacks to vote. A third victim was a fourteen-year-old boy, Emmett Till, a visitor from Chicago. Till had said "Bye, Baby" to a white female clerk in the general store in Money.

Outside the South, *Brown v. Board of Education* was supported by an overwhelming majority of lawyers, public officials and academicians. This decision was so far-reaching in its potential impact on society that the court required a second hearing to receive briefs on procedures for implementation.

On May 31, 1955, Chief Justice Earl Warren, again speaking for a unanimous court, remanded the four cases to the lower courts with directions to take steps necessary and proper "to admit to public schools on a racially nondiscriminatory basis with all deliberate speed the parties to the case." The court assumed that the federal courts would act firmly and with good faith in carrying out this assignment.

Thurgood Marshall and the NAACP praised the court's opinion. They said that the decision furthered the emancipation of the Negro that had commenced during Reconstruction. The black community saw it as a bright ray of hope in the Stygian night of apartheid.

According to legal and political theory one might have expected that this Supreme Court decision would have been implemented by all levels of government. That did not happen. For a large number of government officials in Washington and in the apartheid states the ideology of racism was a stronger determining factor in their actions than the ideology of following legal democratic procedures. It required a thirteen-year nonviolent campaign against the established apartheid system by Americans of African descent to achieve a substantial beginning of desegregation.

II

Nonviolent Activists v. the Establishment

Turning the ship of state 180 degrees from apartheid to democracy was a prolonged process. The first step—reversing the Supreme Court—occupied the NAACP for 40 years, 1915–1955. The *Brown v. Board of Education* decision, 1954–1955, was the dramatic conclusion of that effort. The next necessary step was for that decision to be implemented by the president, the Congress and the apartheid states. But that, too, was a prolonged process. The immediate response of the federal government was inaction, and that of the apartheid states was massive resistance.

From 1955 to 1968, American freedom activists sought to persuade federal and state governments to implement both the Supreme Court's decision and the promise of the Fourteenth and Fifteenth Amendments to the Constitution. Having fought for Europeans' freedom in World War II, blacks were now ready to struggle for their share of American freedom. Using the new-to–America tactic of nonviolent action, they launched a long series of demonstrations against the traditional two-class system.

This chapter presents 50-odd stories of the intercultural confrontations that eventually brought an end to apartheid in eleven states. They show a wide geographical distribution and a variety of tactics and leadership styles. Most were managed by black ministers, conducted by black youths and strongly supported by the black Christian church, the black community, the NAACP and other civil rights organizations.

Students v. Prince Edward County, VA, 1951–1964

Prince Edward County, Virginia, was the site of three notable events in the civil rights revolution. Students planned and implemented a strike at the Farmville High

School in an effort to improve their segregated education. The NAACP Legal Defense Fund sued the Prince Edward county officials to integrate in the name of a 14-year-old student in one of the five cases that eventually were combined as *Brown v. Board of Education*. Prince Edward County also closed all black schools for five years, disrupting the education of 1,500 African American youngsters.

The school strike occurred in 1951, in Farmville, at the Moton High School. Moton was a typical black school: it was severely overcrowded and it had no cafeteria or gym. Tar papered wooden shacks accommodated the overflow and the highest paid teachers earned less than the lowest paid white teacher in the county. Demands for a new school by parents and ministers were rejected or ignored by the county school board.

In April 1951, Barbara Rose Johns, a 16-year-old junior at Moton High, decided that radical action was needed to get the school board's attention. She called a meeting of the student body. The students recounted a list of the school's deficiencies and then they voted to strike the following day. On the third day of the strike the students held a special meeting and listened to a guest speaker, Spottswood Robinson. Robinson was a graduate of Howard University and represented the NAACP–LDF in Virginia. Robinson and other NAACP had obtained improvements in some black schools and had won equal pay for black teachers in one Virginia county. Robinson went to the meeting with the intention of telling the students that their strike could not succeed and would be counterproductive. In the course of the meeting, however, he changed his mind. Impressed by the students' organization, enthusiasm and determination, he offered his assistance. He told the students that if they could get their parents' support the NAACP would work with them. After two weeks the strike ended without any notable results and the NAACP legal campaign commenced.

On May 23, 1951, Spottswood Robinson filed a case entitled *Davis v. County School Board of Prince Edward County*. The "Davis" was a 14-year-old daughter of a Prince Edward County farmer. In their petition, Robinson and his clients—118 students at Moton High and 68 of their parents—asked the state of Virginia to abolish its requirement of racially segregated schools. The verdict was published in 1953. The three-man Federal District Court ruled against the NAACP and upheld racially segregated schools. Robinson and the NAACP Legal Defense Fund appealed the case to the U.S. Supreme Court. The Supreme Court accepted the case and combined it with four similar cases (from Kansas, Delaware, South Carolina and the District of Columbia) to produce the watershed case of *Brown v. Board of Education of Topeka, Kansas*. The Supreme Court heard the case and reported it twice. In 1954 they announced that "separate but equal" was unconstitutional. In 1955 they announced that school integration should proceed "with all deliberate speed." This oxymoron phrase, plus the absence of any support for integration from the president or Congress, was interpreted by the white segregation establishment in 11 apartheid states as a green light for adoption of a policy of massive opposition. The state of Virginia was a leader in this opposition, and Prince Edward County was a leader in Virginia.

Prince Edward County officials were adamantly opposed to integration and proceeded to adopt an extreme measure to prevent it. They transferred most of the county's school property to newly organized private schools that taught white children only. In this new school system the white children were given tuition grants by the state and local governments. By 1959 the new system was operating and all of the black schools were closed. Nearly 1,500 black children in Prince Edward County received no formal education for five years—from 1959 to 1964. The closing of the black schools attracted wide attention. Some businessmen reported a decline in sales of 20 percent, and business leaders learned that no-schools-for-blacks policy discouraged new businesses. In 1960 a group of whites sought to resolve the education problem, offering to re-establish segregated classes for black students. The NAACP rejected the proposal, and urged the black parents to wait for court action that would force the reopening of public schools on an integrated basis.

Black leaders tried to diminish the hardship on the students; the NAACP opened two training centers, and the Rev. L. Francis Griffin, president of the all-black Prince Edward County Christian Association, conducted a campaign to raise $20,000 to finance training centers throughout the county. Sixteen centers were opened in 1960, providing lessons in math and reading for more than 600 students.

The court cases moved on at a deliberate pace. In August 1961, Federal Judge Oren Lewis ruled that Prince Edward County must stop giving public funds to private schools while public schools were closed. The Prince Edward school board responded by conducting a county-wide survey on desegregation. They polled 1, 400 white families and received 487 replies. Only one family supported integration. In March 1962, the Virginia Supreme Court refused to order Prince Edward County officials to reopen the public schools. The court reasoned that under the state constitution a county was not obliged to operate a school system. The NAACP continued their attack on segregation. In June 1962, NAACP lawyers petitioned a federal court to rule that the closing of public schools was unconstitutional. Gradually—very gradually—through innumerable legal actions the state and federal courts adjusted to the Supreme Court's new direction and school integration gradually became the law of the land. In 1964 the Prince Edward County public schools were opened to African Americans, and the desegregation of America continued.

Autherine Lucy v. University of Alabama, 1952–1988

In 1952 Autherine Lucy and Polly Anne Myers applied for admission to the University of Alabama. Autherine was planning to study library science. Both ladies were turned down by the university because of the color of their skin.

Thurgood Marshall and the NAACP Legal Defense Fund had worked on similar cases for many years. Marshall and his associate, Arthur Shores, a Birmingham lawyer, studied the situation and concluded that it would be a matter of routine procedures to get the university's decision rescinded. They filed a suit against William F. Adams, the dean of admissions. The case was heard by Judge Grooms of the Federal

District Court for the northern district of Alabama. The court's decision was what Marshall anticipated. Judge Grooms found that the ladies had been denied the "equal protection of the laws" guaranteed by the Fourteenth Amendment. He permanently enjoined the dean of admissions "from denying the plaintiffs and others similarly situated, the right to enroll in the University of Alabama … and pursue courses thereat."

This decision was not acceptable to the university. They appealed the case to the U.S. Court of Appeals, Fifth Circuit, where they anticipated a more favorable response. They were not disappointed. The appeals court suspended the injunction. It was now Thurgood Marshall's turn to appeal. On September 13, 1955, he applied to the U.S. Supreme Court for injunctive relief. The Supreme Court reinstated the injunction, citing its earlier decisions in similar cases. It appeared at that moment, after a three-and-a-half-year legal struggle, that the case was won and Autherine Lucy could attend the University of Alabama. Miss Lucy attended her first class at Smith Hall on the Tuscaloosa campus on February 1, 1956. But all did not go well. Lucy was pelted with rocks and eggs and epithets by a mob of university students and Tuscaloosa citizens. She fled the campus with the help of a policeman and his patrol car.

The trustees of the University of Alabama then suspended Lucy for her own safety and "for the safety of the students and faculty members." Thurgood Marshall, who had accompanied her during the violence, appeared again before the Birmingham District Court. He argued that the university had punished his client for obeying the law but had not punished the students who attacked her.

On February 29, 1956, Judge Grooms rendered an opinion favorable to Lucy. He held that the university must reinstate Lucy by March 5. The university trustees reacted quickly. They expelled Lucy permanently. The reason given for the expulsion was statements made by Lucy and her counsel before the court. At this point the case became moot. Lucy had been shaken up by the near-death experience of a mob attack. She flew to New York for rest and medical care and did not make further attempts to enter the university. She was married in Dallas, Texas, on April 22, 1956. The Lucy case provided an opportunity for the state university and the president of the United States to stand up for equal treatment under the law for all citizens. Neither responded. President Eisenhower was advised of the Lucy case but concluded that the federal government should not be involved. A postscript to this case occurred in 1988. The University of Alabama rescinded Lucy's expulsion. In 1989, Autherine Lucy Foster and her daughter enrolled at the university. In 1992, they both received their degrees.

Baton Rouge Bus Boycott, LA, 1953

In 1953, the blacks in Baton Rouge, Louisiana, were sick and tired of the U.S. apartheid system. The buses were a constant reminder of their pain and humiliation. Every public bus had a "colored section" sign in the back and a "white section" sign in the front. When the blacks filled up the colored section they had to stand even though there were empty seats in the white section. Drivers were rude to blacks and often pulled away from a stop when blacks were still boarding. This pain was aggravated by the knowledge that the Baton Rouge bus company was supported 66 percent by black patronage.

In early March 1953, black leaders in Baton Rouge petitioned the city council to enact an ordinance permitting blacks to be seated on a first-come-first-served basis with blacks sitting from rear-to-front and whites from front-to-rear. No seats would be reserved for whites. The city council considered the petition and decided to adopt it. It passed Ordinance No. 222, which authorized the new seating arrangement.

The ordinance went into effect on March 11. However, the white bus drivers refused to comply with the new seating procedure. The city council informed the drivers that the ordinance must be obeyed. The bus drivers' answer was to go on strike for four days. The drivers demanded that the four front seats be reserved for whites and the four back seats for blacks. The strike brought the conflict to the attention of the state's attorney general. He ruled that Ordinance 222 was illegal as it conflicted with Louisiana's segregation laws. The buses started rolling again and the drivers continued to insist that blacks ride in the back.

The Baton Rouge black community was upset. They talked it over and in June they inaugurated a boycott of the segregated buses. The Rev. T.J. Jemison, pastor of the Mount Zion Baptist Church and past president of the local NAACP, led the protest. Jemison and Raymond Scott announced the boycott on the local radio station and asked the blacks to not ride the buses. To manage the boycott, the black ministers organized the United Defense League (UDL). To provide transportation a "free car lift" was developed. Volunteers drove bus routes in their own cars, picking up passengers and taking them to their work places or downtown. The car lift was well organized with a dispatcher and reserve drivers ready to go whenever a transport bottleneck appeared. The passengers paid no fares. If they had paid fares the operation would have been shut down for operating taxies without a license. The drivers were all reimbursed for their gas, routine maintenance, tires and batteries. The money was raised in the mass meetings.

The Rev. Jemison and his colleagues held mass meetings every night. They provided information, inspiration and rejuvenation. There were rousing sermons and soul-searing singing. They also passed the hat to support the free car lift. The meetings were held in the auditorium of the segregated public school. Attendance was as high as 2,500 to 3,000. The boycott leaders had their own "police department"—husky volunteers who acted as bodyguards and patrolled the community to maintain order.

The boycott was 99 percent effective. No blacks rode the buses during the ten days of the boycott. The bus company lost about $1,600 a day. The black community was in full support. Negotiations commenced.

The black and white leaders worked out a tentative agreement. The two side front seats would be reserved for whites while the long rear seat would be reserved for blacks. All the remaining seats were to be filled on a first-come-first-served basis.

The United Defense League considered the proposed settlement and accepted it with a 5 to 3 vote. The boycott leaders took this proposed settlement to a mass meeting attended by 8,000 blacks. After discussion a standing vote showed that a majority approved the settlement. The boycott ended June 25, 1953.

The Baton Rouge experience was a revelation to black activists throughout the South. It was the first time that organized mass economic action was employed successfully to challenge the two-class system. Up to 1953, the NAACP format of working through the courts was the accepted formula. After Baton Rouge, the blacks had a new tactic added to their arsenal.

News of the Baton Rouge success and procedures was quickly disseminated through the black's church/minister network. Several characteristics of that experience, such as the umbrella management organization and free transportation, were copied in Montgomery, Tallahassee, New Orleans and other cities.

The Montgomery Bus Boycott, AL, 1955–1956

On December 1, 1955, a 43-year-old, college-educated, black seamstress, returning home after a day of work and Christmas shopping, refused to give up her seat on a bus to a white man when so ordered by the bus driver. The police were called and Rosa Parks was arrested and taken to jail. Mrs. Parks was charged under a 1945 Alabama apartheid law that mandated segregation on buses and gave drivers the power of enforcement.

Mrs. Parks' arrest brought a quick response from two groups. The NAACP decided that she would be an ideal plaintiff for a suit to end bus segregation. The Women's Political Council, associated with Dr. King's Dexter Street Baptist Church and led by Jo Ann Robinson, decided that blacks should boycott the bus companies. Both groups proceeded to implement their plans. Jo Ann Robinson and her council members met at midnight at Alabama State College under the pretext of grading exams. They drafted a flyer that reported Parks' arrest and called for a protest boycott of the buses on Monday. The flyers were distributed through the black churches.

A mass meeting of black leaders was held at the Dexter Street Baptist Church to organize the boycott. Fifty black Montgomery ministers attended. Martin Luther King Jr., a 26-year-old assistant pastor, was elected to lead the boycott. The Montgomery Improvement Association (MIA) was organized to manage the boycott.

From its inception the boycott was based on a small but significant modification of Mahatma Gandhi's precepts. The first mimeographed flyer of the MIA's position stated, "This is a movement of *passive resistance*, depending on moral and spiritual forces. We, the oppressed, have no hate in our hearts for the oppressors, but we are, nevertheless, determined to resist until the cause of justice triumphs." In a later position statement the term "passive resistance" was replaced by the term "nonviolent action." The MIA goals at the beginning of the boycott were very modest. They were not seeking desegregation but only courteous treatment and "fair" segregation. As time passed, however, the goals grew to include desegregation generally.

With King's strong leadership, the Monday boycott became a year long boycott on a citywide scale. The MIA purchased 19 station wagons to haul workers to their jobs. Lloyds of London insured these vehicles when Alabama insurance companies refused to do so. Black churches became pick-up and transfer stations. Phone banks were established to connect riders with drivers. As many as 20,000 rides were provided in one day. There were 350 cars in the volunteer car pool. Two thousand to 5,000 people attended frequent mass meetings to hear how the boycott was doing. At the height of the boycott an estimated 45,000 riders stayed off the buses and "walked for freedom." The bus companies raised their fares 50 percent and still lost $3,200 a day. Downtown merchants felt the decline in sales and put pressure on city officials to settle.

The first meeting of the two sides was held December 8, 1955. M.L. King and two other black leaders met with the Montgomery city commissioners and Jack Crenshaw, the bus company lawyer. Crenshaw refused the demand that the bus companies hire Negro drivers for predominantly Negro routes. He also asserted that desegregated bus seating would be illegal according to Alabama law.

A second meeting was held on December 17, 1955, in a chamber of commerce conference room. Dr. King was encouraged when he saw three prominent white ministers in the room: a Methodist, a Presbyterian and a Baptist. King had met many white ministers during his college years at Crozier and Boston University and he felt that he could communicate with them with a common set of values and assumptions. King began the discussion by making a concession. He said that the demand for black drivers could be considered a long-term objective instead of an immediate requirement. His concession was ignored. The three clergymen spoke. They associated themselves with humanistic values but then came down on the side of maintaining the status quo.

At a third meeting the Establishment team included Luther Ingalls, secretary of the Montgomery White Citizens Council, an avowed racist organization. The meeting was dominated by acrimonious exchanges between white and Negro delegates. King was surprised and saddened to learn that the whites sincerely believed that morality was neutral on the issue and the White Citizens Council was considered a natural counterpart to the Montgomery Improvement Association as both interest groups were racist! There were no more attempts at negotiation. It was clear to King that the Establishment was opposed to change. The bus company, the white clergy, the White Citizens Council and the local media presented a united front in support of segregation and in support of the use of the police and court systems to maintain it. This situation required a revision of tactics.

The MIA shifted its focus from the local Establishment to the national Establishment and tried to use the media to tell the story to the American public who in turn would let their congressmen and president know that segregation was in violation of the Constitution. This was a decision taken on the basis of faith and hope.

There was no indication that help would come from Washington. President Eisenhower was not a civil rights advocate and J. Edgar Hoover was strongly opposed to civil rights for blacks. The mood in Congress was demonstrated by the release of the "Southern Manifesto" which equated integration with subversion of the Constitution and pledged the entire region to fierce resistance. Ninety southern congressmen and all the southern senators except Estes Kefauver, Albert Gore and the Senate majority leader, Lyndon Johnson of Texas, signed this document.

The white Establishment also reassessed its position after the negotiations broke down. They closed ranks and proceeded to launch a series of offensives against the blacks. Their campaign included spreading false rumors, illegal arrests, bombing of homes and continued incivility, segregation, exploitation and harassment. To outside observers these tactics appeared to be a reign of terror but to native Alabamians it was close to life as usual. The three city commissioners, Mayor Gayle, Frank Parks and Clyde Sellers, held a special meeting to see what could be done. They decided to implement a scheme that would divide the blacks and end the boycott. Mayor Gayle invited three black ministers to a meeting at City Hall to discuss "insurance matters." The three ministers were from country churches. One was a Baptist, one a Presbyterian and the third from a Holiness Church. None was a member of the MIA.

When they arrived Mayor Gayle presented them with an agreement to end the boycott and asked them to sign it. The "agreement" proposed (1) courtesy from the bus driver, (2) "All Negro" buses during rush hours and (3) continuation of existing seating arrangements on normal bus runs. This was much less than the MIA was demanding. The ministers signed.

The commissioners then had the *Advertiser* carry a feature story in its Sunday edition. It said that a delegation of "three prominent Negro ministers" had ratified an agreement to end the boycott and all Negroes should return to the buses on Monday. On Sunday morning, January 22, the commissioners read their story in the *Advertiser* and smiled at their clever hoax, completely unaware of what was happening in the black community.

The previous evening, Saturday, January 21, a black reporter, Carl Rowan, read an item on the Associated Press wire in Minneapolis, Minnesota. It stated that the Sunday *Advertiser* in Montgomery would break the news that the Negroes had agreed to end the boycott. It reported the content of the agreement and referred to "three prominent Negro ministers." Rowan, who had already written about the boycott, was incredulous. He felt sure that the black leaders wouldn't accept a segregationist solution. He called Dr. King. King was surprised and flabbergasted. In a few moments he recovered his composure and went to work. He called an emergency meeting of the MIA leadership. In half an hour they were convened in his living room. They soon discovered that the "three prominent ministers" were not MIA members but country pastors who had been used. King's team wrote an announcement about the hoax and a call to continue the boycott on Monday morning. They broke up to distribute this announcement to all of the black ministers in Montgomery, and to the Rev.

Goetz, a white Lutheran minister with a black congregation. King and others spent half the night visiting dives and juke joints to tell the revelers about the attempted hoax and to urge them to continue the boycott.

On Sunday morning all the blacks who attended church got the message the revelers received earlier. On Monday morning the Montgomery buses ran nearly empty as usual. When the three city commissioners realized how they were outmaneuvered they were furious. They declared a new "get tough" policy, which was immediately put into effect. The Montgomery police harassed the carpool drivers regularly. They stopped them, checked their headlights and windshield wipers and then wrote a traffic ticket for some minor violation if they found one, for an imaginary violation, if they didn't. Jo Ann Robinson, the lady whose group started the boycott, was the recipient of 17 traffic tickets in a two-month period. The traffic fines hurt. They transferred to city coffers money that might have gone to support the carpool or bought groceries.

On January 26, Dr. King finished his work at the Dexter Church office and started home driving one of the car pools. As he picked up passengers, two motorcycle cops followed him. At the next pick-up station they pulled up to the driver's window and said, "Get out, King. You're under arrest for speeding 30 miles an hour in a 25 mile zone." The cops radioed for a police cruiser, which soon arrived and took King to the Montgomery City Jail. News of King's arrest and incarceration spread by word of mouth nearly as fast as the cops' radio communication. While Ralph Abernathy was busy scrounging up bail money, carloads of Dexter members and MIA supporters began arriving at the jail. King heard the angry crowd and realized that his jailer was in more danger than he was. The jailer also heard the crowd and had the same thought. He quickly escorted King out the front door of the jail and released him. News and rumors of the arrest and release spread all over Montgomery. All the blacks wanted to hear the details and rejoice in the liberation. That night, instead of one mass meeting to report on the boycott, it was necessary to hold a series of seven mass meetings to make a full report to the people. After that incident, King's friends decided to provide him with a bodyguard.

Police harassment in Montgomery provided a model that other cities copied. Juliette Morgan was a white, highly educated, city librarian. After watching the empty buses roll by for a few days she wrote a letter that was published in the Montgomery *Advertiser*. In her letter she lauded the attitude of the boycotters and compared them to Gandhi. She recommended that her fellow white citizens read Edmund Burke's speech "Conciliation with the American Colonies" and warned them against "pharisaical zeal." Morgan's letter brought down upon her a prolonged harassment by young people. They threw rocks through her windows, insulted her on the streets and played tricks on her in the library. A little more than a year later she was found poisoned in her house. The white culture concluded that she had mental problems and committed suicide. The black culture concluded that her own people harassed her to death.

Harassment was supplemented by threats. Dr. King went to bed late one night.

His mind was on the plans for the next day. Coretta, his wife, was asleep. The telephone rang. King picked up the receiver. "Listen, nigger," said the caller, "we've taken all we want from you. Before next week you'll be sorry you ever came to Montgomery." King endured incidents like these with strong support from his faith and from his people.

Commissioner Seller's announcement of a new "get-tough" policy was taken by extreme racists, such as some members of the White Citizens Council, as a green light to do their thing. Dr. King was speaking at a mass meeting of 2,000 people at Abernathy's church. He was reporting the day's events and rallying support for the boycott and the lawsuit when he noticed an agitated group of MIA ministers. He called Abernathy over and asked, "What's wrong?"

"Your house has been bombed," said Abernathy.

"Are Coretta and the baby all right?"

"We are checking on that," was the reply.

In semi-shock, King kept his calm. He told the assembly what had happened and left by a side door. As he approached his house he found a near-riot situation. White policemen were trying to hold a barricade. Some Negroes were confronting the barricade brandishing knives and guns and shouting for the police to leave. Little boys were breaking the tops off Coke bottles to prepare for a fight. Flanked by MIA leaders King walked across broken glass on his porch and into the living room which was jammed with Dexter church members and a few whites, officials and a reporter. He found Coretta and ten-week old Yoki unharmed in a back room. King then returned to the living room and received crime scene reports from Sellers and the mayor. Both assured him that they would do everything possible to find the bombers.

A crowd of several hundred angry and armed Negroes now surrounded the house. King went to the front porch and raised his hands for silence and spoke in a moderate tone. "Don't get panicky. Don't do anything panicky. Don't get your weapons. If you have weapons, take them home. He who lives by the sword will perish by the sword. Remember that is what Jesus said. We are not advocating violence. We want to love our enemies. Be good to them. This is what we must live by. We must meet hate with love ... I did not start this boycott. I was asked by you to serve as your spokesman. I want it to be known the length and breadth of this land that if I am stopped, this movement will not stop. If I am stopped, our work will not stop. For what we are doing is right. What we are doing is just. And God is with us."

King paused. The crowd responded with "amens!"

Sellers tried to speak. The crowd booed him. The policeman tried to shout them down. The crowd booed louder. King quieted the crowd and asked them to hear the commissioner. Sellers spoke promising full police protection for the King family. Mayor Gayle seconded him and announced a $500 reward for information leading to the arrest of the bombers. King then asked the crowd to go home and they did. King took his family to a friend's house. A few days later another bomb exploded in the yard of E.D. Nixon, a black civil rights activist. It drew another angry and frustrated but peaceful crowd.

Simultaneously with all of these violent episodes a legal case was making its way through the court systems. The NAACP brought a case on Rosa Parks' behalf. It led to a decision by a district court that the segregation of buses was unconstitutional. The Alabama Establishment appealed the decision. On November 13, 1956, the U.S. Supreme Court settled the issue. The court ruled that the state and local laws in Alabama that required bus segregation were unconstitutional. On December 20, 1956, the Montgomery city officials received official notice of this decision. The next day the boycott was over. The buses were desegregated and the blacks rode again.

Rosa Parks became a folk hero. Martin Luther King won recognition as a civil rights leader. The Rev. Abernathy, E.D. Nixon, Fred Gray, Jo Ann Robinson, 50 black Montgomery ministers and thousands of nonviolent boycotters became heroes in the nonviolent black revolution. Martin Luther King Jr. summed up the accomplishments of the boycott in a speech at the final mass meeting of the Montgomery Improvement Association. He said that Negroes had discovered that they could stick together, black leaders did not have to sell out, threats and violence did not overcome strongly motivated nonviolence, black churches were becoming militant, black people had gained a sense of dignity and destiny and nonviolent activism was a powerful weapon.

Tallahassee Bus Boycott, FL, 1956–1958

On May 26, 1956, Wilhelmina Jakes and Carrie Patterson of Florida Agricultural and Mechanical University (FAMU) boarded a bus in Tallahassee. The bus was filled except for two seats in the "white" section. The co-eds took those seats. The bus driver, Max Coggins, asked them to move to the rear of the bus where there were no unoccupied seats. The ladies refused but offered to leave the bus if the driver would return their fares. The driver refused their counteroffer, stopped the bus at a service station and called the police. The two students were then arrested for "inciting a riot."

Jakes and Patterson were quickly released on $25 bonds and remanded to the FAMU authorities. The charges were then dropped but the confrontation continued. The same night a cross, a symbol of the Ku Klux Klan, was burned on the lawn at the co-eds' residence. FAMU officials moved the girls to a dormitory to assure their safety. The next day FAMU students held a mass meeting and the Student Government Association president, Broadus Hartley, called for the boycott of the Tallahassee buses. The students approved the proposal and agreed to refrain from riding the buses for the two remaining weeks of the school term. The Negro community supported the boycott and made it into a communitywide project.

Three days later the Tallahassee Ministerial Alliance met at the African Methodist Episcopal Church. The alliance called a meeting that same night, May 29. Four hundred and 50 people attended. The events of the previous days were discussed and then a proposal was made and adopted to form an Inter-City Council (ICC) to manage the bus boycott. The Rev. Charles Kenzie Steele was elected president. The ICC agreed to employ nonviolent tactics. Their immediate goal was to eliminate bus segregation. The boycott would be terminated when three conditions were met: (1) bus seating on a first-come-first-served basis, (2) courteous treatment of Negroes by bus drivers and (3) Negroes were to be hired to drive routes that traversed the black community. The ICC also made plans to operate a carpool to transport workers to their jobs. The ICC made its demands known to the city officials and to the bus companies. The immediate reaction of the white Establishment was to ignore the blacks' demands.

The boycott progressed according to the ICC plan. Ten days after it started the bus company petitioned the city council to permit it to cut all bus service to the Negro neighborhoods. The petition was granted. By that time the carpool was operating with 73 cars. The boycott was about 90 percent effective. The president of the Tallahassee Bus Company, J.S.D. Coleman, said that he suffered a 60 percent loss of revenue. After a month, Coleman requested and received a fare increase from the city commission. The commission also reduced the company's franchise tax to an unprecedented low of one-and-one-half percent to help keep the company solvent. However, the fare hike and tax cut failed to keep the buses rolling. On June 30, 1956, bus services were suspended.

Coleman continued to press for a settlement. He offered the ICC a proposal that was much less than its demands. The ICC refused it. A month later, on August 2, 1956, Coleman reestablished the bus service and launched a campaign to increase ridership. He even offered free coffee on one route. He also hired some Negro drivers. But the seating conditions demanded by the ICC were not met and the boycott continued.

During the remainder of 1956 the Establishment tried again and again to break the boycott by a series of tactics. In early September 1956, the Ku Klux Klan held a parade in Tallahassee and marched past the Rev. Steele's parsonage on Tennessee Street. The parade was followed by a rally of 400 KKK members just west of the city. The Establishment also tried police harassment. On May 10, 1956, the Rev. Steele was arrested and charged with running a stop sign. By June 6, 1956, six carpool drivers and 22 other blacks had been stopped and hauled to police headquarters where they were questioned and forced to sign statements of which they knew neither the contents nor the purpose. The city commission and the bus company published letters in the local press stating their position and placing blame for the controversy on the ICC. The local paper, the *Tallahassee Democrat*, attempted to discredit protest leaders, especially the Rev. Steele. Throughout the confrontation the white press continuously railed against "outsiders." There was one truth in this claim. The Rev. Steele was born in West Virginia.

Since they shared the same city, the Florida Legislature was constantly reminded of the boycott. They decided to do their part in guaranteeing the continuation of a segregated society. In July 1956, the Legislature passed four new segregation bills. In August 1956, the Legislature established a permanent watchdog committee to monitor NAACP activities in the state and look for illegalities. Since the Rev. Steele was the president of the Tallahassee NAACP, he was the prime target of the committee. The legislative committee held hearings on the ICC but found nothing incriminating.

By mid–July 1956, the city commissioners realized that the boycott was a serious matter and the Establishment's efforts had not dented the blacks' resolve. The commissioners decided to wage an all-out attack on the carpool. The carpool at that time consisted of 63 cars, two station wagons and more than a score of volunteer drivers. To implement this new policy, the police arrested 21 carpool drivers. The ICC and the drivers were charged with conducting a taxi business in violation of the for-hire tag law. The trial was set for October 17, 1956. The ICC attorney, Theries Lindsay, worked hard. He sought a dismissal on grounds that the trial was the result of discriminatory legislative action based on race. Request denied. Lindsay then sought at injunction from the federal court. The federal judge refused to take any action. Lindsay presented evidence that the ICC did not make a profit from the carpool and was not a for-profit business.

The black community was extremely worried about the outcome of this trial as they were aware that the Florida system of "justice," like that of other southern states, did not dispense justice to blacks. The Rev. Steele, hoping or gambling that Governor Collins might be fair minded, sent him a telegram asking him to intervene on behalf of the carpool defendants. The governor declined, thus giving tacit support to the court proceedings. After three days of the hearing the expected verdict was pronounced: "guilty." Each of the defendants was fined $500 and sentenced to 60 days in jail. The jail sentences were suspended but the fines, totaling $11,000, had to be paid.

Henry Gitano, editor of *The Militant*, wrote a summary of the trial:

"The 21 Negroes were victimized in the car pool trial ... City Judge Rudd tossed out as irrelevant a motion by defense attorney Francisco Rodriguez, which stated that boycotters were not engaged in a business activity but a protest movement; that the right of free speech cannot be licensed by public authority; that the requirement of racial segregation on the city's buses is a bill of attainder; that the action of the city denies equal protection of the law." Gitano's article also noted that the city of Tallahassee had retained an outsider, Mark R. Hawes of Tampa, for a $4,000 fee to prosecute the case. The verdict was successful in stopping the organized carpooling but walking and informal carpooling continued. The Rev. Steele and the ICC responded to the court decision by holding a mass meeting at which they reasserted their determination to desegregate the buses and encouraged the black community to continue the boycott.

On December 24, 1956, three black ministers, the reverends Steele, A.C. Reed and H. McNeal Harris, demonstrated their resolve. They boarded a bus and sat in the "white" section. They were not arrested. However, the city commission reacted quickly and angrily. They revoked the transit company's franchise. They arrested nine drivers and manager Charles L. Carter and placed them under $100 bond on the charge that Negroes had been allowed to ride up front. Then it was the turn of the bus company to be angry with the commissioners. The company filed a suit to test the validity of the segregated seating ordinance and obtained a court restraining order to prevent the city commission from interfering with its operation. In the meantime a *Life* magazine photographer persuaded the Rev. Steele to board a bus and sit in the "white" section to provide a photo opportunity.

On January 1, 1957, Governor Collins decided to intervene in an effort to provide a cooling-off period. He suspended all bus services until a court decision was made on the segregated seating ordinance. However, instead of cooling off the situation heated up. The Steele family was at home on January 1, 1957, when a large stone landed on the front porch. Mrs. Steele gathered the children together in the middle of the house fearing that a bomb had been thrown. When bricks came crashing through the windows Steele moved to a bedroom window where he could see the street. He saw a late model car. Mrs. Steele put the children to bed and retired. The reverend had a premonition that the car might return so he stationed himself at the window armed with a .38-caliber revolver. After 15 minutes the car returned. Steele watched a white male get out of the car and commence to throw stones on the parsonage porch. The man yelled, "You black goddamned son of a bitch." Steele did not fire his weapon because of his commitment to nonviolence and the fear that if he did it would escalate the violence. On January 3, the KKK burned a cross in front of Steele's church. On January 15, a shotgun blast shattered the windows in a store owned by the Rev. Dan Speed, a member of the ICC.

As the violence increased, Governor Collins became concerned and threatened to step in again if the violence was not stopped. The Tallahassee police chief, Frank Stoutamire, supported the governor's statement and announced a crackdown on acts of violence and vandalism. Violence and vandalism decreased.

In January 1957, the bus company, desperate to reestablish its former income flow, took the initiative and with the support of the city commission, instituted a new bus seating policy. Some seats were reserved. Other seats were numbered and assigned to passengers by the driver. The penalty for noncompliance with this policy was a $500 fine and 60 days in jail. Passengers who were dissatisfied with their seat assignment could have their fare refunded and leave the bus. The Rev. Steele and the ICC rejected this seating policy, as it did not satisfy the ICC's requirement of desegregation.

A group of students from Florida State University and FAMU tested this seating policy by refusing to accept their assigned seats. Three of the students were arrested. Their case was tried before City Judge John Rudd with no possibility of a fair trial. They were all convicted and fined $500 and 60 days in jail. The ICC lawyer, Francisco Rodriguez, appealed to the U.S. Supreme Court, which declined to review the case. The students served 45 days of their sentences. Following this student action the State Board of Control issued a policy statement prohibiting students from participating in the civil rights protest movement. However, students of both universities ignored this directive, sometimes at great personal cost such as being denied a diploma.

While the bus boycott was being contested in the courts, on the buses and in the legislature, another civil rights campaign was in progress. It was a voter registration drive. In Tallahassee, as in many other places in the South, civil rights activists were working hard to register voters. The drive started July 5, 1956, when Edward D. Irons proposed that the ICC support a voter registration program to supplement the boycott. While the annual voter increase was small it was continuous and so it implied that eventually segregation might be eliminated. The KKK paraded in an effort to scare blacks from registering to vote. Instead the parade had the opposite effect. Due to the Rev. Steele's leadership there was a surge in registrations. There was another increase in the rate of registrations after the violent incidents in January 1957. The local paper, *The Tallahassee Democrat*, reported the increased registration and acknowledged that the Negro vote was becoming increasingly powerful.

By February 1957, the boycott was winding down. A CBS reporter interviewed a number of white citizens and found that many of them believed that desegregation was inevitable and they were ready to accept it. In March, April and May 1957, the Tallahassee Establishment tried to defang the boycott by means of a news blackout. Local news outlets were encouraged to deemphasize the protest. The ICC countered this tactic by holding a newsworthy celebration of the first anniversary of the FAMU co-eds' courageous act. Guest speakers were Bishop D. Ward Nichols, Congressman Charles Diggs and Dr. Martin Luther King Jr. During the remainder of 1957 the confrontations became fewer. Bus service was resumed in the Negro neighborhoods. Negroes began to sit wherever they wished. Some sat in the back from habit or fear. Others sat in the front. There were no reprisals. The boycott confrontations were over but not the campaign. The ICC still had to raise funds to pay fines. In one 13-day period, the Rev. Steele spoke at 26 fund-raising meetings in Rhode Island, New York and Massachusetts.

By May 1958, two years after the co-eds' challenge, the buses in Tallahassee were completely integrated. It was a great victory for the Rev. Steele and the ICC. But it was a qualified victory. Schools, hotels, motels, restaurants and other public facilities were still illegally segregated and the blacks had no representation in city, county or state government or in Washington, DC.

The Baton Rouge, Montgomery and Tallahassee bus boycotts were models and inspirations to others. In a press conference, the Southern Regional Council stated that by January 7, 1957, 21 southern cities had ended compulsory segregation on local buses without difficulty. They said that in every case the desegregation took place without court action—usually by a change in policy by bus company management.

Virginia v. The NAACP, 1956

The Supreme Court's *Brown v. Board of* Education decision was a cataclysmic event for both the blacks and the southern whites. It led the blacks to explode in revolution with many outbursts by many leaders throughout the apartheid states. It led the white Establishment, which was much more centrally organized into powerful states, to coordinate and intensity its efforts to maintain the two-class system. The apartheid states quickly reacted with three initiatives: (1) massive resistance, (2) declarations of interposition and (3) legal attacks designed to deactivate the NAACP.

Interposition was a claim that the state could interpose itself between its citizens and the national government if the state believed that the national government was acting unconstitutionally. Within two years of *Brown*, Alabama, Georgia, Louisiana, Mississippi, South Carolina and Virginia adopted interposition resolutions. As soon as this concept reached the Supreme Court it was thrown out.

Attacking the NAACP through legislation was attempted by Virginia, Alabama, Texas and South Carolina. The Virginia case is a good example of this ploy. In 1956, the Virginia General Assembly enacted five statutes that required the registration of all persons or corporations who rendered financial assistance in litigation and who engaged in the public solicitation of funds for that purpose. The statutes also established a procedure for the suspension and revocation of licenses of attorneys who violated the law.

The NAACP's Legal Defense Fund moved quickly. It brought actions for declaratory and injunctive relief on its own behalf and on behalf of the NAACP against the state's attorney general and five state attorneys. A three-judge federal court declared three of the five statutes void. It held that the two remaining statutes must be authoritatively construed by the state's courts.

The case was then appealed to the U.S. Supreme Court as *Harrison v. NAACP et al.* 1959. Thurgood Marshall and his team of Legal Defense Fund Lawyers argued the case. They argued that the laws violated the "due process" clause of the Fourteenth Amendment. In a 6–3 decision—with Chief Justice Warren and justices Douglas and Brennan dissenting—the court vacated the judgment of the district court and remanded the case for further consideration.

During the next three years the lower court reconsidered the case and declared most of the laws unconstitutional. One law which was directed against persons who solicit business for lawyers was not declared unconstitutional at that time. A year later, in the case of *NAACP v. Button* (1963), this statute was also declared invalid.

In the short run—from 1956 to 1963—it can be said that the Establishment won. It harassed the NAACP, tied up a lot of time of the blacks' best legal team and so postponed the evolution to desegregation. In the longer run, the blacks won. They established the superior authority of the Supreme Court in Virginia and the NAACP lawyers became expert at handling this issue—an expertise they employed in other states.

Alabama v. The NAACP, 1956

On June 1, 1956, the attorney general of Alabama filed a complaint against the

NAACP alleging that the association had failed to comply with Alabama state laws that required the registration of foreign or out-of-state corporations.

In the litigation before the state court that followed, the judge ordered the NAACP to produce its records, including its membership lists. The association agreed to produce its papers but not its membership lists on the grounds that such a disclosure would result in harassment of individual members. The judge's response was to find the association in contempt of court, to fine them $10,000 and to threaten a fine of $90,000 if the lists were not produced within five days.

The NAACP again refused to give up the lists and appealed to the Alabama Supreme Court. The court upheld the earlier decision and imposed the full $100,000 fine.

The NAACP then took the case to the U.S. Supreme Court as *NAACP v. Alabama ex rel. Patterson*. Thurgood Marshall, Robert Carter and Arthur Shores argued the case for the NAACP. They argued that the State of Alabama was depriving them of their right to freely associate and express ideas without the "due process of law" required by the Fourteenth Amendment. Friend of the court briefs were filed by the American Baptist Convention Committee on Christian Social Progress, the Anti-Defamation League of the B'nai B'rith and the Japanese American Citizens League. The Friends argued that Alabama's actions violated the First, Fifth, and Fourteenth Amendments.

On June 30, 1958, a unanimous Supreme Court reversed the decision of the Alabama Supreme Court. Associate Justice Harlan, speaking for the court, reasoned that "the deterrent effect on the free enjoyment of the right to associate" violated "due process of law" as protected by the Fourteenth Amendment. The court dismissed the charge of contempt, the $100,000 fine and sent the case back to the state Supreme Court for "proceedings not inconsistent with this opinion."

If court decisions were governed by law and logic this would have terminated the case, but this did not happen. The state Supreme Court reaffirmed the contempt citation and reimposed the fine. Once again the NAACP's Legal Defense Fund took the case to the U.S. Supreme Court with Thurgood Marshall arguing the case.

On June 8, 1969, the U.S. Supreme Court again reversed the decision of the lower court and remanded the case for reconsideration. Again the Alabama Supreme Court adamantly refused to decide the case on its merits. It took another five years and two more decisions by the U.S. Supreme Court before the matter was finally settled in favor of the NAACP.

The Ku Klux Klan v. Black Activists, AL, 1956–1963

Throughout U.S. apartheid—from Reconstruction to the 1960s—the ultimate enforcement of Jim Crow was not through the courts and "justice" system but by organized and Establishment-condoned terrorists. The terrorists were ordinary citizens by day and terrorists by night. Their tactics were lynching, arson, beatings, cross burning, torture and murder. Following is a sample of a dozen news items that give a picture of apartheid enforcement as practiced in one state, Alabama, from 1956 to 1963. These news items are from the *New York Times*, *Jet Magazine* and *My Soul Is a Witness*.

January and February 1956, Montgomery

Bomb blasts shattered windows in the homes of Martin Luther King and E.D. Nixon, leaders of the bus boycott. No one was hurt in the explosions (*My Soul Is a Witness*).

December 25, 1956—Christmas Day, Birmingham

The home of the Rev. Fred Shuttlesworth, a civil rights leader, was bombed and more than 40 people were subsequently arrested for attempting to ride local buses on a nonsegregated basis (*My Soul Is a Witness*).

January 28, 1957, Montgomery

A bomb exploded at the home of a black resident, injuring three people. Another bomb on the porch of Martin Luther King failed to detonate. King told those who gathered, "Don't get your guns. Don't shoot back—but fear no one. We won't stop our fight for justice. They'll have to blow up God himself" (*New York Times*).

March 21, 1957, Birmingham

The car of Lamar Weaver, a white supporter of the anti-segregation campaign, was attacked by a mob of whites while the Rev. Frank Shuttlesworth sat in a "white" waiting room in the railroad terminal. When police prevented the mob from reaching the Rev. Shuttlesworth, they turned on Weaver, who was waiting in his car (*Jet Magazine*).

March 28, 1957, University of Alabama

Seventy hooded Ku Klux Klansmen disrupted a forum on race relations being held at the University of Alabama Methodist Student Center. The KKK spokesman read a statement that said, "The University of Alabama is a white man's school. It has always been that way and we intend for it to stay that way." After the Klansmen left, Dr. Paul Ramsey, who organized the forum, continued the program (*Jet Magazine*).

September 1957, Birmingham

The Rev. Fred Shuttlesworth attempted to enroll four black children at an all-white school. Violence erupted. This was the third time in less than a year that Shuttlesworth had been attacked by white mobs opposed to any attempt to desegregate public accommodations in Birmingham.

November 1, 8, 1957, Birmingham

Six white men accused of castrating a black man, J.E. Aaron, were convicted by an all-white jury and given sentences of 20 years maximum. The six were members of the local Klan chapter (*New York Times*).

December 8, 1957, Birmingham

The home of Robert Greer was bombed before he and his family were able to move in. Located in the predominantly white Fountain Heights section, this was the latest in a series of bombings aimed at black residents in the city (*New York Times*).

March 11–12, 1958, Mobile

A cross was burned in front of the home of the Rev. J.T. Parker, a white minister who had signed a statement in support of a petition of 36 black ministers calling on city officials to desegregate public transit in the city. The next day, crosses were burned in front of the churches of three white clergymen who had also supported the black ministers' petition (*New York Times*).

May 1958, Birmingham and Bessemer

After the bombing of a Jewish community center in Birmingham and the homes of Ernest Coppins and Dora Maudlin in Bessemer, black and white citizens contributed money toward a $15,000 reward for information leading to the conviction of the person responsible for the bombings. In July, the Justice Department issued a report that documented 44 racially and religiously motivated bombings in eight southern states during the previous 18 months (*My Soul Is a Witness*).

December 18, 1962, Birmingham

The Bethel Baptist Church, formerly the church of civil rights leader the Rev. Fred Shuttlesworth, was bombed. Although once the hub of antisegregation campaigning, the church remained relatively quiet since his departure. The blast also damaged two nearby houses (*The New York Times*).

September 15, 1963, Birmingham

Segregationists in Birmingham continued their reign of terror. Four black girls were killed when a bomb exploded at the Sixteenth Street Baptist Church. Other bombings occurred in black neighborhoods and at the homes of civil rights activists in September and October, and strong opposition to desegregation continued to the end of the year (*My Soul Is a Witness*).

Prayer Pilgrimage for Freedom, Washington, DC, 1957

In early 1957 militant segregationists dropped all pretense of resisting the Supreme Court's desegregation decision through legal maneuvers and began to employ violence at an unprecedented level. There were midnight bombings, arson and sniper fire at integrated buses, as well as dynamitings and KKK cross burnings. The southern racist-dominated governments were determined to maintain apartheid and the Eisenhower administration in Washington appeared unconcerned.

The leaders of the civil rights movement felt that some new tactic was needed to awaken the president to the fact that blacks' rights were being violated with no restraint or legal recourse. On January 11, 1957, Dr. King convened a conference in the Ebenezer Church in Atlanta to decide what nonviolent protests could be conducted to democratize America's political system. Negro leaders, mostly ministers, came from ten states to participate in the planning. As a first order of business the conferees founded an organization. They called it the "Southern Negro Leaders Conference on Transportation and Nonviolent Integration." This name was eventually changed to "Southern Christian Leadership Conference" or SCLC. The SCLC was led and run by black Christian ministers. It functioned as the action arm of the black church in the South. It provided a basis for cooperation and mutual support in their common struggle to activate the Fourteenth and Fifteenth Amendments to the Constitution and implement *Brown v. Board of Education.*

The conferees also took some action. They sent a telegram to President Eisenhower that said, "A state of terror prevails in the South." They asked the president to "come immediately" and make a "major speech in a southern city asking all persons to abide by the Supreme Court's decision as the law of the land." They also requested a meeting with Attorney General Herbert Brownell. The SCLC ministers were very disappointed when both the president and the attorney general declined their invitation, but they persevered.

On February 14, 1957, the SCLC held another strategy planning conference in New Orleans. Ninety-seven black leaders met at the New Zion Baptist Church. The first order of business was election of officers. They elected Dr. M.L. King Jr. president, the Rev. C.K. Steele of Tallahassee first vice president, the Rev. A.L. Davis of New Orleans second vice president, Samuel Williams of Atlanta third vice president, T.J. Jemison of Baton Rouge secretary, Medgar Evers assistant secretary and the Rev. Ralph Abernathy treasurer. The conference then considered a march on Washington. It was a new tactic and it provoked intense discussion. It was a break with the long established NAACP policy of working through the courts. Dr. King argued that the blacks "must not get involved in legislation and fights in lower courts." That was "exactly what the white man wants the Negro to do." We must move to mass action … in every community in the South, keeping in mind that civil disobedience to local laws is civil obedience to national laws."

At the end of the deliberations, Dr. King held a press conference and announced that they would march on Washington to get the president to speak out in support of *Brown* and school desegregation. He said that the march would not be politically partisan but a march "rooted deep in spiritual faith." By calling the march a "Prayer Pilgrimage for Freedom," they hoped to arouse the conscience of the nation and prod the president and Congress to action. Plans for the march attendance, speakers, meeting place and other arrangements were developed by A. Philip Randolph, Ralph Abernathy, Fred Shuttlesworth, Roy Wilkins of the NAACP, Dr. King and Bayard Rustin, King's secretary.

On April 5, the SCLC held a third conference in Washington to finalize the march details and programs. In attendance were more than 70 representatives of supporting groups and churches. It was decided that the Prayer Pilgrimage would take place on May 17, the third anniversary of the Supreme Court's historic desegregation decision. Dr. King announced that the pilgrimage had five objectives: (1) to demonstrate black unity, (2) to invite northerners to demonstrate their support for civil rights, (3) to protest the ongoing illegal attacks on the NAACP in southern states, (4) to protest racial violence in the south and (5) to urge passage of civil rights legislation.

On March 17, 1957, the Prayer Pilgrimage for Freedom proceeded as planned.

The headquarters was the Metropolitan Baptist Church in Washington, DC. Estimates of the number of "pilgrims" varied from 15,000 to 30,000. In any case it was, at that time, the largest civil rights demonstration in American History. The main event was an exuberant three-hour rally on the steps of the Lincoln Memorial. Randolph was the emcee. Mahalia Jackson sang. Several ministers, including William Holmes Borders and Fred Shuttlesworth, spoke. Entertainers Sammy Davis Jr., Ruby Dee, Sidney Poitier and Harry Belafonte entertained.

Dr. King spoke last. Dr. King criticized both political parties, the Congress and President Eisenhower for their inaction on civil rights. He said: "We come humbly to say to the men in the forefront of our government that the civil rights issue is not an ephemeral, evanescent domestic issue that can be kicked about by reactionary guardians of the status quo. It is, rather, an eternal moral issue which may well determine the destiny of our nation in the ideological struggle with Communism. The hour is late. The clock of destiny is ticking out. We must act now, before it is too late." King's rallying cry of "Give us the ballot!" was echoed in cadence by the crowd and provided a heading for the next day's papers. His speech ended with a rousing ovation.

Press coverage of the pilgrimage reflected the editorial policies of each news organ. The *New York Times* reported it on its front page. *Newsweek* and *Time* magazines did not report on it. *The Nation* and the *Christian Century* reported it. *Ebony* and the *Amsterdam News*, a New York Negro journal, said that King emerged from the Prayer Pilgrimage to Washington as the number one leader of sixteen million Negroes in the United States.

Some considered the pilgrimage a failure as attendance was disappointing and President Eisenhower did not hear the prayers. He continued to avoid meeting with black leaders and made no statement in support of the Supreme Court's desegregation ruling. Others hailed the pilgrimage as a tactical success as it demonstrated black solidarity, it supported congressmen who were working on the first civil rights bill since Reconstruction and it exposed the president as ill-informed or ill-advised in regard to civil rights in America. It increased the tempo and sophistication of demonstrations and presaged a second and more successful march on Washington in 1963.

Daisy Bates v. Governor Faubus, AR, 1957–1959

In 1954, Little Rock, Arkansas, gave no indication that it was a potential site for a soap opera theater of the absurd involving mobs, paratroopers, the U.S. president and nine students. At that time it was a liberal city by southern standards. Arkansas had integrated more school districts than any other southern state—two. The University of Arkansas Law School in Fayetteville and the Medical School in Little Rock were integrated. Half the students at the University of Arkansas Graduate Center were black. There were even some blacks on the Little Rock police force and some neighborhoods were integrated. When *Brown v. Board of Education* was pronounced, the Little Rock school board was the first in the South to issue a statement that it would comply. Daisy Bates, president of the Arkansas NAACP was optimistic. Virgil T. Blossom, superintendent of Little Rock schools, drew up a plan for the progressive integration of all schools.

On May 24, 1955, the school board rejected the Blossom plan and adopted one that provided for very slow integration; then racial politics entered the equation. In 1954, Orval Faubus had been elected governor for a two-year term. In 1955, his focus was not on school integration but on his own reelection. He saw a poll that said that 85 percent of Arkansans opposed integration and he decided to run as an anti-integrationist.

Meanwhile, Daisy Bates, disappointed with the school board's go-slow plan for integration, decided to accelerate the process through legal channels. Wiley Branton, chairman of the NAACP Legal Redress Committee, and U.S. Tate, NAACP regional attorney, filed a suit in federal court to require immediate integration of all schools. The suit was filed in the name of 33 Negro children and their parents. Judge John E. Miller dismissed the suit, saying that the school board plan was adequate evidence of its intentions to integrate the schools. Then Thurgood Marshall of the NAACP Legal Defense Fund joined Branton and appealed the case to the Eighth Circuit Court of Appeals in St. Louis. The St. Louis court agreed with Judge Miller but ordered that there should be no delays in implementing the school board plan.

In early 1957, the Arkansas State Legislature made its position clear. It enacted four anti-integration bills. The laws allowed school boards to hire lawyers, made school attendance voluntary, required anyone "challenging the authority" of government officials to register and created a "Sovereignty Commission" to protect the sovereignty of Arkansas from encroachment by the federal government.

The school board proceeded to implement its plan. It required all black kids who wanted to attend white schools to register. Then the NAACP lawyers cut their list of more than 75 students down to nine and the drama of the "Little Rock Nine" commenced. During August and September 1957, the confrontations at the school, in the courts, with Washington and in Mrs. Bates' home produced a media extravaganza. It began on August 22 when a rock was thrown through Daisy Bates's living room window. An attached note said, "Stone this time, Dynamite next."

On August 27, the Mothers' League of Little Rock Central High—a segregationist group organized by Governor Faubus—appealed to the Pulaski County Chancery Court for a temporary injunction against school integration. The reason they gave was that Governor Faubus told them that both white and black students were buying guns and knives and preparing for gang warfare. An investigation by the Justice Department found no evidence to support that claim. However, Chancellor Reed believed the claim and granted an injunction against integration.

On August 30, Thurgood Marshall and Wiley Branton went to the federal district court and asked Judge Ronald N. Davies to nullify the injunction. Judge Davies agreed and canceled the injunction that was blocking integration. He said that integration must proceed.

On September 2, Governor Faubus spoke on statewide TV. In defiance of Judge Davies' order he announced that he would have the National Guard surround the school because of the threat of violence and the school would remain segregated. The next day— the first day of school—250 National Guardsmen surrounded Central High. No students were allowed to enter. The school board asked the Negro students not to attempt to go to school and asked Judge Davies how to proceed. Judge Davies responded by immediately ordering the school board to proceed with its integration plan. The school board then advised Daisy Bates that the nine black students could attend school the next day.

On September 4, Daisy Bates tried to take the students to school but was rebuffed by the National Guard. One black student, Elizabeth Eckford, went to school on her own and was harassed by the mob around the school until she was rescued and taken to Mrs. Bates's house by a policeman.

On September 5, Judge Davies asked the U.S. Department of Justice to investigate the noncompliance with his order to follow the desegregation plan. Simultaneously, Governor Faubus sent President Eisenhower a telegram asking him to modify the extreme demands of the federal courts. President Eisenhower wired Governor Faubus that the Justice Department was investigating the failure to comply with Judge Davies's order to follow the integration plan.

September 6–8: Governor Faubus continued his defiance of the federal court and kept the National Guard at the school. The school board asked the federal court to suspend the segregation plan. The court refused. Thurgood Marshall said that the problem was a conflict between the state and the federal government—rather than between Bates and the school board. President Eisenhower was reluctant to clash with Governor Faubus to enforce federal law. Governor Faubus was trying to orchestrate the disagreement to produce voted for himself in the upcoming election.

September 9: The U.S. Justice Department finished its investigation. It concluded that (1) Governor Faubus had no evidence of impending trouble if blacks enrolled in the school, and (2) when the governor called out the National Guard he was enforcing segregation.

September 10: At the request of Judge Davies, the Justice Department filed a petition for an injunction to force Governor Faubus to comply with the desegregation order and to remove the National Guard from the school. A hearing on this petition was scheduled for September 20.

September 11–14: Governor Faubus did not remove the National Guard which was continuing to block students from entering the school.

September 14: President Eisenhower met with Governor Faubus at the president's summer home in Newport, Rhode Island. They had a non-meeting of minds. President Eisenhower said that the federal courts must be obeyed. Governor Faubus suggested a one-year delay in the desegregation process. There was no agreement but Eisenhower, accustomed to having a general's wishes carried out, thought that his recommendation was understood and would be followed.

September 14–20: Governor Faubus kept the soldiers at the school and the students out.

September 20: At the hearing, Governor Faubus challenged the jurisdiction of Judge Davies. The judge rejected the challenge and proceeded with the case. He ordered Faubus to remove his armed forces from the high school immediately. That night Faubus went on TV and announced that he would remove his National Guardsmen. He also asked blacks to stay away from the school until he could arrange for peaceful integration.

September 23, Monday: Daisy Bates gathered the nine students at her house along with four black journalists. The journalists drove to the school. The Little Rock police took the students to school and escorted them in by a side entrance. The four journalists were not so fortunate. They were met at the school by an angry white mob. (The Guard had been withdrawn and the police did not control the mob.) One newsman was hit in the head with a brick. A *Life* reporter and two photographers were harassed and beaten. The photographers' equipment was smashed. By noon the mob was 1,000 strong. Police Chief Gene Smith, unable to control the mob, decided to remove the students. The police took the scholars back to Mrs. Bates's house. Mrs. Bates told the reporters that the students would not return until the president could assure their protection. Little Rock's mayor, Woodrow Mann, was concerned. He called the Justice Department and suggested that the president send troops to enforce Judge Davies' order to keep the school open. Dr. M.L. King of the SCLC and Roy Wilkins of the NAACP also sent telegrams to Eisenhower calling for enforcement of constitutional law in Little Rock. President Eisenhower responded with an emergency proclamation ordering all Americans to cease and desist from blocking entry to the school and obstructing the federal court order to desegregate Central High.

September 24, Tuesday morning: Governor Faubus again permitted a mob of segregationists to congregate at the high school. Mayor Mann again telephoned the Justice Department and pointedly requested that federal troops be sent to maintain order. This time President Eisenhower acted like a general. He sent more than 1,000 members of the 101st Airborne Division to the Little Rock Air Force Base. They arrived by nightfall. He also nationalized the Arkansas National Guard—removing them from Governor Faubus's control. The Guard was ordered to protect the black students. President Eisenhower spoke on national TV to explain his use of federal troops in a state problem. He said that he could not allow a continuation of mob rule and demagogic extremists overruling a federal court order.

September 25: With the 101st Airborne in control the situation was changed. The Little Rock Nine met at Daisy Bates's house. They were then escorted to school in a convoy of jeeps with machine guns fore and aft. At the school, 350 paratroopers of the 101st lined the streets in front of the high school. Once in the school, each student was assigned a soldier as a bodyguard. At day's end, paratroopers escorted the nine back to Daisy Bates's house.

September 27: Governor Faubus spoke on statewide TV. He said that Little Rock was "occupied."

September 30: The 101st Airborne Troops were withdrawn to Camp Robinson and the federalized Arkansas National Guard was left to maintain order at the school The mob was gone.

October: The Little Rock "crisis" appeared to be over but Governor Faubus still refused to cooperate. He falsely accused federal troops of entering the girls' restrooms at Central High. Six hundred segregationists who were Faubus supporters met at the Central Baptist Church to pray for the governor and for troop withdrawal.

At first, the nine students experienced some friendliness as most of the more racist students had withdrawn to protest integration. When they returned, harassment returned and bothered the nine for the whole school year. There were anonymous phone calls to the students' homes threatening violence. The nine suffered oral abuse, spitting and threats from racist students. They refused to react, with the exception of one student. In December, Minniejean Brown was in the cafeteria line in front of a white student who had been following her saying, "Nigger, Nigger, Nigger." Minniejean took her chili bowl and dumped it over the boy's head. There was a moment of silence and then the help—all black—broke into applause. At another time a white girl called Minniejean a "nigger bitch" and she called the white girl "white trash." For these improprieties Minniejean was suspended and then expelled. Minniejean transferred to a high school in New York City with much publicity unfavorable to Arkansas. The other eight students completed the 1957–58 school year with no major incidents.

Governor Faubus's prime agenda continued to be getting reelected. Toward that end he continued to joust against the federal government. He said, "I stand now and always in opposition to integration by force or at bayonet point." In July 1958, he succeeded. He won the nomination for a third term as governor with 69 percent of the vote. In September 1958, the U.S. Supreme Court ruled that Little Rock must continue to desegregate its schools.

A few days later, Governor Faubus closed down the schools to assert his opposition to federal intervention. Little Rock public schools remained closed throughout the 1958–59 school year. The Supreme Court ruled again that closing the high school was unconstitutional and "evasive schemes" could not be employed to avoid integration. The schools were reopened on an integrated basis in August 1959.

The Little Rock confrontation was the first on-site news extravaganza of twentieth century television. Faubus is remembered for his racist extremism and his use of the National Guard to bar students from class. The names of Daisy Bates and the nine courageous students are less well known. On November 9, 1999, President Clinton awarded the Congressional Gold Medal to the nine: Melba Patillo Beals, Ernest Green, Jefferson Thomas, Carlotta Walls Lanier, Minniejean Brown Trickey, Thelma Mothershead Wair, Gloria Ray Karlmark, Elizabeth Eckford and Terrance Roberts. The NAACP honored Daisy Bates and all nine students with their Spingarn Medal.

Miami Lunch Counter Sit-Ins, FL, 1959

In September 1959, the Congress of Racial Equality conducted a 16-day workshop in Miami on the theory and tactics of nonviolent action. It was called the September Action Institute. Dr. M. L. King assisted in the training at one of the sessions. During the workshop the students inaugurated a sit-in at the lunch counter of the Jackson-Byron's Department Store. After a week of the sit-in, the management closed the lunch counters while they decided what to do.

On September 19, 1959, the Jackson's-Byron's representative informed CORE that Negroes would be served beginning September 21. On September 21, four black CORE activists went to the store's lunch counter and were refused service! On September 23, the CORE reactivated their sit-in. The lunch counter had 40 seats. CORE had 40 sitters from 10:00 A.M. to 3:00 P.M. On September 25, the Miami police began to harass and arrest the CORE sitters and local white racists attacked some of the protestors. The sit-in was disrupted.

The students at the institute also sat in at the lunch counter of Grant's Department Store. As many as 40 activists sat from three to six hours daily until the institute ended on September 20. The Grant's Store closed rather than serve blacks.

In addition to Miami, there were sit-ins in the late 1950s in 15 other cities—mostly in border states. There were sit-ins in St. Louis, Missouri; Wichita and Kansas City, Kansas; Oklahoma City, Enid, Tulsa and Stillwater, Oklahoma; Lexington and Louisville, Kentucky; Charleston, West Virginia; Sumter, South Carolina; East St. Louis, Illinois; Nashville, Tennessee; Atlanta, Georgia; and Durham, North Carolina. These sit-ins were planned and conducted by (1) NAACP Youth Councils, (2) the CORE working with the NAACP, (3) the Fellowship of Reconciliation and (4) the Durham Committee on Negro Affairs. Many of the advisors to the NAACP Youth Councils were women.

These 16 sit-ins of the late '50s worked out the most effective procedures and led to another long series of sit-ins in 1960. The black communities throughout the country knew about these sit-ins through their networks of black news media, the activist organizations, and their ministers and churches. The white culture became aware of the sit-in movement primarily with news of the Greensboro Four.

Greensboro Lunch Counter Sit-Ins, NC, 1960

In January 1960, four freshmen in the black Agricultural and Technical College (A&T) in Greensboro, North Carolina, had another bull session. The four, Ezell Blair, Franklin McCain, Joseph McNeill and David Richmond, discussed the situation of blacks in American society and what could be done about it. They ended the bull session by challenging each other to translate their beliefs into action. Each one accepted the challenge. The next morning, February 1, the four dressed up and went downtown to the Woolworth's variety store in Greensboro. They bought some toothpaste and school supplies and kept the receipts. Then they took seats at the whites-only lunch counter and awaited service. The store patrons and employees were amazed to see such a flagrant violation of Jim Crow mores. The waitress said: "Fellows like you make our race look bad" and refused to serve them. The young men asked why Woolworth's would sell them toothpaste but not coffee. They sat at the counter long enough for a forewarned local reporter to observe the confrontation and write an item for the local paper.

News of the incident spread quickly. The next day, 23 more A&T students joined the sit-in. On the third day there were 80 protesters. By the end of the week there were 400 demonstrators including students from Bennett, the black women's college, and Dudley High School. There were even some students from Greensboro's white colleges. A second sit-in was launched at S.H. Kress—the other downtown variety store with a lunch counter. A Student Executive Committee for Justice was organized to manage the protest.

The four students were knowledgeable about apartheid from the black's point of view. They had been educated by their parents, ministers and teachers to understand the importance of the struggle for freedom. The Greensboro NAACP had proactive leadership. The NAACP youth group met weekly to discuss the movement. Students from Little Rock, Arkansas, had told them about their experiences. The Montgomery, Alabama, boycott was discussed. In 1959, Dr. King visited Greensboro and stimulated the students' enthusiasm for action. Thurgood Marshall, national counsel for the NAACP, spoke at Bennett College, a women's school in the heart of the Greensboro ghetto. He also stimulated the student activists and warned them against accepting any offer of "token integration."

The sit-ins raised the issue of segregation and prominent officials and groups were prompted to comment. North Carolina Governor Luther Hodges said that sit-ins were counterproductive and a threat to law and order. Attorney General Malcolm Seawell urged store owners to invoke trespass laws and arrest the demonstrators. McNeill Smith, chairman of the State Advisory Committee of the Civil Rights Commission, urged equal treatment of all lunch counter customers. Frank Graham, former president of the University of North Carolina, said that "in sitting-in demonstrators are standing up for the American dream." The presidents of two black colleges, Warmoth Gibbs of A&T and Willa Player of Bennett, were able to resist white pressures to "discipline" the student activists and supported their right to demonstrate. The North Carolina AFL-CIO passed a resolution in support of the sit-ins at their state convention. The North Carolina Council of Churches endorsed the sit-ins and commended the Negro citizens for their self-restraint. In Greensboro the sit-ins were supported by the Greensboro Council of Church Women, the YWCA, the Unitarian Fellowship and two ministerial associations. Even the *Greensboro Daily News* supported the sit-ins. The movement had broad support from Greensboro blacks and from the Congress of Racial Equality (CORE) which began to organize sympathy boycotts of Woolworth and Kress stores in northern cities. The store managers refused to serve the students but they did not call the police. Whites heckled the students but the students maintained their decorum.

On April 2, the two stores closed their lunch counters. The students responded by organizing a consumer boycott of the stores. They picketed the stores and they also increased their demands to include desegregation of all eating places in Greensboro. The pickets attracted Ku Klux Klan counterpickets but there was no violence. The Kress manager tried a new tactic. He reopened his lunch counter but tried to control access to it within the store. It didn't work. The activists moved in and sat down. The manager called the police and 45 students, including three of the original four, were arrested and taken to jail. However, they were all quickly released without bail.

As the sit-ins continued, pressure on the mayor to "do something" increased. In February, Mayor George Roach appointed a special committee headed by Edward R. Zane of Burlington Industries. The committee consisted of representatives of the Merchants' Association, the Chamber of Commerce and the city council. Zane's committee was in general agreement with the Woolworth's argument that the store should "abide by local custom" and not change its practices until the majority of the community agreed. In accord with that reasoning, Zane sent out 5,000 letters to citizens asking their opinion. By mid–March he had received 2,000 replies with 73 percent favoring equality of service. The committee saw this response as evidence that there was no massive public support for integrating lunch counters.

The negotiations continued for several months with no progress. The two sides had quite different understandings of the situation. Many members of the white Establishment strongly believed in "good race relations" and they mistook ritualistic deference as an authentic expression of blacks' attitudes toward them. They did not understand that the students were serious, had the full support of the black community and would not compromise their constitutional rights. The students saw that progress was not being made and intensified their demonstrations and tightened their boycott.

The sit-in formula included several tactics: arousing public opinion against segregation, challenging government officials to enforce the constitutional rights of citizens, threatening the "good name" of the city and economic pressure. In Greensboro, as in many other cases, it was the economic pressure that finally opened the lunch counters. The sit-in plus boycott was effective. Woolworth's manager C.L. Harris estimated that blacks were only five percent of his customers but their loss was multiplied several times by the number of white customers who were scared away by picketing. In 1960, Woolworth's sales in Greensboro declined 20 percent and profits declined by 50 percent.

In June, C.L. Harris called Mayor Roach and told him that something had to be done as his business was going to pot. The manager of Kress had also suffered financially and was ready to capitulate. The manager of the third largest store, Meyer's Department Store, also agreed to settle. An agreement was made that without public notice a few Negroes at a time would be served at their counters. On July 25, 1960, the first black ate a meal at Woolworth's. Within a few weeks, hundreds were served at the three stores and no one protested.

The Greensboro sit-ins were well reported by both the black and white press and were followed by an explosion of similar protests. The Southern Regional Council (an organization of blacks and whites that promoted improved race relations) reported on sit-ins in 1961. During 1960 there were approximately 70 sit-ins in southern cities. All southern and border states had been affected by these demonstrations and 70,000 people had participated in them. They were primarily students from nearby black colleges. High school students also participated in Greensboro and High Point, North Carolina, and Nashville, Tennessee. Following are some of the 1960 sit-ins and their leaders:

1. Winston-Salem, North Carolina. Leaders were: Floyd McKissick, the Rev. Douglas Moore and Gordon Carey.
2. High Point, North Carolina. Leader: the Rev. B. Elton Cox.
3. Rock Hill, South Carolina. Leader: the Rev. C. A. Ivory.
4. Orangeburg, South Carolina. Leader: James McCain.
5. Sumter, South Carolina. Leader: James McCain.
6. Petersburg, Virginia. Leader: the Rev. Wyatt Walker.
7. Montgomery, Alabama. Leader: the Rev. Ralph Abernathy.
8. Marshall, Texas. Participants came from Bishop and Wyler Colleges.
9. Birmingham, Alabama. Leader: the Rev. Fred Shuttlesworth.
10. Little Rock, Arkansas. Leader: Daisy Bates.
11. Tallahassee, Florida. Leader: Patricia Due.
12. Raleigh, North Carolina. Student leader: William H. Peace.
13. Nashville, Tennessee. Leaders: the Rev. James Lawson and the Rev. Kelly Miller Smith.

The Greensboro sit-in was frequently referred to as the "beginning" of the youth-led sit-in movement. Actually, it was not the first. There were more than a dozen lunch counter sit-ins in 1959 conducted by NAACP Youth Councils, CORE and the FOR. Those sit-ins were studied by movement leaders and their tactics were refined. That is how the Greensboro four knew how to dress, how to react to harassment, how to use the press, how to express their demands and how to plan, expand and maintain their pressure on the store owner. If the Greensboro Four had not "started" the 1960 sit-in series when they did, it would have been started the following week by Nashville students.

Nashville Lunch Counter Sit-Ins, TN, 1960

Nashville, Tennessee had four Negro colleges: Fisk University, Tennessee State, Meharry Medical and the Baptist Seminary. It also had a center for training in nonviolent action with three civil rights leaders in residence: James Lawson, Diane Nash and John Lewis. Lawson was a native of the north, the son of a Methodist minister.

During the Korean War he spent time in prison as a conscientious objector. He visited India and studied the nonviolent methods of Mohandas K. Gandhi. He was a member of the Fellowship of Reconciliation (FOR). In 1957, at age 27, he went to Nashville as the FOR's southern field secretary. Nash was an English major at Fisk University. John Lewis, the son of an Alabama farm family, was a student at Baptist Seminary.

Lawson called a meeting at the First Baptist Church to share information on the Greensboro sit-in. About 500 students showed up. Their mood was one of impatience to get going. Lawson tried to caution them to go slow, to build up a bond fund first and to get more training in the techniques of nonviolent action. The students would not agree to any delay so Lawson gave them a quickie course in nonviolent action. He told them how to dress, how to avoid arrest for loitering, how to react to taunts and threats. He also explained the logistics of a sit-in, how to schedule shifts and move participants in and out, etc.

The next morning, February 6, 1960, the Nashville sit-in was launched. Volunteer drivers picked up the students from the four colleges and brought them to the First Baptist Church 500 strong. They marched to the downtown stores, sat down at the lunch counters and waited for service. For them, there was no service.

It was a standoff for a couple of weeks and then, on February 26, 1960, the Nashville chief of police announced that the grace period was over. If the sit-ins were not stopped the participants would be arrested for trespassing and disorderly conduct. This announcement forced the activists to shift gears. John Lewis worked all night to prepare lists of do's and don'ts to help the students prepare for incarceration. The list ended with the admonition, "Remember the teachings of Jesus Christ, Gandhi, Thoreau and Martin Luther King Jr."

The next morning the students marched downtown to their assigned stores, each one clutching a copy of Lewis' nonviolent action guide. Racist white youths taunted the students with calls of "nigger." The police allowed some of the whites to attack the unresisting students with rocks, fists and lighted cigarettes, and then moved in and arrested 75 Negroes, including John Lewis, and five whites. The students appeared before a judge on February 29, 1960. Diane Nash, the civil rights activist from Chicago, was the students' spokeswoman. She said: "We feel that if we pay these fines we would be contributing to and supporting the injustice and immoral practices that have been performed in the arrest and conviction of the defendants." Nash, Lewis and 14 students were then led off to jail. Then the rest of the students decided to take jail instead of paying a fine that supported the apartheid system they detested.

Negro observers were shocked to see their city imprison some of the best students in the area instead of the racist hoodlums who attacked them. James Bevel, a nonviolent action instructor, reacted by organizing another wave of student protestors who followed the same route to the same jail.

The Nashville mayor, Ben West, decided to resolve the impasse. He offered to release the jailed students and appoint a biracial committee to make recommendations about apartheid practices in stores if the students would halt the demonstration.

It was agreed. Diane Nash, John Lewis, James Bevel and all of the students emerged from jail as local heroes. They had forced a southern city to concede on one of the major goals of the civil rights revolution. But their celebration was short. They read in the *New York Times* that the trustees of Vanderbilt University had expelled James Lawson from their divinity school without a hearing and without faculty approval. Nearly 400 Vanderbilt faculty members resigned in protest. Lawson was reinstated. Nash celebrated the victory by leading a band of activists to the lunch counter of the Greyhound bus terminal, which had not been covered in the agreement with the mayor. To the surprise of everyone, the students were served without incident. Another victory!

Greensboro and Nashville were well publicized and set the pattern for those that followed: good preparation, surprise action, mass meetings in churches, well-disciplined activists, wise use of the media and adherence to the principles of non-violent action. The Greensboro and Nashville sit-ins led the wave of direct-action protests that marked the early 1960s. By the end of 1960, sit-ins had been staged by civil rights activists in about 70 southern cities. About one-third of them led to the desegregation of lunch counters. It is estimated that 60,000 to 70,000 activists participated in sit-ins, making this campaign the most massive demonstration of opposition to U.S. apartheid that the country had yet seen. Greensboro and Nashville continued a generational shift in the black campaign for democracy. Although they received the endorsement of both the NAACP and CORE, both the Greensboro and Nashville sit-ins were student initiated and student implemented.

Tallahassee Lunch Counter Sit-Ins, FL, 1960

Two co-ed sisters, Patricia and Priscilla Stephens, attended a CORE workshop in Miami, Florida, in 1959. They learned the tactics and psychology of sit-ins and practiced them at the Royal Castle lunch counter. In the fall they returned to Tallahassee to attend the Florida Agricultural and Mechanical University (FAMU). They now had a mission to accelerate the process of desegregation.

In Tallahassee they joined Daisy Young, NAACP campus advisor, James T. McCain and Gordon Carey, CORE field secretaries; C.K. Steele, leader of the Tallahassee bus boycott; three local clergymen; and two FAMU professors. They organized a CORE chapter with 20 charter members. The chapter's first action was to test the status of bus desegregation that the Rev. Steele had sought for 18 months. A group of students boarded a bus and took seats up front. Nothing happened! The bus was desegregated.

The next CORE project was to study segregation practices in Tallahassee to provide a basis for their intended action. The study verified what they all knew from personal experience—segregation, although illegal, was widespread.

CORE's next move was a "dress rehearsal" sit-in to show sympathy with the Greensboro students and to finalize their protest training program. On February 13,

1960, ten FAMU students and two high school students, all neatly dressed and carrying books, entered Woolworth's and sat at the lunch counter. Signs on the wall advertised sundaes for 25¢ and a roast turkey dinner for 85¢. The students ordered cake. Their reception was what they had trained for—cool and insulting. The waitress expressed surprise and refused to serve them. While some whites passed by, other hoodlum whites taunted the students with threats, challenges and the epithet of "nigger." The sitters kept their noses in their books and refused to react. The hoodlums' threats intensified and the store manager closed the counter. The students continued to sit until reporters came by to see what was going on—and then they left.

The second sit-in was held a week later—also on a Saturday to accommodate the students' class schedules. On February 20, 1960, at 2:00 P.M., 19 people entered Woolworth's. There were fourteen FAMU students; two high school students (Charles and Henry Steele, sons of the Rev. C.K. Steele); Mary Gains, a citizen activist; and two white observers. They mounted the stools and awaited service.

The waitress was distraught. A crowd of white men gathered and commenced abuse. They taunted the sitters and threatened and called them "niggers." After about 45 minutes the observers left. Then the mayor of Tallahassee, several city commissioners and five policemen arrived. The mayor asked the sitters to leave. Six students left. Priscilla Stephens, the group's designated spokesperson, responded that they would leave after they were served.

The police arrested the remaining eleven activists for "engaging in riotous conduct" and marched them to the police station. The protestors were fingerprinted and processed by the officers who taunted and tried to intimidate them. Bail was set at $500 per person. There was no local attorney who would represent the group, but the CORE obtained legal assistance from the ACLU and the NAACP in Miami. The trial was first set for March 3, but when FAMU students voted to skip classes to attend the trial, the judge postponed it to March 17.

The CORE tried again to negotiate desegregated lunch counters with Woolworth's and McCrory's but made no progress. On March 12, 1960, they launched a third sit-in aimed at both stores. On this attempt, the CORE was assisted by white students from Florida State University (FSU). Twelve students—both black and white—went to the Woolworth's lunch counter. They were all immediately arrested and marched to the police station in interracial pairs. Onlookers jeered the file and called the whites "nigger-lovers." The FAMU-CORE sent a replacement group of students to Woolworth's. They were met by an armed group of White Citizens Council members who threatened them and prevented them from entering the store. The students stood in front of the store and chanted "no violence, no violence." It was a stand-off.

Another group of students was dispatched to McCrory's lunch counter. The police were waiting and arrested them and took them to the police station. When this setback was reported to the FAMU-CORE headquarters, they implemented an alternative tactic. They launched a march to protest the arrests of the students. Several hundred students commenced a two-mile march from the FAMU campus to the downtown. They carried placards that read: "No Violence," "We Will Not Fight Mobs," We Are Americans Too" and "Give Us Back Our Students."

At the railroad tracks the marchers were met by a line of police officers with anti-riot gear. The police halted the march and then attacked the marchers with tear gas. The march was thrown into confusion. There were shouts, screams, cries and sobbing. The students, most of whom had no training for this treatment and were now blinded, sought refuge in a nearby church. Many were treated at the FAMU hospital. The police arrested 35 of the demonstrators and took them to the police station.

On March 17, 1960, the trial of the eleven activists arrested after the second sit-in was held. The Stephens sisters and nine others were charged with "disturbing the peace." By any measure the trial was more a farce than a search for truth. The judge made racist remarks and accused the students and CORE of being Communists without mention of any evidence. It was a typical segregated trial in the segregated South. All the activists were found guilty and given a choice of a $300 fine or 60 days in jail. Three defendants paid their fines. The Stephens sisters and six other students chose not to pay the fines and so support the apartheid system. This was the first time in the student sit-in movement that students refused to pay fines to protest the unjust system. The eight pioneers were Patricia and Priscilla Stephens, Henry M. Steele (age 16), Barbara and John Broxton, Angelins Nance, Clement Carney and William Larkins.

Once in prison the group was not forgotten. Dr. Martin Luther King Jr. sent a telegram congratulating them on their courage and willingness to suffer in the cause of freedom. Hundreds of Tallahassee residents—Negro, white, students and community members—visited the jail to express their support. In March, Jackie Robinson, the baseball hero, published a letter from Patricia in his weekly column in the *New York Post*. To protest the jailing, the Tallahassee CORE sponsored a boycott of downtown businesses that supported apartheid.

In the meantime, the white Establishment continued its vendetta against blacks. The Rev. Dan Speed and the Rev. T.S. Johnson suffered vandalism. Supplies were cut off to Speed's grocery store. Johnson's car windshield was smashed by a concrete block. In jail, the activists kept their spirits up by singing.

On May 5, 1960, after 49 days in Leon County Jail, the remaining five were released. Two Stephens sisters, John and Barbara Boxton and William Larkin were free from detention but not free to eat at Tallahassee lunch counters, which were still segregated. The CORE immediately signed Patricia and Priscilla to a summer-long national publicity and fund-raising tour. In the short run, the Tallahassee lunch counter sit-ins were a failure. In the longer run, they were successful. In 1963, Tallahassee's lunch counters were desegregated. It takes a few years for a culture to reverse its fundamental concepts and values.

Baton Rouge Lunch Counter Sit-Ins, LA, 1961

In the spring of 1961, 16 students in Baton Rouge, Louisiana, decided to do their part in the black peoples' campaign for civil rights. They dressed in their Sunday best and went to three lunch counters to get a bite to eat and do their bit for democracy. They challenged the lunch counters in the Kress Department Store, a drug store and in a bus station. At all three counters the results were the same. They were refused service. The proprietor asked them to leave. They refused. They were arrested and hauled off to jail. They were charged with violating a state law and forbid any act that "would foreseeably disturb or alarm the public." The court combined the cases into one called *Garner v. Louisiana*, named for the alleged ringleader of the students. The 16 students were found guilty and each one was sentenced to 30 days in jail and a fine of $100. They appealed their case to the Louisiana Supreme Court, which upheld their conviction.

And then Thurgood Marshall and the NAACP Legal Defense and Educational Fund took charge of the case. Marshall and Company submitted a petition for a writ of certiorari to the U.S. Supreme Court. In their brief they argued that the state Supreme Court's decision affirmed a criminal conviction based on no evidence of criminal actions and was therefore in conflict with the recent U.S. Supreme Court decisions. They argued that the 16 youths were convicted under a statute that was so vague, indefinite and uncertain as to offend the concept of "due process of law" that was protected by the Fourteenth Amendment. Marshall's team also attacked the use of the state statue concerning "disturbing the peace" to enforce racial segregation in public facilities. The U.S. Supreme Court considered Marshall's argument and on December 11, 1961, rendered its decision. The convictions of all 16 students were unanimously reversed.

This case illustrates a pattern that was frequently repeated. It was started by spontaneous action by black students. The Establishment's initial reaction was to use its legal system to deny justice. The NAACP's legal arm took the case to a higher, nonracist court and justice prevailed. This was the last case in which Thurgood Marshall participated as the leader of the NAACP Legal Defense and Educational Fund team.

Desegregation of Savannah, GA, 1960–1963

Savannah, in 1960, was Georgia's oldest city, one of its largest and certainly its most beautiful. It was known for its gracious old mansions (General Sherman spared the city in his destructive march) and its mignon municipal parks. It was also known for its attitude of self-assurance and its conscious enjoyment of beauty. But, like the rest of Georgia, it was an apartheid society overdue for transformation to democracy. When young blacks learned about the lunch counter sit-ins in Greensboro, North Carolina, they were stimulated to action.

On March 16, 1960, several black students sat down at eight lunch counters in downtown stores. They announced that they would not move until they were served. Three students were arrested. Black leaders met and planned a desegregation push. They called for a total boycott of downtown stores. They demanded (1) service to all customers, (2) employment of blacks above the menial level, (3) desegregation of drinking fountains and rest rooms, and (4) addressing blacks with courtesy titles. On Easter, the blacks wore last year's clothes rather than patronize local stores. The boycott was continued from March 1960 to July 1961.

Meanwhile, the students were busy challenging all segregated facilities. They conducted "wade-ins" at all-white public beaches, "kneel-ins" at all-white Christian churches, "ride-ins" on municipal buses and "stand-ins" at theaters. Some blacks took a "plunge-in" at the all-white swimming pool in Daffin Park. They even had "piss-ins" at segregated restrooms.

Six youths did a "play-in" at a basketball court in Daffin Park. They were all immediately arrested and convicted. The convictions carried a fine of $100 and five months in prison. A lawsuit was filed that challenged the boys' convictions. The case went to the U.S. Supreme Court, which found the convictions unconstitutional.

In June 1961, there was a break in the Establishment's previously solid front. The Savannah bus company promised to hire black drivers for some of its routes. The boycott continued, however, and five major stores that refused to integrate went bankrupt. By October 1961, the downtown merchants had had enough. They persuaded the city officials to negotiate with the blacks. The officials agreed to desegregate buses, golf courses and restaurants in return for the blacks lifting the boycott. The movie theater was also desegregated but the manager was subject to so much pressure from his patrons that he resegregated it in June 1963.

In August 1963, city officials announced a second desegregation agreement. This agreement was followed and the NAACP canceled a planned Christmas season boycott. School desegregation followed. In September 1963, 12 black students enrolled as seniors at Savannah High School and seven entered the Robert W. Groves High School in West Chatham County. The long campaign for civil rights and civil freedom was finally over—but it had not been a picnic. Several protestors had faced police dogs and tear gas; some were roughed up; some were jailed with very high bonds. One activist leader, Hosea Williams, spent 65 days in jail. One store was burned. Seventy-five arrests were made in one night in July. At one time the city banned all marches and Governor Carl Sanders placed the National Guard on alert. Most tragic was the case of Benjamin Van Clark. He was a 19-year-old who headed the youth division of the Chatham County Crusade for Voting (CCCV). He led as many as three marches downtown in one day. He was jailed 25 times, then after a march in July 1963 he disappeared.

The Savannah desegregation campaign won a significant number of civil rights without the help of Dr. King. King had offered to help but he was asked to stay away as the local leaders were making good progress. Neither was there any assistance from Washington, which did not offer to help. The question arises, "How did they do it?" One answer is strong leadership.

The blacks had a strong leader in Westley Wallace Law, head of the Savannah chapter of the NAACP. His job as a postal worker put him in touch with people throughout the city and he worked nights and weekends to guide the campaign. He used a telephone tree to maintain contact with his community. Another key leader was Hosea Williams, a chemist with the U.S. Department of Agriculture. He delivered inspiring speeches and kept the black community working as a team. He led night marches in 1963 and led the CCCV. A second reason was that the whites also had superior leadership. The mayor was Malcolm Maclean, a moderate who was elected with the help of a block of black votes. He recognized that support and appointed a black to each city council board or commission. A third reason was economic power. The purchasing power of the blacks was that of one-third of the city population—sufficient to make a business fail if it was withheld. A fourth reason was voting power. In 1960, 57 percent of eligible black citizens were registered to vote—a higher percentage than among whites.

Desegregation went so well—in comparison with some other southern cities—that when Dr. Martin Luther King Jr. gave a New Year's address in Savannah Municipal Auditorium in 1964 he praised Savannah as "the most desegregated city south of the Mason-Dixon line."

Desegregation of Atlanta, GA, 1960–1961

Students at Atlanta University and Morehouse College in Atlanta, Georgia, learned about student sit-ins in other cities and decided to do the same. Their first step was to ask their professors for guidance. They recommended a low-key, diplomatic approach. The students agreed and two of them, Rosyln Pope and Julian Bond, drafted an "Appeal for Human Rights" which they delivered to Atlanta city officials.

The officials did not reply so the students decided to try nonviolent action. During March 1960, the students, led by Lonnie King, drew up plans for a civil rights campaign focused on lunch counter sit-ins and boycotts of segregated downtown stores. The spring of 1960 was spent in organizing the students, conducting nonviolent action training and in making trial runs. In the fall they were ready to roll. They launched a sit-in and boycott campaign designed to desegregate Atlanta.

As the campaign proceeded, a generation gap appeared in the black society. Older black leaders were opposed to the campaign. Many of them had received small favors or courtesies from the Establishment and, like the university and college professors, they advocated go-slowism. This opposition from their own people dismayed the students. They decided to ask Dr. King for assistance. They knew that he was the spiritual leader of the movement and believed that he could lead them to victory. Dr. King was reluctant to help the students. He had multiple demands on his time and his own father, Daddy King, was one of the old guard that opposed the campaign. But they pleaded and he relented and agreed to support them. When he joined them he explained to the press that the protest was student planned and student implemented. King's first month with the students was much more energy- and time-consuming than he had anticipated. On October 19, 1960, Dr. King and 75 students launched what one reporter called "the Second Battle of Atlanta." They set up boycott picket lines and established sit-ins at major downtown stores. King joined the sit-in at Rich's Snack Bar. The police were called and they arrested Dr. King and the students for trespassing. The students were shoved into a paddy wagon and taken to jail. King was put into a cell with Lonnie King, Bernard Lee and several students in Fulton County Jail.

King refused to post a $500 bond. He told a *Life* reporter: "In order to serve as a redemption agent for the nation, to arouse the conscience of the opponent, you go to jail and you stay. You don't pay the fine and you don't pay the bail. You are not to subvert or disrespect the law. You have broken a law which is out of line with the moral law and you are willing to suffer the consequences by serving the time."

The nation knew of King's incarceration and many were concerned. Senator John F. Kennedy telephoned Atlanta Mayor Hartsfield and asked if King's constitutional rights were being observed. The mayor then announced that he had talked with Senator Kennedy and on his recommendation he had reached an agreement with the student leaders. King and all of the other imprisoned Negroes would be released, the students would cease demonstrations and the mayor would negotiate the desegregation of lunch counters with the Atlanta stores.

This announcement was an attempt to finesse an agreement. It didn't quite work. The protests stopped temporarily and the students were freed. But Dr. King was not. Officials in neighboring DeKalb County intervened. They asked that Dr. King be transferred to KeKalb County to be tried for violation of probation. He had been convicted of a minor traffic violation by a racist judge, Oscar Mitchell, several months earlier. KeKalb County was known as being KKK infected. Negroes there had gone to jail and were never seen again.

On Monday morning, October 24, Dr. King was picked up by DeKalb County sheriff's deputies and taken to face Judge Mitchell again. On October 25, the judge found King guilty of violating his parole and sentenced him to four months at hard labor in a Georgia public works camp. Bail was denied and the judge said that any appeal had to be quick as he was going on a fishing vacation. Dr. King's colleagues, family and supporters throughout the country were stunned by the severity of the punishment.

That night several men went into the cell where Dr. King was sleeping with other prisoners. They told him to get dressed. They put handcuffs on his wrists and chains on his legs and took him out to a sheriff's car. The car drove off into the night. King asked the deputies where they were going but they did not answer. After several hours they pulled up at the gates of a prison. A sign announced "Reidsville Penitentiary." The deputies took King to a small room and outfitted him with a prison uniform with green stripes on the pant legs. Then they took him down a long corridor and shoved him into a cell reserved for dangerous criminals. King had cockroaches for cellmates. The food was bad. He caught a cold and lay shivering and hacking on his bunk.

Meanwhile, the Kennedys were busy. Senator Kennedy phoned Coretta King and promised that he would do what he could to help her husband. Robert Kennedy phoned Judge Mitchell and discussed the adverse publicity surrounding King's imprisonment. After the conversation Judge Mitchell reversed his decision and ordered King to be released on bond. King was released on October 28. At the Fulton County line his motorcade was stopped by a welcoming party of a hundred students, veterans of the Atlanta sit-ins. King greeted the students and they sang *We Shall Overcome*. The next stop of the motorcade was at Atlanta's Ebenezer Church, where 800 people and press representatives greeted King with songs and prayers.

The students managed the sit-ins and boycotts with discipline. The Atlanta police did not employ excessive violence. Many Atlanteans were concerned about the image of a city "too busy to hate." The blacks' campaign was effective. White owners of 13 corporations closed more than 70 downtown stores for three months, December 1960 and January and February 1961. About 500 Negroes were laid off. Pressures for a settlement were strong on both sides.

When Mayor Hartsfield failed in his attempt to broker an agreement, he stepped aside to let the white businessmen do the negotiating. The black leaders who negotiated were old guard, including Daddy King. The white negotiators represented the all-white chamber of commerce and lawyers who represented 50 downtown stores. Two students attended the negotiations. On March 7, 1961, a proposed agreement for the desegregation of Atlanta was published. It was in the form of a contract. The agreement, worded in legalese, was designed to promise desegregation without admitting that segregation existed. The agreement provided that the stores would desegregate their lunch counters within 30 days after Atlanta schools began to accept Negroes in September. The boycott would cease immediately. Students in jail would be released and all charges against them would be dropped.

When they learned the details of the contract, the students and their supporters in the black community were disappointed and angry. They felt that they had demonstrated, been arrested and jailed and lost jobs all for the goal of immediate desegregation, not for legalistic promises. They knew that seven years after *Brown v. Board of Education* Atlanta schools were still segregated. A mass meeting was held in a black church to discuss the agreement. Daddy King explained and defended the contract. Some student leaders rejected the contract and called for a resumption of demonstrations. There were boos and hoots as the old guard blacks lost control of the meeting. The agreement appeared doomed. Just then, a late arrival took the pulpit. Dr. King looked over the audience for a full minute and then began to speak in his rhythmic and compelling tones. He praised the endurance and contributions of his father's generation. He praised the students for their initiatives and discipline. Then he presented his reasons for accepting the agreement. It was the first written contract Atlanta Negroes had ever extracted from the white man. They had waited

100 years for justice, so maybe they could wait five more months. "If the contract is broken, it will be a disaster and a disgrace. If anyone breaks the contract, let it be the white man." King then walked out leaving the crowd becalmed and thoughtful. The boycotts stopped. The sit-ins stopped. That fall, the Atlanta schools accepted Negroes and the downtown stores and hotels desegregated their lunch counters.

The Atlanta students' desegregation campaign was a success. It effectively dismantled the apartheid system as required by the supreme court decision. Atlanta police played their role without excessive violence. Dr. King received rough treatment but that was in another county known for excessive racism. The awakening interest of Washington was notable. Political analysts say that Senator Kennedy's telephone calls saved King from a sentence of hard labor on a questionable traffic violation. This help won a large percentage of the black vote which helped Kennedy win a close race against Vice President Richard M. Nixon.

Desegregation of College Station, TX, 1959–1961

College Station, Texas, the home of Texas A&M University, had separate and inferior schools for blacks. The University was de facto segregated. It did not encourage attendance by blacks, Hispanics or women. In 1958, the YMCA assigned a new secretary, Carl Zitlow, to its College Station office. Zitlow and his wife, Madge, were white progressives and sensitive to the bifurcated society and wished to help heal it. They worked hard in an effort to establish a community improvement association with a broad base of membership. They succeeded in organizing a small interracial group with an interest in promoting desegregation. They were joined by the Rev. L.W. Flowers, the pastor of the College Station Black Baptist Church, two of his deacons, two white clergymen and one white university professor.

The Rev. Flowers provided the group with spiritual leadership, encouragement and continuity. He told the group, "After you pray it is necessary to get up off your knees and start moving toward the goal that you were praying for." The group met in members' homes to plan action. They decided to attend Sunday services at segregated churches as black and white visitors. They chose the Lutheran Church as the first target. The Lutheran minister was then the white co-chairman of the activists. Everything went smoothly. It seemed that desegregation had been successful. Not so. A fortnight later there was a meeting of the board of directors of the Lutheran Church and they voted to terminate the contract of their minister.

This was a surprise and disappointment but the project continued. The Lutheran minister was replaced by the Episcopal minister as the group's co-leader. They then went as a black-white group to the Episcopal Church on Sunday. Everything appeared to go well. But it didn't. A few days later the board of directors of the Episcopal Church voted to terminate their minister's contract! The group was disappointed but under the Rev. Flowers' leadership they were not about to quit. Instead, they elected a Texas A&M professor, F.O. Sargent, as the third white co-leader within one year and the project continued.

The Flowers group proposed to the white Baptist church, the largest white church in College Station, that it desegregate its summer bible school. The board of directors of the church listened to the proposal and then, to everyone's surprise, voted unanimously and without discussion to open the bible school to black children. They even provided a bus to haul the black children from their corner of town to the Baptist church. On the back of the bus was a large hand-painted sign: "All God's Children!"

The next target was the Catholic Church. The interracial group attended mass. Everything went smoothly but they did not desegregate the church for a very good reason. It was not segregated! Next, Flowers and company desegregated a public park. It was a part of the Texas A&M campus and was used by the white faculty and students for picnicking and cookouts. The university's director of buildings and grounds gave the group permission to use the park for a biracial watermelon bust. They brought a pick-up truckload of watermelons and invited the whole black community. Participants said that desegregation was never more relaxed and enjoyable.

Another significant success came with a minimum of effort. A white member of the group called the U.S. Post Office and asked if mail could be delivered to the black neighborhood just as it was to the white neighborhood. The Post Office manager agreed that it could and the mail delivery commenced.

Professor Sargent, the third white co-chairman of the group, sought to bring some desegregation to the university. At a professional biracial meeting at Prairie View, the black A&M College 40 miles south of College Station, he made a gesture. At lunchtime he joined the black professors in the blacks' dining room instead of going with his white colleagues to the whites' dining room. The black professors welcomed him and told him of their problems of inadequate funding. When he returned to College Station, Sargent reported the blacks' complaints to the dean of the university. His actions and reporting were not appreciated.

Dr. Tyrus R. Timm, Ph.D., Harvard, the chair of Sargent's Department of Agricultural Economics, called him in for a little talk. Dr. Timm suggested to Sargent that he conform to acceptable practices or move on. Unknown to Dr. Timm, Sargent was engaged in economic and historical research that documented illegal treatment of Hispanic settlers in Texas and the discriminatory treatments of black farmers. Sargent recognized that he was out of step with Texas A&M and accepted a position at the University of Guelph in Ontario, where he published his research on black Texas farmers.

A major desegregation occurred in 1961. One night, the dilapidated and poorly furnished black primary school mysteriously went up in flames. The white school officials decided that it was a propitious time to comply with *Brown v. Board of Education*. They quickly made arrangements to bus the black kids to the attractive, well furnished but previously all-white primary school. It was accomplished with no difficulty. Two years later, Texas A&M University began to admit blacks.

The desegregation of College Station was not reported in the regional and national media. Without arrests, violence or legal maneuvers it was not considered newsworthy. However, it was representative of many quiet, nonviolent desegregations that occurred throughout the country.

Sharecroppers Seek to Vote, TN, 1960–1961

Passage of the Civil Rights Act of 1957 stimulated blacks in many southern states to attempt to register to vote. They were under the impression that the 1957 law guaranteed them that right. In Fayette and Haywood counties, Tennessee, a number of blacks attempted to register. They ran into the usual roadblocks: rejection by the registrars by a number of ruses. They complained to the new Commission on Civil Rights, established by the 1957 Act. Some federal agents visited the counties to investigate the complaints. In March 1960, several white election aides in Fayette County resigned in protest against what they called unwanted probes by the FBI of blacks' registration complaints.

Two weeks later, the Civic and Welfare League recruited 70 blacks who registered to vote. Immediately the white merchants retaliated by launching a campaign to "starve out" 10,000 black sharecroppers by refusing to sell them gasoline to operate their tractors. This campaign and its effect were reported to the NAACP. The NAACP responded by asking its 350,000 members to boycott the gasoline companies; Texaco, Amoco and Esso-Standard. The NAACP also sent food and clothing to the farmers. The FBI began an investigation of the situation.

In August 1960, those blacks who had succeeded in registering voted for the first time and helped to elect Estes Kefauver, a pro-democracy politician, to the Senate. After that election, the NAACP negotiated with the oil companies and ended the boycott. The white merchants, however, continued to punish the blacks. They fired large numbers of black employees and evicted their black sharecroppers. In September, the Justice Department filed civil rights suits based on the 1957 Civil Rights Act against 27 white merchants and banks in Haywood County.

In December 1960, a delegation of Haywood and Fayette County black leaders appealed to President Eisenhower to send emergency food and gasoline to 300 sharecropper families who had been evicted from the land they worked. The evicted sharecroppers moved into Freedom Village, a tent city. During 1960 and 1961, thousands of pounds of food and clothing were sent to the evicted families by both black and white non-governmental organizations. Among the donors were the Chicago Greater Harvest Baptist Church, the AFL-CIO Executive Council, the United Packinghouse Workers of America and the NAACP.

The sharecroppers' experience in Fayette and Haywood counties provides examples of (1) the failure of the federal government to enforce federal laws, (2) the inhumane tactics employed by the Establishment and (3) the large number of segregated, exploited and disenfranchised black citizens under the apartheid system.

Hunter and Holmes Desegregate the University of Georgia, 1961

In 1957, the U.S. Congress established the U.S. Commission on Civil Rights. In November 1957, President Eisenhower appointed the commission members. The job of the commission was to implement the Supreme Court's school desegregating decision of *Brown v. Board of Education*. Unfortunately, the first commission members lacked the ethical values or the political savvy or both to carry out their assignment. Three years later, President Kennedy named Erwin Griswald and Spottswood Robinson III to the commission. Robinson was an NAACP lawyer and the dean of the Howard University Law School. These two appointments were calculated to provide a majority of commissioners with the will to implement the Supreme Court decision.

Establishment of a federal commission with a genuine interest in enforcing civil rights was one step toward school desegregation. Another requirement was the appearance of black students with academic qualifications and abundant courage to challenge the American institution of segregation. The candidates were forthcoming. In the fall of 1960 Charlayne Hunter and Hamilton Holmes applied for admission to the lily-white University of Georgia in Athens. The University of Georgia did not accept their applications but, fortunately, there was a federal commission with new blood. In Washington, DC, the Federal Commission on Civil Rights accused the federal government of using its own funds to perpetuate segregated colleges in six southern states. The commission also proposed a solution. They said that all federal funds should be withheld from any publicly supported college that practiced racial discrimination. Further support for Hunter and Holmes came from the judiciary. On January 6, 1961, District Court Judge W.A. Bootle ordered the University of Georgia to admit Hunter and Holmes immediately. In his order, the judge stated that the black students were qualified and would have been admitted except for their ethnicity.

These two incentives—the threat of federal funds being cut and the judge's order—forced Georgia governor Ernest Vandiver to rethink his opposition. He decided to renege on his promise to preserve segregation in all Georgia schools and permit the integration of the University of Georgia. Following the judge's order, Hunter and Holmes arrived at the University of Georgia campus on January 9, 1961. They were given a racist reception. The students' protest was massive and violent. Police were forced to use tear gas to break up 2,000 rioting students. To calm things down, the university administration suspended Hunter and Holmes "for their personal safety."

When the two students left it was the faculty's turn to take a stand. Three hundred faculty members signed a petition demanding that the administration reinstate the two students and give them full protection. The university administration agreed. Hunter and Holmes returned one week later to a more salubrious climate. The crowds were no more. They were treated with civility. Fifty University of Georgia student leaders distributed a handbill urging their colleagues to treat Hunter and Holmes with kindness. The student's attorney, Donald Hollowell, asked Judge Bootle to complete the desegregation of the university. The judge agreed and issued orders for the university to desegregate the dining rooms, the swimming pool and other facilities. Both Hunter and Holmes graduated two years later in 1963.

Charlayne Hunter is now Charlayne Hunter-Gault, a prominent TV journalist. Hamilton Holmes became a physician in Atlanta. He died in 1995.

At the time of their matriculation, the national media did not give the event much notice. It was peaceful, i.e. no one got killed, and so it was not very newsworthy. However, university administrators throughout the country did take notice and many followed suit. By the fall of 1961, the list of newly desegregated institutions included Georgia Tech in Atlanta; the University of Miami in Coral Gables, Florida; Wake Forest College in Winston-Salem, North Carolina; Duke University in Durham, North Carolina; the University of the South in Sewanee, Tennessee; Texas Technological University in Lubbock, Texas; and Guilford College in Greensboro, North Carolina. In 1962, Florida State University in Tallahassee and the University of Florida in Gainesville integrated. In 1963, Texas A&M University in College Station was integrated.

Freedom Riders—First Echelon, 1961

In 1946, the U.S. Supreme Court outlawed segregation on interstate buses and trains. In 1960, the court extended that ban to include bus and train terminals. However, the white Establishment of the country did not move to implement that decision. The nation's chief executive officer, the president, deferred to state authorities. Southern governors, sheriffs, judges and mayors continued to practice and enforce segregation. It was the established system that they preferred.

In May 1961, James Farmer, founder of the Congress of Racial Equality (CORE), decided to test compliance with the supreme court ruling. He planned a series of Freedom Bus rides through the South to physically desegregate bus stations. On May 4, a group of 13 blacks and whites boarded two buses, a Greyhound and a Trailways, and headed south. The first day they passed through Fredericksburg, Richmond and Petersburg, Virginia with no trouble. The second day they passed through Farmville in Prince Edward County, Virginia, where the county officials had transferred public schools to private operators to avoid desegregation. The black kids had no school for two years. All 13 riders obtained service without incident. They then went on to Lynchburg and Danville. At Danville they were not allowed in the bus waiting room but there was no violence and no arrests.

The next day, however, they ran into trouble. When the Freedom Riders stopped at the Greyhound terminal in Rock Hill, South Carolina, a gang of thugs set upon John Lewis and Albert Bigelow when they exited the bus. They punched and kicked and beat the non-violent riders. After two or three minutes, the local police captain moved in and stopped further beatings and asked Lewis and Bigelow if they wanted to press assault charges. They said, "No, it would not be in the spirit of nonviolence." The next stop was Atlanta, Georgia, where the riders enjoyed dinner with Martin L. King and Wyatt Walker, who congratulated them for completing more than half of their trip to New Orleans.

On May 14, the buses departed Atlanta and headed west with great concern. Both the bus drivers and CORE scouts reported that a white mob awaited the riders in Anniston, Alabama. When the bus arrived at the Greyhound dock in Anniston, the rumor was confirmed. A crowd of men with clubs, bricks, iron pipes and knives were waiting. The nine Freedom Riders and five other passengers were scared breathless when the mob shouted for them to come out. Two mobsters tried to force the door open. This brought two Alabama state investigators out from their cover as bus passengers. They ran to the front of the bus and held the door shut. The mob began to pound on the bus. The passengers told the driver to leave while he could. He revved the engine and backed up. Immediately Anniston police moved in from the back of the mob and guided the bus out of town.

The Greyhound raced down Highway 78 with about 50 cars carrying 200 men in hot pursuit. Just outside of Anniston the bus began to list to one side. The driver realized that a slashed tire was going flat. He steered the bus off the road, cut the engine, jumped out and ran like hell. The mob's cars screeched to stops, the mob poured out and surrounded the bus. Axes and bricks were used to break bus windows. One mobster threw a firebomb through the back window. Flames ran along the floor and seats caught fire. The black smoke was choking the riders and passengers, who were near panic.

One of the passengers, E.L. Cowling, an undercover state investigator, was up front. He saw that the mob wasn't trying to force entry but rather to keep the door shut to incinerate the whole lot. Cowling threatened the mob with his revolver and they fell back. Cowling pushed the door open and the riders and passengers stumbled out. The mob attacked them as they came out until some Alabama state troopers appeared. They fired warning shots and stopped the attacks. The mob retreated, the bus burned and the troopers took the beaten and wounded to the Anniston hospital. Photographs of the burning bus were put onto national and international wires and distributed throughout the civilized world.

The second bus, the Trailways bus, arrived at Anniston an hour later than the Greyhound. It was met by a bunch of KKK or mob members who entered the bus and beat the riders with fists and kicks and clubs until they were all incapacitated or subdued. Then a policeman and the thugs jumped off and the bus and driver headed out of town on back roads, trying to avoid the bus-burning mob on the highway to Birmingham.

Fred Shuttlesworth had reported to King for two weeks that the Ku Klux Klan planned to ambush the Freedom Riders at the Birmingham bus terminal. Gary T. Rowe, an FBI informant, had told his FBI handlers that the Birmingham police had agreed to give the Klansmen 15 unmolested minutes to beat up the riders. The FBI special agent in charge of the Birmingham office had reported the police–Klan agreement to FBI headquarters in Washington several times. The planned ambush by the KKK was so well known by the media that half a dozen reporters, photographers and TV camera crews and CBS's Howard K. Smith awaited the bus at the Birmingham terminal. The whole white Establishment knew about the coming ambush and supported it actively or tacitly.

When the Trailways bus pulled into the Birmingham terminal, the mass mob assault materialized as predicted. With the police in the background the white, sadistic Klansmen proceeded to beat up the riders with fists, kicks, pipes and clubs. The FBI informant was one of the attackers! The attack continued for 15 minutes and then the police moved forward to "restore order." One rider, Jim Peck, required 53 stitches to close six head wounds, including a four-inch gash on his forehead. The stitching was done at the Hillman Hospital after the ambulance carrying Peck was turned away from the Methodist Hospital. The KKK mob got so excited in the attack that seven bystanders were hurt badly enough to be hospitalized.

The ambush and beatings were so cowardly and vicious that the local Establishment papers were sympathetic to the riders. The *Birmingham News* editorialized: "People are asking, Where are the police?" The president of the Birmingham Chamber of Commerce, Sidney Smyer, was in Tokyo, Japan, leading the city's business delegation at the International Rotary convention. He was embarrassed and at a loss for an explanation when the photographs of the police-assisted bus station riot appeared in the Japanese papers. Smyer, a segregationist, told his Birmingham colleagues that something must be done about Bull Conner. Conner was the Birmingham police commissioner who made no secret of his contempt for black citizens.

After the 15 minutes of mayhem the riders, bloody and beaten, gradually re-assembled at Fred Shuttlesworth's house. They were physically beaten but not spiritually. They all decided to continue. Shuttlesworth led 18 Freedom Riders down to the Greyhound terminal so they could board the three o'clock bus to Montgomery. But there were problems. Bull Conner refused to provide police protection. Governor Patterson said, "I refuse to guarantee their safe passage." Greyhound couldn't find a white bus driver willing to make the trip. There were nearly continuous radio bulletins on the exact position and the size of the mob waiting to attack the riders. There were also frequent reports about the discussions going on with Washington.

A spokesman for the governor said that angry whites had been seen all along the highway from Birmingham to Montgomery. Shuttlesworth was repeatedly on the phone to Washington trying to get protection for the riders. Kennedy was not helpful. He didn't wish to admit that there was a crisis that required federal intervention. The Freedom Riders were hostages in a trap. They felt that they were public targets for racist mobs that were supported by the local sheriff and the governor and a president who deferred to a racist governor rather than enforce the supreme court decisions. The 18 riders began to talk among themselves about diminishing returns and increasing costs. They had already called national and international attention to the apartheid-style transportation practices in the southern states. Further beatings by racist mobs would add very little to their accomplishments.

The Freedom Riders notified Shuttlesworth that they had decided to take a plane to New Orleans. This decision was immediately broadcast and led the mob to shift its focus from the bus station to the airport. Every time the riders were ready to take off a bomb scare was called in and the departure was canceled. Meanwhile, Washington was still loath to recognize any crisis that would require federal intervention. Shuttlesworth talked to President Kennedy six times but was unable to persuade him to help.

Finally they tricked the mob. The riders boarded a plane and took off without any prior announcement. And that was the end of the story of the first group of Freedom Riders of the nonviolent black revolution. The story of the second group of Freedom Riders begins immediately.

Freedom Riders—Second Echelon, 1961

On Tuesday, May 16, 1961, Diane Nash of Nashville called the Rev. Fred Shuttlesworth and told him, "The Nashville students have come to Birmingham to continue the Freedom Rides."

"Young lady," replied Shuttlesworth, "do you know that the Freedom Riders almost got killed here?"

"Yes," said Nash, "that's exactly why the ride must not be stopped. If they stop us with violence the movement is dead. We're coming. We just want to know if you can meet us."

The next morning, ten Freedom Riders boarded a bus for Birmingham. The group was made up of James Bevel, leader, accompanied by John Lewis, who had just returned from New Orleans; six Negro male students; two female Negro students; a white boy, Jim Zwerg; and a white girl, Selyn McCollum. All were trained and experienced in nonviolent action. All went well for 200 miles to Birmingham, and then the police flagged the bus down.

The white boy, Zwerg, and a black boy, Brook, were arrested for sitting together and so violating Alabama apartheid law. The police then examined all the tickets. All tickets marked Nashville to New Orleans via Montgomery and Jackson, Mississippi, were identified as Freedom Riders and held on the bus. Selyn McCollum had purchased her ticket in Pulaski. She said, "I'm not with this group," and was permitted to exit. She ran to a telephone and called Diane Nash in Nashville. Nash called Washington and asked why the Freedom Riders were being held.

After an hour of waiting the nine riders were allowed to leave the bus and enter the terminal to await the bus for Birmingham. Helmeted policemen, who protected them from a mob of angry white people, surrounded them. After three hours, the riders were about to board the bus when Bull Conner appeared. He arrested the seven riders, handcuffed them and took them off to jail. Conner announced that he was placing them under "protective custody." While the riders sat in jail there was a long discussion among representatives of the riders, Washington and the local

Establishment. All of the participants in this bicultural debate suffered various value conflicts that made negotiation and compromise difficult.

Alabama's Governor Patterson refused to guarantee the safety of the riders. He faced a dilemma. If he guaranteed their safety, he would violate Alabama apartheid law. If he refused to guarantee their safety, he would be admitting that state sovereignty had limits and federal assistance was needed. Attorney General Robert Kennedy faced a dilemma. He was sworn to enforce federal laws, including the equal treatment clause of the Constitution, but he knew his brother's narrow election victory was due to the votes of southern racists and he didn't want to displease them. President Kennedy also had a value conflict. He had urgent business with Canada, the USSR, and other foreign nations and wished to keep embarrassing domestic issues off the front pages. He was impatient with the small band of faceless, nameless, half-suicidal pacifists who had seized the attention of the media and embarrassed him both nationally and internationally. He was also learning a great deal from his brother about how apartheid was actually operating in the U.S.

During this debate about their future, the Freedom Riders were being held illegally, without charges and with lawyers demanding their release. This standoff was suddenly broken by Bull Conner in the middle of the night. He had his men drag the limp, protesting Freedom Riders out of their cells and into unmarked police cars. He told federal officials that he would personally "escort" the riders through the state under cover of darkness to avoid the mobile white mobs and dump them in Tennessee. Conner's convoy left Birmingham and headed north on U.S. Highway 31. Near the tiny town of Ardmore, Tennessee, he halted the police convoy and dumped the riders and their baggage beside the road in the dark. He told them to follow the railroad tracks to a station and then catch a train back to Nashville. Conner and his men made a U-turn and headed back to Birmingham.

Groping in the dark, the riders found no train station but they found a telephone. They called Diane Nash in Nashville and reported their situation. Then, still in the dark, they found a Negro home in the country. The old Negro couple was first terrified by night visitors but after some black culture talk they warmed up, invited them in and fed them. (They hadn't eaten in more than a day.) Nash sent a car that picked them up and took them back to Birmingham to recommence their Freedom Ride. Back in Birmingham, they found that little had changed. The bus drivers still refused to take them to Montgomery because of the awaiting mobs. While they spent the night, under guard, in the bus station, the argument continued between Washington officials and Alabama officials over what to do with the riders. Finally, an agreement was reached. The riders would be protected, or so Washington thought, on their ride to Montgomery.

Early the next morning the riders boarded a Greyhound bus that was heavily guarded by state troopers and headed for Montgomery. In Montgomery, the local police were supposed to pick up the protection, but there was a double cross. When the bus pulled into the Montgomery station, there were no police in sight. As the riders descended from the bus a white mob of KKKers and similar types attacked them with clubs and chains. It was another police-condoned beating spree. The mob beat the riders, unmolested, for 15 minutes. Then the local police arrived to "restore order." Three riders had been beaten severely and Justice Department representative John Seigenthaler was knocked unconscious. Ralph Abernathy and other members of the Montgomery Improvement Association (MIA) rescued the riders as they were able to crawl or stumble away from the fracas.

In Washington, Robert Kennedy was furious, as he had believed that state and local officials had broken their promise to provide rider protection. He immediately ordered federal marshals to Montgomery and obtained a federal injunction barring the Ku Klux Klan and other hoodlums from harassing the riders.

Dr. King was in Chicago when he learned of the attack. On Sunday, May 21, he flew to Montgomery where the MIA was rehabilitating the riders. King and company immediately scheduled a public meeting at Abernathy's First Baptist Church. By early morning, over 1,000 people were waiting to hear him speak. King told them that unless the federal government acted forthrightly in the South to assure every citizen's constitutional rights the nation would be plunged into a dark abyss of chaos. He also promised a full-scale nonviolent assault on the system of segregation in Alabama. As King spoke, some of his listeners were distracted by a commotion in the churchyard. A mob of hostile whites had gathered outside the church. Federal marshals were using tear gas but the mob was beyond their control. They had set fire to a car and there were threats that the church might be torched.

Inside the church, the crowd was calm. King went to the basement and called Attorney General Kennedy in Washington. The federal officials told King that national guardsmen were on the way to reinforce the marshals. In the meantime, no one dared leave the church. In the early morning hours the guardsmen arrived. The trapped prisoners were now safe even though the mob was still milling about. Finally, between 5 and 6 A.M., the mob began to disperse and the guardsmen commenced to escort the church people to their homes.

Later that day, the Nashville Riders told King that they were ready to depart Montgomery and continue their ride to Mississippi. Deputy Attorney General Byron White told King that the riders should not continue as the students could expect much worse treatment in Mississippi.

Tuesday was another day of waiting and preparing. The National Guard continued to keep the peace and protect the riders. New volunteers, including several northern whites, came to Montgomery to join the Rides for Freedom. In the afternoon King, Abernathy, James Farmer, John Lewis and Diane Nash called a news conference. They announced that the Nashville Riders would continue their bus trek from Montgomery to Jackson, Mississippi.

Early Wednesday morning, the riders ate breakfast at the Montgomery bus station. Then they boarded a special bus for Jackson. A second bus set out later. Both buses were accompanied by police cars. Both buses made an uneventful run to Jackson. However, all of the riders were arrested and incarcerated when they tried to use facilities at the Jackson bus station. That was the end of riding for the Nashville Freedom Riders. At the time it seemed to be a failure or a standoff. The riders failed to ride the buses to New Orleans and the Establishment failed to resolve the contradiction between enforcement of supreme court decisions and support of state apartheid laws.

In fact, that very same afternoon there was a high-level discussion that led to a more satisfactory conclusion. King and Bobby Kennedy had another long and sometimes acerbic exchange on the subject of Freedom Rides. Kennedy called for a temporary halt to the rides for a cooling-off period. King told Kennedy that the heavy protection given the two buses had made the ride to Jackson meaningless. Kennedy said that he was trying to get the arrested riders out of prison. King told Kennedy that the protesters vowed to remain in jail as "part of the philosophy of the movement." Both were irked at the other's failure to adequately understand his point of view. The next morning, King returned to Atlanta and told reporters that the rides would resume in full force on either May 29 or 30. King told reporters that there would be a temporary lull but no cooling off of the rides. King added that he was hopeful that something would be done which would make any continuation of the rides unnecessary, such as a federal order banning segregation in bus terminal facilities. Guess what happened next.

On May 29, Attorney General Robert Kennedy made the precise move that King had asked for. He announced that he had requested the Interstate Commerce Commission, which had responsibility for interstate travel facilities, to issue regulations banning all segregation in such facilities. The ICC issued the requested regulations in September to take effect on November 1, 1961. That announcement ended the urgency for Freedom Rides. CORE continued small-scale recruitment of volunteers to ride to Jackson where they were immediately jailed. During the summer, more than 300 people were arrested for testing transportation facilities in Jackson. The Student Nonviolent Coordinating Committee that had supplied volunteers and the Southern Christian Leadership Conference that had supplied public relations both stopped promoting the rides as the struggle had been won in Washington. The Freedom Riders are generally and correctly credited with ending segregated bus facilities. King pronounced the issuance of the ICC regulation "a remarkable victory," and so it was.

The Albany Campaign, GA, 1961–1962

On September 22, 1961, the Interstate Commerce Commission published an order that prohibited segregated facilities for interstate travel effective November 1, 1961. In Albany, Georgia, a group of black ministers decided that they would assist in the implementation of that ruling. They wrote a letter to Albany's city officials requesting a biracial meeting to discuss how Albany could comply with the ICC ruling and desegregate the bus station. The response of the Albany officials was rude and violent. James Gray, owner of the *Albany Herald* published an editorial condemning the ministers for making such a proposal and the home of one of the min-

isters was bombed. The ministers were not cowed. They organized the "Albany Movement" with the goal of desegregating the bus station. Their leader was Dr. William
Anderson, a local osteopath. The membership included several community associations, ministers and NAACP members. To start their campaign, Dr. Anderson called
the Student Nonviolent Coordinating Committee in Atlanta and asked if some SNCC
activists could come to Albany to lead their challenge. The SNCC agreed.

In early November, just after the ICC ruling became effective, six SNCC students
boarded a bus in Atlanta bound for Albany. Upon arrival at the Albany bus station
they proceeded to use the whites-only waiting room. They were immediately arrested and jailed by Police Chief Laurie Pritchett's men. Students at the nearby black
Albany State College heard about the arrests and volunteered to replace the SNCC
six. When they attempted to enter the whites-only waiting room Pritchett arrested
and jailed them. And then another group of students made the same attempt with
the same results. This process was repeated over and over again in the following days
and weeks. By mid–December more than 500 demonstrators had been jailed. Some
of the students were bailed out for health or personal reasons, but the majority refused bail in order to make a statement of opposition to the Establishment system
of "justice" that violated the ICC ruling and the U.S. Constitution.

At the beginning of the confrontation, the goal had been simply to obtain conformance with the ICC ruling. But as time passed this goal was expanded. By December, the Albany Movement sought the desegregation of all public facilities in
conformance with the 1954 supreme court decision.

The Albany officials were not cooperative. They refused to even talk to the black
leaders about any change in the segregation system. The confrontation was stalemated. To try to get things moving, Dr. Anderson invited his Morehouse College
classmate, Martin Luther King Jr., to come to Albany and give them a lift. King agreed
and arrived in Albany on December 15 with his associate, the Rev. Ralph Abernathy.
Dr. King spoke at mass meetings at two black churches. His audiences included
NAACP activists. SNCC activists, students and a hundred or so victims of U.S.
apartheid. King's voice, spirituality, phrasing, logic and message were spellbinding.
The next morning, King and Abernathy led 200 followers to the Albany City Hall to
pray for freedom. The whole group was immediately arrested and taken to several
jails by Chief Pritchett's deputies.

The arrests of King, Abernathy and Dr. Anderson got the attention of the national press. A number of stories were published about the Albany Movement but
King was unable to benefit from the publicity, as he was incommunicado in jail. In
fact, the Movement leaders were beginning to realize that they were dealing with a
formidable adversary. Other Southern sheriffs had been sadistic and uncommu-
nicative, but Pritchett was worse. He was also smart and employed new tactics to defeat the protestors.

Pritchett was a studious police officer. He studied the performance of the Alabama authorities during the Freedom Rides and concluded that they had erred in
permitting police violence to be seen on TV. It drew unfavorable attention and

brought federal intervention. He developed a better strategy. Pritchett told his deputies to follow four policies: (1) Avoid the use of violence before the media. This keeps public opinion from siding with blacks. (2) Make arrests for trespassing or disturbing the peace rather than for violating Jim Crow laws. This makes it easier to prosecute. (3) Incarcerate, incarcerate, incarcerate. When the black leaders and their followers are in jail their activities cease. (4) Don't negotiate. No negotiation means no concessions.

Pritchett's strategy enjoyed strong support from the Albany Establishment. City officials refused to negotiate and the "judicial" system incarcerated as fast as Pritchett would arrest with no concern for the validity of charges. When the Albany jails were crowded, Chief Pritchett made deals with sheriffs in neighboring counties for the rent of their jails. He bused his prisoners to Sumter, Terrell and Baker counties where jail conditions were harrowing and the sheriffs untrained in nonviolence.

Pritchett also courted the press. He combined a good-old-boy friendliness with a sophistication that impressed the northern reporters. In December and again in July, several influential news media carried laudatory stories about Laurie Pritchett. It was reported that he had studied Martin Luther King's concept of nonviolence and that he believed in nonviolent law enforcement.

Pritchett had another secret weapon: informants, some paid and some volunteers. He paid one black man to report on the efforts to organize young people. He persuaded two blacks that he was really a moderate and it would help their cause if they told him the demonstrator's plans. Most helpful were the reporters. Pritchett conned several of them into sharing the tapes they recorded at mass meetings or interviews. All of this intelligence helped him keep prepared and implement his plan.

Pritchett's policy of no violence before reporters or cameras was generally followed. Threats, violence or maltreatment of prisoners, their relatives or activists was confined to times and locations where no media people were present. Out of view of cameras and reporters, however, the treatment of blacks was inhumane. One example: King, Abernathy and Anderson were taken to the jail in Americus in Sumter County, a jail that was infamous as a hellhole for blacks. Jail conditions were so bad that several of the activists had to be bailed out as they could not stand the abuse and discomfort. King's group had not anticipated that they might go to jail for a prayer meeting and so they were not prepared. Many wore only light jackets or even shirt sleeves. After they were jailed, a cold wave hit. King asked the Americus sheriff, Chappell, for blankets for his colleagues. Instead of blankets, Chappell turned the heat off, removed the few blankets available, opened windows and turned on fans. King said that Chappell was "the meanest man in the world."

The confrontation between the Albany Movement and Chief Pritchett and the Albany officials continued in the pattern of demonstrations, arrests and incarcerations until July 1962. Protestors were arrested until they filled the jails in several counties. It is estimated that over 1,500 were jailed. Pritchett's men refrained from public violence and the Albany officials refused to even talk with the movement leaders. Repeated jailing (three times) and constant "legal" harassment by the "justice" system prevented the Rev. King from leading protests and from taking his cause to the public.

King was very unhappy. He had been called in to resuscitate a poorly planned campaign. He tried hard to persuade President Kennedy to take positive action in support of the civil rights that had been established on paper by the Constitution and Supreme Court cases but he had not succeeded. In late July 1962, the Albany confrontation wound down. King and his Southern Christian Leadership Conference moved on to work in other areas. The Albany campaign was looked on as a failure even though the participants learned a lot about goals, training, communication, the media and Washington that was useful in subsequent campaigns. The City of Albany was not a winner either. The city officials conceded the bus terminal desegregation but held the line on all other aspects of apartheid even though many of them could see that it was a rear-guard action in a losing struggle.

The Albany campaign is a classic example of the differences that may occur between prime-time media reports and the historian's analysis 40 years later. The media described a charismatic Sheriff Laurie Pritchett, who used nonviolent methods to maintain law and order and black activists who were poorly organized. They reported a failed campaign. The historians, by contrast, are describing a clever, racist sheriff who wooed the media and kept police violence out of the public eye. Today a civil rights museum in an Albany church celebrates the bravery and sacrifices of hundreds of blacks and portrays the campaign as a significant contribution to the eventual success of the nonviolent revolution and the introduction of desegregation and democracy to Georgia.

Meredith Matriculates at Ole Miss, MS, 1961–1962

The desegregation of Mississippi's universities required several attempts. In 1958, Clennon Washington Jr., a black instructor at Alcorn Agricultural and Mechanical College, applied for admission to the lily-white University of Mississippi. He arrived on campus alone with no U.S. marshal to protect him. The Mississippi Establishment's response to his application was to get him declared insane and committed to Whitfield, a segregated Mississippi asylum. (His brother succeeded in getting him released.) In 1959, Clyde Kennard attempted to enroll at the University of Southern Mississippi. The local law officers planted some chicken feed in his car and then arrested him for the theft of chicken feed. He was sentenced to seven years in prison. In January 1961, James Meredith tried again. He applied for admission to the all-white University of Mississippi. He was a nine-year veteran of the air force and a student at Jackson State College, a black institution. When Meredith informed the registrar that he was black, he was informed that registrations were closed.

Undaunted, Meredith immediately applied for the summer session starting in June 1961. On May 25, 1961, he received notification that his admission was denied. Meredith contacted the NAACP and its Legal Defense Fund assigned Constance B.

Motley to help him. Motley filed a civil suit in the hope of getting Meredith admitted for the summer session. The court, however, upheld the decision of the university registrar. Motley appealed that ruling. This took another year. On June 25, 1962,
the U.S. Fifth Circuit Court of Appeals ruled that the University of Mississippi should
admit Meredith. The State of Mississippi took the case to the Supreme Court. Justice Hugo Black consulted with other members of the Supreme Court and then upheld the ruling of the Court of Appeals in Meredith's favor.

Governor Ross R. Barnett immediately issued a proclamation claiming state
sovereignty in matters of public education. Barnett also directed university officials
to defy the order of the Supreme Court. The State of Mississippi also charged Meredith with the crime of moral turpitude. Barnett called a special session of the legislature and obtained passage of a bill that denied admission to institutions of higher
learning to anyone charged with that crime. The governor then had himself declared
the registrar of the University of Mississippi and announced that Meredith would be
arrested if he appeared to register. The governor's statement stirred up anti-black hatred. Newspapers across the state encouraged white citizens to support the governor.
The Kennedy administration was monitoring the events. Attorney General Robert
Kennedy telephoned Barnett. The governor agreed not to arrest Meredith but refused
to allow him to register.

The first time Meredith tried to register he had U.S. marshals at his side and a
court order, but it wasn't sufficient. Barnett and a company of state troopers turned
them away. The second time that Meredith and the marshals tried to register they
had a federal court order that specified admission on September 30, 1962. Governor
Barnett led a crescendo of opposition. In a televised address he pledged that no
school would be integrated on his watch and that those who agree with him should
be prepared to go to jail before drinking "from the cup of genocide" that integration
represented. Retired General Edwin Walker, who had commanded the U.S. Army
troops that President Eisenhower sent to Little Rock, Arkansas, Central High School
in 1957, announced that he had changed his mind about segregation and called for
a showdown at Oxford. The showdown came.

On Sunday, September 30, white racist crowds began to gather around the university. Cars bedecked with rebel flags and "Dixie" blaring from their radios, circu-
lated through town. At 4:15 P.M., U.S. marshals from Memphis lined up in front of
the Lyceum where they attracted the gathering crowd and acted as a decoy. Meanwhile a small armed guard sneaked Meredith into a dorm room at the rear of the campus. The ruse worked but it also brought a crowd of rowdies to the Circle. The crowd
threw epithets at the marshals and then, as their excitement grew, they threw bricks
and bottles. Then the Mississippi Highway Patrol withdrew from the area while
shouting encouragement to the mob. The mob, reinforced by large numbers of outsiders, grew more hostile. While President Kennedy was delivering a televised speech
calling for calm the angry crowd was beginning to riot. By nightfall, the riot was in
full force and several federal marshals were injured.

Attorney General Robert Kennedy ordered the army units waiting in Memphis to go to Oxford. The troops arrived at 2:00 A.M. and relieved the exhausted marshals. The army occupied the entire campus and town of Oxford. Order was restored. There was no clear account of how the riot progressed as there were no objective observers present, but the body count at the end tells a sad story. Two people were killed. A French journalist, Paul Guihard, was shot in the back and Ray Gunter, a jukebox repairman, was shot in the head. One hundred and 60 marshals were injured. Two hundred rioters were arrested, less than one-sixth of whom were from Ole Miss. A showcase campus was littered with tear gas canisters, three burned-out cars and other riot rubbish.

The next day, October 1, 1962, James Meredith registered at Ole Miss. When he attended classes, he was accompanied by three U.S. marshals who tracked his every move in person and by radio. At night, three marshals kept guard in an adjacent room; an alert platoon bivouacked behind the dorm, ready to respond to any call. The University of Mississippi was traumatized. Thirty-seven professors resigned! Student enrollment dropped. Twenty thousand troops, more than the population of Oxford, patrolled the campus and the town for the remainder of the year. Total cost to the taxpayer was estimated to be $2.5 million.

As time passed, the atmosphere of race hatred and wounded pride largely evaporated. The university became accustomed to the presence of one black student. In June 1963 a second black student enrolled in the law school without incident. Meredith graduated in August 1963, also without incident. After his graduation, Meredith had little direct involvement with the black revolution until 1966 when he launched his march against fear—the last of the revolution's marathon marches. Meredith's matriculation at Ole Miss was a significant accomplishment. It shattered the academic barriers in one of the most segregated and racist states. It showcased the incredible courage of blacks who defied the quasi-sacred institutions of U.S. apartheid and it was a turning point in the ideological shift in the U.S. culture from racism to equality and democracy in the state of Mississippi.

COFO and Moses v. Extreme Apartheid, MS, 1961–1964 (The Mississippi Campaign)

The Mississippi civil rights campaign was conducted by an agency specifically set up for that purpose—the Council of Federated Organizations (COFO). Founded in 1961 and revitalized in 1962, the council was a coalition of four agencies: the Student Nonviolent Coordinating Committee (SNCC), the Congress of Racial Equality (CORE), the National Association for the Advancement of Colored People (NAACP) and the Southern Christian Leadership Conference (SCLC). COFO's objective was to eliminate interorganizational competition for funds distributed by the Voter Education Project (VEP), and to register black Mississippians to vote. In practice, the SNCC dominated the coalition and provided most of the staff and operating funds for COFO.

A special organization was required for Mississippi because the state had a special form of apartheid: extreme apartheid. Among apartheid states, Mississippi had the worst record on racial violence, education, infant mortality and living standards for black citizens. The state had a reputation, even in the South, for its brutal enforcement of apartheid. Statistics on lynching up to 1955 and racial murders during the black revolution confirmed this reputation. In 1955, black Mississippians launched a major voter registration drive. It was defeated by the white Establishment with the use of economic reprisals against activists and by physical violence and murder of black leaders.

To check the civil rights movement, the Mississippi legislature passed several new apartheid laws. Voting requirements were increased to a two-year residency and a $2 poll tax. A breach of the peace law prescribed a $1,000 fine and six months in jail for violators. It also required libraries to carry white supremacist literature. One law required the names of new voters to be published in the newspaper for two weeks prior to acceptance. With the phone company, the post office, the police and the courts in the hands of the white Establishment, it was very difficult for the SNCC to operate. To send a letter, get a ride, or hold a meeting was a major operation. Fear kept most Negroes from attending meetings. A turnout of 20 sharecroppers was considered a big success.

The legislature established Sovereignty Commissions to help maintain the status quo. At the same time, the White Citizens Councils became active in persuading businesses, creditors and suppliers to cut services to anyone pushing for a change. Any whites sympathetic to the black cause were harassed out of town.

The structure of both the black and white cultures differed from other states. The blacks had proportionally fewer educated activists and minister-leaders. The whites had fewer businessmen who were moderate racists and realized that segregation was bad for business. As a result, the demonstration marches, boycotts and sit-ins that were employed in other states were not effective in Mississippi. The COFO replaced them with emphasis on education and voter registration.

The efforts of SNCC and COFO to reform Mississippi society were met with immediate and extreme opposition. The result was that they could not conduct a single coordinated campaign but had to rely on a series of efforts continuously frustrated by violent acts. Following are three newsworthy stories from that campaign: Moses' attempt to register voters, Moses' legal action against Attorney General Robert Kennedy and the Establishment's tactic of food denial.

Bob Moses, a black, was born in New York City, the son of a janitor. His grandfather had been a Baptist circuit preacher in Tennessee, South Carolina and Virginia. Bob earned a degree in philosophy at Harvard and then taught mathematics at a New York school. When he read about the Greensboro sit-ins in 1960 he decided to go south. He joined the Student Nonviolent Coordinating Committee (SNCC) and was assigned to investigate the possibility of a civil rights campaign in Mississippi.

When Moses went to Mississippi in July 1961, he met C.C. Bryant, chairman of the Polk County NAACP. Bryant asked Moses to conduct a voter registration project in McComb and Moses agreed. As a preliminary step, Moses and Bryant visited churches and homes in the area to explain voter registration and to raise money for the project through $5 and $10 donations.

In August, Moses held the first voter registration class in the Masonic Hall in McComb. After the class, Moses took four of his students to Magnolia, the Pike County seat, to test their registering skill. Three students completed the registration. Two weeks later, Moses took two more students to Liberty, the county seat of Amite County, to repeat the procedure. A sheriff's deputy stopped them in the street and beat Moses with the butt of a knife. Moses did not resist. Nine stitches were required to close the wound. The deputy was acquitted of criminal charges.

That encounter was the beginning of a series of violent attacks and murders that were intended to stop the registration of blacks. Travis Britt was beaten while trying to register to vote in Liberty. John Hardy was pistol-whipped for doing the same in Tylertown. Some students challenged the segregation practices of the McComb Woolworth's and Greyhound bus terminal. They were jailed for 30 days for their efforts. On September 25, 1961, E.H. Hurst, a white member of the Mississippi legislature, shot dead a black farmer and registration worker, Herbert Lee, in Amite County. Louis Allen, a black logger witnessed the murder. Hurst was not prosecuted. Allen received many threats on his life and on January 31, 1964, he was shot dead outside the gate of his house. On October 4, 1961, students led a mass march for civil rights—the first one in McComb. The police arrested 116 of them. Bob Zeller, a white SNCC worker, had his eyes gouged by a member of the white mob. On October 31, the marchers were convicted and sentenced to four to six months at Pike County Jail in Magnolia.

While the few voter registrations they managed were gratifying, they were not enough to offset the high price that the activists and innocent blacks were paying. The COFO leaders were disappointed. In December 1962, Moses conceded that "we are powerless to register people in significant numbers anywhere in the state." He listed three changes which were necessary: (1) removal of White Citizen Councils from control of Mississippi politics, (2) action by the U.S. Department of Justice to assure safe registration for Negroes and (3) a mass uprising by the unlettered, fearful Negroes, demanding their constitutional right to vote.

On January 1, 1963, Moses tried another tactic. With the support of the Gandhi Society and the endorsement of Martin Luther King, he filed a federal suit in Washington against Attorney General Robert Kennedy and FBI director J. Edgar Hoover. Moses and his co-plaintiffs sought an injunction ordering Kennedy and Hoover to enforce six sections of the Federal Code that made it a crime to harass or intimidate those trying to vote. He wanted to force the attorney general and the FBI to face up to their responsibilities to enforce voter protection statutes.

Kennedy saw the lawsuit as a threat to the prestige of his brother's administration. U.S. Justice Department lawyers maneuvered to block the lawsuit as a nuisance or crank suit. While the suit failed, the point was made in legal terms that the attorney general had responsibility for enforcing civil rights laws and it put some pressure on Kennedy to move in that direction.

Meanwhile, the Mississippi Establishment also tried a new tactic—food depravation. They shut off distribution of federal food surpluses to Delta counties. The cutoff affected Sunflower County, the home of Senator James Eastland, and LeFlore County, where Emmitt Till had been lynched and where the White Citizens Council of Mississippi had its headquarters. In LeFlore County, the cutoff stopped food relief to 22,000 people—nearly half the county population, mostly Negroes, fully a third of whom had annual incomes of less than $500. In Greenwood, more than 6,000 sharecroppers stood in a line outside the Wesley Chapel hoping to receive some food. A sharecropper in Mississippi at the time was similar to a slave in anti-bellum days except for the absence of ownership and a slave market. He was tied to the land and plantation owner by poverty, the plantation accounting system that kept him perennially in debt and the KKK which would pursue him if he fled.

COFO and SNCC workers were suddenly confronted with a famine in their project area. They sent out a nationwide appeal for donations of food and money. There was an immediate and strong response—but not commensurate with the magnitude of the deficiency. Civil rights groups, Freedom Ride veterans and students drove south with carloads of donated canned goods. SNCC held a fund-raiser at Carnegie Hall in New York City on February 1. Harry Belafonte and the Albany Freedom Singers performed. In Chicago, Dick Gregory chartered a plane and flew seven tons of food to Mississippi.

A prime objective of the black revolution was to persuade the president of the United States to follow the U.S. Supreme Court's leadership and abolish apartheid and promote democracy and freedom. The food cutoff brought this issue squarely before President Kennedy. On February 12 at a Lincoln's birthday reception, members of the U.S. Civil Rights Commission met with the president. They told him that they felt an urgent duty to investigate racial conditions in Mississippi. Chairman John Hannah said that he was embarrassed that during the commission's five years in existence it had never held hearings in Mississippi, the one state most in need of the commission's services of fact gathering and public education. Hannah knew that this was a morally and politically sensitive issue. He knew that the U.S. Department of Justice had lobbied to keep the commission out of Mississippi.

President Kennedy responded that he thought that hearings in Mississippi would serve no purpose. This statement signified that the president was not ready to break his tacit political agreement with the Mississippi state establishment that they would deliver Democratic votes in national elections and he would close his eyes to apartheid.

In 1964, the SNCC mounted another attempt to register Mississippi citizens to vote. The Pike County Establishment met it with another surge of terror. There were three house bombings and attacks on volunteers, their homes and black churches. Police harassed volunteers by hauling them in for "questioning" several times a day. By October, the local paper wrote that it had lost track of the number of violent attacks on activists. Its guess was 24. The editor of the *Enterprise Journal* called for calm. His plea brought him smashed windows, crosses burned on his lawn by the KKK and a boycott by whites. Any whites that showed friendliness to blacks were hounded out of town. The total number of blacks registered was miniscule. This experience would have discouraged most reform leaders but the COFO and SNCC and their black accomplices would not quit, as shown by the stories of the Freedom Schools, the mock election and the Mississippi Democratic Party.

Harvey Gantt Desegregates Clemson University, SC, 1963

Harvey Gantt was born and grew up in Charleston County, South Carolina. His father enjoyed job security as a mechanic at the Charleston Navy Shipyard. His mother raised four daughters and one son in a disciplined and happy home environment. As a teenager, Harvey joined sit-ins and protest marches with his parents' support. After graduating from Charleston High School, Harvey looked for a college that taught architecture. Black colleges usually lacked that program and white colleges in the South were segregated. He chose Iowa State University. After a year, however, he decided that he would like to study in his own state.

In January 1961, Harvey Gantt applied for admission to Clemson University, the state land grant university in Clemson, South Carolina. When he submitted his transcript, the Clemson registrar noted that he had gone to a black high school. That disqualified him and his application was denied in accord with Clemson policy. A year later, in January 1962, Harvey again applied for admission to Clemson. There was no response to his application so after six months, in July 1962, he filed a suit against Clemson in a federal court.

In the meantime, the white Establishment was thinking about *Brown v. Board of Education* and how to respond. Led by Governor Ernest F. Hollings, they were more concerned with doing what was good for business and in following the law than in maintaining apartheid. They were aghast at what had happened in the desegregation of Ole Miss in Oxford, Mississippi—two people killed, another 50 injured in rioting—and were determined to avoid that scenario. During the summer and fall, the Clemson University administrators drew up a procedure to be followed when the court ordered them to admit Gantt. The procedure was designed to be dignified and without violence. Local business leaders were advised of this plan and agreed to use their influence to support civil obedience and order. In January 1963, the court ordered the administrators of Clemson University to admit Harvey Gantt. The university followed its prearranged procedure.

At 1:30 P.M., a black sedan drew up to the Clemson administration building. Gantt got out and walked into the building while cameras clicked to record the historic event. He emerged a few minutes later as a formally enrolled student in the School of Architecture. Unobtrusive federal marshals protected Gantt for six weeks and then were withdrawn. Clemson U. had desegregated without violence and without a riot. Both Governor Hollings and Harvey Gantt went on to new challenges and opportunities. Hollings went on to the U.S. Senate and Gantt became an architect and later the mayor of Charlotte, North Carolina.

William Moore, the Postman, April 1963

William Moore, a hulking ex–Marine, was a white postman in Baltimore, Maryland. He had authored a book—*The Mind in Chains*—which told of his treatment in a psychiatric hospital. His postal co-workers considered him a peculiar but likeable fellow who did his job. His family lived in Binghamton, New York. Moore grew up in Mississippi where he had learned Golden Rule Christianity. He believed that if the world did not conform to the Christian ideal of nonviolence, then the world was wrong and must change. He would maintain his faith in that ideal.

Moore read about the incipient black revolution and decided that he must do his part to bring justice and humane treatment to African Americans. Moore wrote a letter to President Kennedy and told him that he planned to take a ten-day vacation from his postal route and walk from Chattanooga, Tennessee, to Mississippi to promote brotherly love. He would wear two signboards. One would say "End Segregation in America" and the other, "Equal Rights for All Men." He added, "If you have any letters for anyone on my line of travel, I would be happy to deliver them for you."

Moore went to Washington to deliver his letter personally to the president. He got as far as the White House gates. The guards stopped him and refused to accept his letter. He put the letter in a mailbox and took a bus to Chattanooga to start his walk. He added "Mississippi or bust" to one of his signs and took to the road on April 21, 1963. Moore wore his signs and pushed a mail cart holding his belongings. He soon wore out his shoes and walked barefoot except when he went into a store for provisions. The reception he received along the route varied. Some bystanders threw angry epithets and even rocks at him. At another place a feature writer asked him for an interview.

Moore made steady progress from Tennessee through a corner of Georgia and into Alabama. He had gone 70 miles when a reporter from radio station WGAD in Gadsden stopped him on the road for an interview. In response to a question about his goal he said, "I intend to walk right up to the governor's mansion in Mississippi and ring his doorbell. Then I will hand him my letter." The letter, he explained, was a plea for civil rights and a request that Governor Barnett "be gracious and give more than is immediately demanded of you." The reporter said "goodbye" to Moore on a lonely stretch of U.S. Highway 11 near Atlanta.

On April 23, 1963, Moore's body was discovered by a motorist a mile down the road. He had been shot two times in the head at close range. A telephone call was made from a farmhouse and police and reporters rushed to the murder scene. Moore lay in the grass, still wearing his signboards. In his pocket was $51, his letter to Governor Barnett, his diary and postal receipts for the money he had mailed ahead to himself at planned stops along his route. Beside him was his postal cart with his shoes and clothes and copies of his letter to President Kennedy. His diary told of a mongrel dog joining him in his walk for a number of miles and then leaving him to go with a small boy.

News of the roadside execution was flashed across the country. In Washington, Moore's letter to President Kennedy had been delivered to Lee White who briefed Kennedy on the story before his news conference. At the news conference a reporter asked if there was some merit in the case for federal action to establish the rights of Negroes in Mississippi. The president referred to the Moore case and said, "We have offered to the State of Alabama the services of the FBI." A grocer from California who had accosted Moore on the road twice was arrested but he was not indicted for murder.

A week later on May 1, 1963, ten activists left the Greyhound bus station in Chattanooga to complete Moore's walk. There were five from CORE and five from SNCC. One wore a copy of Moore's sandwich board message. On May 3, they were arrested and taken to DeKalb County Jail in Fort Payne. They were held for 31 days on a charge of breaching the peace and were fined $200 each. However, upon appeal their sentences and fines were overturned.

The impact of Moore's assassination was varied but considerable. The CORE was somewhat embarrassed as Moore had been a CORE member but had acted on his own initiative without the blessing and support of the veteran activists. For the blacks, Moore's death was a new stimulus to nonviolent action. One columnist raised the question: Who was crazy? Moore? his assailant? or the society?

The Mock Freedom Vote, MS, 1963

Bob Moses had worked in McComb, Mississippi, for two years trying to get blacks to register but with little success. The tactics of the Establishment to prevent blacks from registering had been successful. Cutting food supplies, murders, police harassment and brutality supported by the courts, the legislature and the KKK had discouraged blacks from registering. Moses and the SNCC leaders decided that to break the pattern of oppression they must educate the blacks about their rights as citizens and convince the Establishment in Washington and in Mississippi that voting rights must be enforced. The Mock Freedom Vote was a new attempt at this task.

Volunteer students from Yale and Stanford assisted in the project. Polling places were black churches and businesses in the black neighborhood. The registration procedure for the Mock Freedom Vote was simple: name, age, address. This was in contrast to the white system for registering blacks, which included a 21-question registration form and a requirement to interpret any one of 285 sections of the state constitution to the satisfaction of the white registrar. The Mock Freedom Vote registration provided a list of possible candidates for regular voter registration in the Freedom Party's campaign the following year.

The mock ballot listed candidates for governor and lieutenant governor from the Democratic Party and from the Freedom Party. The Freedom candidates were Aaron Henry, a Negro pharmacist from Clarksdale, Mississippi, and the Rev. Edwin King, a white chaplain at the Negro Tougaloo College near Jackson, Mississippi. The Mock Freedom Vote was conducted simultaneously with the traditional election. While only whites could vote in the traditional election, all adults could vote in the Mock Freedom election. The mock election brought out hundreds of new "mock" voters in the primary and a surprising 83,000 black votes in the run-off. In the unofficial Freedom Vote, the overwhelming winners were Aaron Henry for governor and the Rev. Ed. King for lieutenant governor.

The mock vote served four purposes. First, it protested the Democratic Party's exclusion of blacks. Second, it educated hundreds of blacks in the procedures of registering and voting. Third, it answered the oft-repeated charge that the blacks "were content with the way things are" and had no interest in the electoral process. Finally, it sent a message to the Kennedy administration in Washington that the FBI and the U.S. attorney general should enforce the voting rights that were already on the books.

The "Battle" of Birmingham, AL, 1963

In January 1963, Martin L. King announced that he was going to Birmingham and that he would lead demonstrations there until "Pharaoh lets God's people go." While King spoke for black revolutionary activists, a newly elected governor of Alabama spoke for the white Establishment. George Wallace, in his inaugural address in Montgomery, said, "From the cradle of the Confederacy, this very heart of the great Anglo-Saxon southland, I draw the line in the dust and toss the gauntlet before the feet of tyranny. And I say, segregation now! Segregation tomorrow! Segregation forever!"

In February 1963, King went to Birmingham with his staff and installed the Southern Christian Leadership Conference (SCLC) command post in Room 30 of the Gaston Motel in the Negro section of Birmingham. His announced intention was to awaken the moral conscience of America. Wyatt Walker, a King lieutenant, proceeded to organize committees and enlist volunteers. One of King's first jobs was to raise money for bail bonds, which would be needed as soon as the demonstrations began. He went to New York to Harry Belafonte's apartment where he explained his proposed Birmingham campaign to lawyers of the NAACP Legal Defense Fund and 70 celebrities, activists and politicos who agreed to help raise funds.

The nonviolent action campaign began on April 13, 1963, with sit-ins by 65 Negroes at five downtown department stores and the simultaneous issuance of the "Birmingham Manifesto." This document stated the three goals of the demonstrations: (1) desegregation of all lunch counters, restrooms and drinking fountains in downtown stores, (2) hiring of Negroes in local businesses and industry and (3) establishment of a biracial committee to work out a schedule for desegregation of other areas of city life.

The first day of protests brought critical reviews. The mayor-elect, Albert Boutwell, blamed the sit-ins on outsiders. In Washington, Robert Kennedy spoke as a typical "moderate." He called the campaign "ill-timed." The *Washington Post* and most of the national press echoed Kennedy's "moderate" point of view. While the sit-ins and boycotts continued, King worked to keep and enlarge his support from black businessmen and professional people. He pleaded with Negro ministers to stop preaching "the glories of heaven" while ignoring the "earthly hell" in Birmingham.

By April 10, small groups of Negroes paraded before City Hall and picketed downtown stores. The police responded with police dogs and mass arrests. In the first week of demonstrations 300 Negroes were put in jail. On April 10, the sheriff, Bull Conner, served King with a state court injunction which prohibited him, Abernathy, Walker, Shuttlesworth and other leaders from conducting demonstrations. This injunction was designed to cripple the movement. It very nearly succeeded. But King, after wrestling with his conscience, decided to follow his principles and defy the injunction. He led 50 volunteers on a march downtown. Hundreds of supporters followed the march and the police were everywhere. When the marchers came face to face with Conner, King and Abernethy knelt in prayer. The police grabbed them and shoved them and the 50 marchers into paddy wagons, which took them to the Birmingham jail.

At the jail, King was put into solitary confinement in a small cell without a mattress or pillow. His attorneys were not allowed to visit him. He was depressed. The next day A.D. King, Martin's brother who pastored a church in Birmingham, led more than 1,500 Negroes on the largest march of the campaign. The situation changed abruptly. King was given a pillow and mattress. His lawyers were allowed to visit him. He was allowed to call his wife, Coretta. Coretta told him that she had called Attorney General Robert Kennedy in Washington and he had called Birmingham to see why King was in solitary confinement. In the meantime, Harry Belafonte's group had raised $50,000 for bail bonds.

While in jail, Dr. King wrote one of the most famous letters in U.S. history—his "Letter from Birmingham Jail"—that told the white culture what it was that bothered the blacks (see next controversy).

On April 20, 1963, King and Abernathy posted a $300 cash bond and walked out of the jail together. They were happy to learn that northern civil rights groups were starting nationwide boycotts of chain stores with branches in Birmingham. Later in the week the judge dropped the civil contempt charges and found the defendants guilty of a lesser charge. The local business leaders had decided that they didn't want King in their jail with a national campaign to free him. It would be bad publicity.

By late June, the campaign was running out of steam. It was difficult to find new volunteer marchers when there were no indications of real progress. A new strategy was needed to recruit new volunteers and to further awaken the conscience of America. And just then a new strategy evolved.

James Bevel, Bernard Lee and Dorothy Cotton had been working on educating local college and high school students on the principles and practices of nonviolent action. They said, "Why not ask the students to march?" It was agreed and the students were invited to participate. The response was nearly overwhelming. Hundreds of high school students swarmed into SCLC workshops at the churches, all raring to march. They were accompanied, however, by hundreds of little brothers and sisters who also wanted to march.

Bevel and Lee tried to dissuade the younger kids, but in vain. They kept coming back. Bevel and Lee took their problem to King. King deliberated. Letting children march for freedom would invite criticism, but filling the jail with kids would attract media attention and put pressure on the white Establishment. King decided to let the children march. On May 1, he announced to his staff that the next day would be "D-day," the start of a children's crusade to save the soul of Birmingham.

The next day, more than 1,000 youngsters from six years on up assembled at King's 16th Street Baptist Church. From there, adults and experienced march marshals guided the children downtown two abreast, column after column, singing freedom songs. When they encountered Conner, he ordered his men to arrest them and lock them up. The police arrested more than 900 youths. They had to borrow school buses to haul them off to jail.

But that did not dampen the youth's enthusiasm. The next day, 2,500 youngsters turned out to march. The columns were formed and the marchers headed downtown. Conner was waiting for them with a line of police and firemen with batons, attack dogs and high-pressure fire hoses. The sheriff called on the marchers to return to their church. They refused. "Let 'em have it!" he shouted. The firemen turned on the hoses which shot jets of water crashing into children and adults, knocking them down, smashing them into buildings, flushing them down the street and driving them soaked, crying, bruised and blooded into the park. When Negro bystanders threw bricks and bottles Conner ordered a dog attack. They bit three children severely. The final score was 250 nonviolent protesters arrested and an unknown number injured.

The whole event was well covered by the media. Millions of readers and TV viewers learned how minority children signing hymns were treated in Birmingham. It was labeled "Birmingham's day of infamy." A wave of indignation and criticism swept the country. Senator Wayne Morse of Oregon declared that Birmingham "would disgrace the Union of South Africa." Washington was also watching and reacting. Burke Marshall, Robert Kennedy's assistant attorney general for civil rights, flew to Birmingham to see if he could facilitate a settlement.

The next day, May 5, the Rev. Charles Billups and other Birmingham Christian ministers led more than 3,000 young people on yet another prayer pilgrimage to the Birmingham jail. As they marched they sang *I Want Jesus to Walk With Me*. King and his aides were in the streets managing the march with walkie-talkies.

As Billups's column approached the police barricade, the column halted, then knelt in prayer. Conner ordered them to return to their churches. The marchers continued to pray, then sing, then pray again. Suddenly the Rev. Billups stood and faced the police and said, "We're not turning back. We haven't done anything wrong. All we want is our freedom. How do you feel doing these things? Bring on your dogs. Beat us up. Turn on your hoses. We're not going to retreat." Then he stepped forward, followed by the other ministers and hundreds of children. Conner yelled, "Turn on the hoses!" His men just stood. "Damn it, turn on the hoses!" he reiterated. But they didn't. As the blacks marched through their ranks, the firemen and cops fell back as though hypnotized or as though they were responding personally to Billups's plea. The Negroes continued their march unimpaired, prayed for their imprisoned comrades in front of the jail, then headed back to the Negro quarter singing, *I Got Freedom Over My Head*. It was an unusual incident. King remarked, "It was one of the most fantastic events of the Birmingham story. I saw there, I felt there, for the first time the pride and the power of nonviolence."

On Monday, May 6, more than 3,000 Negroes were in jail and some 4,000 more were still parading and picketing. Birmingham was being condemned in the court of world opinion, the Birmingham economy was hurting from the racial disorder but the Birmingham Establishment still refused to negotiate. King decided to apply more pressure on the business leaders.

On May 7, while 175 of the city's business leaders met downtown, he executed a new tactic. Guided by King and his marshals on walkie-talkies, thousands of students headed downtown. They avoided Conner's police lines and infiltrated the downtown area. They flooded it with bodies. They tangled up traffic for several blocks and disrupted store after store with sit-ins and stand-ins.

When the 125 business leaders broke for lunch they faced a sea of marching, singing, clapping Negroes. They saw Conner call for his fire hoses and attack dogs. A blast of water knocked one leader, Fred Shuttlesworth, unconscious against a building. He was carried away in an ambulance. The 125 businessmen were horrified at what was happening. They all thought that it was abominable and something must be done. They agreed on a plan to bypass city officials and reach a settlement with King on their own.

Meanwhile Conner asked Governor George Wallace for help. By nightfall Colonel Al Lingo had 250 of his state troopers in Birmingham with 575 more just outside the city. That night, the businessmen's committee began to negotiate with the blacks. They negotiated very long hours for three days. At last, on May 10, the two groups produced an agreement that met all of King's manifesto objectives. Within 90 days, lunch counters, restrooms, fitting rooms and drinking fountains in downtown stores would be desegregated. Within 60 days, Negroes would be hired as clerks and salespersons. Within two weeks, a biracial committee would be established to improve black and white relations in Birmingham. City officials would be pressed to release all incarcerated Negroes on bonds or on their own recognizance. Reuther's United Automobile Workers and other unions provided huge sums of money needed for bail.

For nearly 24 hours it seemed that some semblance of sweetness and light and civil manners were returning to Birmingham. But the very next day, May 11, some whites (presumed to be Ku Klux Klanners) detonated two bombs. One was at the home of A.D. King, Martin's brother and also a freedom activist, and the other at the Gaston Motel, King's headquarters. A.D. King and his family escaped injury but several people were injured in the motel.

The two KKK bombings triggered violent black retaliation. Blacks stabbed a cop and set a taxi and two stores on fire in their riot. This riot in turn triggered a police riot. Lingo's state troopers stormed the Negro district and beat up people indiscriminately with clubs and rifle butts. Dr. King went to the scene himself to quiet things down.

The Kennedys in Washington were watching, learning and taking positive action. On May 12, President John F. Kennedy announced to the nation that he would not let extremism imperil the peace pact in Birmingham. He ordered 3,000 troops into position near the city and made plans to federalize the Alabama National Guard. The president's actions put an end to KKK involvement.

While the city officials resisted bitterly, desegregation was gradually introduced in Birmingham. A new city administration rescinded Birmingham's apartheid ordinances. Under strong Negro pressure, the city desegregated the library, municipal golf courses, public buildings and schools. Local merchants removed the "white" and "colored" signs on drinking fountains and restrooms and opened downtown lunch counters to all citizens and even hired some black clerks.

According to black leaders, the Birmingham campaign was a major victory. It showed that when the whole black community pulled together it could demolish the apartheid system. The nonviolent tactics prevailed against the brutality of fire hoses, attack dogs and club-wielding policemen. The success of the campaign stiffened the backbone of Negroes throughout the country. Most significant, perhaps, it marked a turning point in the thrust of the federal government from apartheid-as-usual to an attempt to implement the Supreme Court's decision of *Brown v. Board of Education* and the Constitution's civil rights amendments.

Dr. King Answers Eight White Clergymen, AL, 1963

On April 16, 1963, Dr. King was in jail for the thirteenth time. He had come to Birmingham to help direct the demonstrations at downtown department stores, marches, lunch counter sit-ins and white church kneel-ins. On Good Friday, King was arrested, charged with "parading without a permit," and put into solitary confinement in the Birmingham jail. After a few telephone calls to and from Washington, King's jail conditions were improved. He was allowed to see his lawyer, who smuggled him a pen and a copy of the *Birmingham News*.

First King read the good news. A letter called for blacks to support King and for whites to begin negotiations on desegregation of public facilities. It was signed by 60 local Negro leaders. Then he read the bad news—a headline stated: "White Clergy-men Urge Local Negroes to Withdraw from Demonstrations." The headline was fol-lowed by a second letter that was signed by C.C.J. Carpenter, the Episcopal bishop of Alabama, six white Christian clergymen and one rabbi.

The eight clergymen objected to the civil rights protests. They called them un-wise, untimely and instigated by outsiders. They advised Birmingham Negroes to withdraw their support from his struggle. They advised Dr. King to wait for a better moment to push his case.

Dr. King was provoked to respond. He took the smuggled pen and proceeded to compose his "Letter from Birmingham Jail" on the margins of the newspaper. He stated, in part:

> We have waited for more than 340 years for our constitutional and God-given rights.... Perhaps it is easy for those who have never felt the stinging darts of segregation to say, "Wait." But when you have seen vicious mobs lynch your mothers and fathers at will and drown your sisters and brothers at whim; when you have seen hate-filled police-men curse, kick and even kill your black brothers and sisters; when you see the vast majority of your twenty million Negro brothers smothering in an airtight cage of poverty in the midst of an affluent society; when you suddenly find your tongue twisted and your speech stammering as you seek to explain to your six-year-old daugh-ter why she can't go to a public amusement park that has just been advertised on tele-vision, and see tears welling up in her eyes when she is told that Funtown is closed to colored children, and see ominous clouds of inferiority beginning to form in her lit-tle mental sky, and see her beginning to distort her personality by developing an un-conscious bitterness toward white people; when you have to concoct an answer for a five-year-old son who is asking, "Dad, why do white people treat black people so mean?"; when you take a cross-country drive and find it necessary to sleep night after night in the uncomfortable corners of your automobile because no motel will accept you; when you are humiliated day in and day out by nagging signs reading "white" and "colored"; when your first name becomes "nigger," your middle name becomes "boy" (however old you are) and your last name becomes "John," and your wife and mother are never given the respected title "Mrs."; when you are harried by day and haunted by night by the fact that you are a Negro, living constantly at a tip-toe stance, never quite knowing what to expect next, and are plagued with inner fears and outer resentments; when you are forever fighting a degenerating sense of "nobodiness"—then you will un-derstand why we find it difficult to wait. There comes a time when the cup of en-durance runs over, and men are no longer willing to be plunged into the abyss of de-spair. I hope, sirs, you can understand our legitimate and unavoidable impatience.

He expressed extreme disappointment in the white "moderates" of the South. He was "the Negros greatest stumbling block in his stride toward freedom." He also expressed disappointment with the white "moderate" church and its leadership. He said, "If today's church does not recapture the sacrificial spirit of the early church, it will lose its authenticity, forfeit the loyalty of millions, and be dismissed as an irrel-evant social club with no meaning for the twentieth century."

The handwritten letter was smuggled out of jail by one of King's lawyers and then typed at the Gaston Motel. It was first published by the American Friends Service Committee and then by the *Christian Century*, *Liberation* and the *New Leader*. It was widely distributed with nearly a million copies circulating in churches and in Washington. It was judged the most eloquent and learned statement of the goals and philosophy of the nonviolent revolution ever written. The eight "moderate" clergymen did not answer it.

Desegregation of Greensboro, NC, 1963

The apartheid states employed a variety of strategies in reaction to the Supreme Court's *Brown* decision. The list includes (1) physical attack on the leaders, (2) defiance of Washington authority, (3) enactment of laws to shut down the NAACP, (4) use of truncheons, water hoses, attack dogs and tear gas against activists, (5) incarceration, incarceration, incarceration, (6) prevent blacks from voting and (7) jiu-jitsu—say "yes" to the principle of integration but require a consensus, go slow and avoid it. Greensboro, North Carolina, used the jiu-jitsu system. To counter it, the blacks resorted to large, repeated demonstrations designed to destabilize business until an agreement was reached.

In 1960, the Greensboro Establishment permitted a token desegregation of two lunch counters. That cut the momentum of the movement for two years. There were a few sporadic picketings of movie theaters by students but nothing sustained and successful. By 1963, the black activists were ready to again mount a major attack on apartheid.

The desegregation campaign started in late September 1962 when hundreds of students picketed two cafeterias in downtown Greensboro, the S&W and the Mayfair, on a daily basis. In October, the picketing was replaced by massive Saturday marches downtown. Fifteen hundred black students marched one Saturday, and 2,000 the next Saturday. The marchers sang freedom songs and carried signs demanding a boycott of merchants that did not integrate. The marchers were ladies from Bennett College and both sexes from North Carolina Agricultural and Technical College (A&T). The marches were followed by a mass rally addressed by James Farmer, national chairman of CORE. In November, there was another 2,000 student march downtown and 48 members of CORE were arrested for sitting-in at the two cafeterias.

These marches upset the downtown businessmen and got the attention of the mayor. The Mayor's Human Relations Commissions (consisting of both black and white business and education leaders) endorsed equal treatment of all people but also emphasized the right of businesses to decide who should enter their premises. This reflected the position of North Carolina governor, Terry Sanford, who held that desegregation should occur but only through voluntary compliance. This standoff lasted until April 1963 when the students again became active.

From April to June 1963 Greensboro blacks and the Greensboro Establishment played out one of the most large-scale and dramatic confrontations of the nonviolent freedom revolution. Following are the highlights of that freedom opera.

April—Demonstrations recommenced against restaurants that excluded blacks. Three students were arrested for a protest at McDonald's.

May 11—Thirty students picketed McDonald's.

May 12, 13—Demonstrations occurred at the other chain stores and two cafeterias, S&W and Mayfair. The KKK set up a counter picket line.

May 14—Three hundred and fifty demonstrators marched downtown and held a kneel-in in front of local theaters.

May 15—Two thousand students from Bennett College and A&T demonstrated at S&W and Mayfair cafeterias and at Center and Carolina theaters. Two hundred were arrested.

May 16—The Mayor's Human Rights Commission, chamber of commerce and merchants association held an emergency meeting and passed resolutions endorsing equal access of all citizens to government and business facilities in the city.

One thousand students marched downtown and then returned to their campuses.

May 17—The S&W Cafeteria and the Center Theatre rejected the recommendations of the C of C and the M.A.

More than 500 disciplined protestors attempted to enter downtown cafeterias and theaters. The police arrested more than 400. Only ten posted bail.

May 18, 19—Two hundred more students demonstrated and were arrested. Filling the jails to put pressure on the mayor became a prime tactic.

May 20—More demonstrators were arrested. A total of 940 were arrested in four days.

May 15—The Greensboro Men's Club, composed of the black male community leaders, wrote Mayor Schenck that they supported the students.

May 19—James Farmer, national director of CORE, addressed a mass rally. Jesse Jackson also spoke. Attendance was 1,200. Farmer said that a second revolutionary war had begun.

May 20—Another rally was held at Trinity AME Zion Church. Attendance was more than 1,000. A resolution prepared by local ministers to boycott white-owned businesses was enthusiastically accepted. They sang *We Shall Overcome* and 400 marched downtown to get arrested. More than 1,000 activists were in city jails. Governor Sanford intervened to solve the problem of overcrowded jails. He called on acting president, Lewis Dowdy of A&T, to take the students back to their campus.

May 21—The first court hearing was held for the jailed students. The judge remanded some of the students into the custody of their colleges. He then released a number of defendants. Two hundred and fifty students were taken from the National Guard Armory to the A&T campus by sheriff's orders.

May 22—The police transferred more than 700 A&T students to their campus. The blacks were thereby deprived of their tactic of filling the jails. So they turned to a new tactic—a super demonstration which they launched that very night. It began with a mass meeting of more than 1,500 blacks at the Trinity AME Zion Church. First they sang *Oh Freedom*, a spiritual that expressed their collective goal. Black ministers then told the assembly that it was time to show the whites how Negro adults felt about civil rights.

The silent march began. Two thousand marched two by twos. The line stretched more than eight city blocks. The marchers included every black school principal, 26 black ministers, black doctors, nearly every schoolteacher and hundreds of average citizens. In silence they marched to the center of the city. They made their point impressively that their nonviolent revolution was not by students only but by the whole black community.

The silent march had its desired effect. It increased the pressure on Mayor David Schenck to act. The *Greensboro Daily News* called for negotiations. There was a heated meeting between the mayor and black leaders and then the mayor agreed to break the deadlock by appointing a new committee: the Evans Committee.

May 23—Another silent march was held. More than 1,200 blacks marched downtown. Most were adults and teenagers. The students were restricted to their campuses.

The coordinating council of the protest organizations presented its list of demands: (1) all charges against demonstrators be dismissed; (2) the city must enact a public accommodations ordinance, (3) schools should be desegregated by September, (4) at least three black police officers should be promoted to detective, (5) blacks should be hired in various city departments and (6) at least one Negro should be appointed to each city board. The new Evans Committee tried to cooperate but the mayor was unable to make a decision to move toward desegregation.

May 24, Saturday—The protest leaders announced a temporary truce. The Evans Committee worked at negotiations.

May 27, 28—The Evans Committee convened meetings of restaurant and theater owners to attempt to get voluntary desegregation. Simultaneously, U.S. Attorney General Robert Kennedy held a meeting in Washington in an attempt to get theater-chain owners throughout the South to desegregate. Governor Sanford asked theater owners to desegregate. The truce continued. Mayor Schenck stuck to his position. He personally favored desegregation but he believed that it should come about by voluntary actions by individual citizens in an atmosphere of reason and calm. It should not be the object of illegal acts. Schenck had broad support. The KKK appeared at each march. Segregationists charged a Communist plot was behind the demonstrations. The White Citizens Council worked to maintain the status quo.

The desegregationists were also active. By June 1, the Greensboro Community Fellowship collected more than 1,300 signatures on a petition to remove the color bar in all public places. The YWCA endorsed desegregation and the Episcopal bishop of North Carolina called on church members to support civil rights for all. There were a few white leaders who would take a public stand for desegregation.

Last week of May—Protest leaders issued an ultimatum demanding action before June 3.

June 2—The activists convened a mass meeting in the afternoon and then they broke the truce and commenced a silent march downtown. The coordinating council of activist organizations presented a revised demand for action to the city council. It called for the city council to endorse equal treatment for all persons and support the immediate removal of the color bar in every business to which the public had access. They also asked the city council to hire workers strictly according to merit.

June 3—The city council met, debated and did not act.

June 4—Greensboro theaters announced that they were ready to work out a plan for desegregation.

June 5—Jesse Jackson led more than 700 activists downtown. They blocked the streets around City Hall. Jackson was arrested and charged with inciting to riot. That night, more than 1,000 blacks gathered at Providence Baptist Church. Their leaders spoke; they sang and danced and then they marched downtown. They were met by 50 state troopers that the chief of police had requested the governor to send. The demonstrators sat in the streets blocking traffic. The police arrested nearly 300 of them and hauled them off to jail. An hour later the last demonstrators left the square singing *Freedom, Freedom, Freedom*.

June 6—Mayor Schenck finally made a decisive move. He convened an emergency meeting of 23 community leaders. With their support he capitulated.

June 7—Mayor Schenck made a statement in which he affirmed that human rights took precedence over property rights. He called on all places of public accommodation to "immediately cease selection of customers purely on the basis of race." For the first time, the black activists had forced the mayor into a clear declaration in support of desegregation.

June 8–13—The mayor's new position led a number of business leaders to speak out in favor of desegregation. By June 13, eight restaurants had agreed to desegregate. Three motels pledged to desegregate, as did four theaters. Mayor Schenck declared that race would no longer be a criterion in hiring city workers. He pledged to appoint blacks to all city boards. He also promised to create a permanent human relations commission.

June 18—The S&W Cafeteria opened its doors to blacks.

July 2—The city council created a Commission on Human Relations and appointed prominent black activists to be members.

In September, four bowling alleys desegregated. Two black policemen were promoted to detective and a black employee in the tax office was promoted to assistant cashier. By the end of 1963, 200 blacks were attending school with whites in contrast to 19 in 1962.

The apparent success of this campaign may be attributed to the leadership which represented the whole black community. It consisted of three student leaders, William Thomas, A. Knighton Stanley and Jesse Jackson; two college presidents, Dr. Willa Player and Dr. Lewis Dowdy; Dr. George Simkins of the NAACP; CORE leaders; McNeill Smith, a white attorney; Dr. George Evans, a school board member; and the Rev. Otis Hairston, a minister.

This partial desegregation of Greensboro was accomplished in a short period without bloodshed or brutality, but the victory should not be overemphasized. The completion of desegregation in Greensboro was a long process with years of contention. The Greensboro schools were not fully desegregated until 1971, 17 years after the *Brown* decision.

Danville Demonstrations and Boycott, VA, 1963

Danville, Virginia, is a small city five miles north of the North Carolina border. In 1963, one-third of the population were blacks. The blacks were disenfranchised, segregated and exploited. The city's largest employer was the Dan River Mills, a textile factory. The mill employed 12,000 people and sold as much as $170 million worth of fabric and yarn in a year. Approximately 1,100 of the laborers were blacks. Most of them had menial jobs. The highest-paid black was a machinist who earned $80 a week.

In May 1963, two black Protestant ministers, the Rev. Lawrence Campbell and the Rev. Alexander I. Dunlop, decided that it was time to act. They led a demonstration at City Hall. They called for equal opportunity in municipal employment, school integration and desegregation of restaurants and hotels. They repeated the demonstration for five days. The Establishment's response was quick. The Virginia state attorney obtained an injunction against demonstrations and the Danville police arrested everyone who violated it. By the end of the week, 200 demonstrators had been arrested.

On June 5, the two ministers and several students sought a meeting with the mayor, Julian Stinson. They were told that the mayor was not in. They said that they would wait and sat down. The police assaulted the group and arrested the two ministers and one student who had bit a policeman. A grand jury indicted the ministers for "inciting to riot." Their bail was set at a very high $5,500 each.

On June 6, the Rev. Campbell telephoned Jim Forman in Atlanta and asked for help from the SNCC. On June 8, Forman sent 14 SNCC workers to Danville for the summer. On June 10, the demonstrations recommenced. Sixty-five civil rights activists marched to City Hall. They were met by a police reception committee with fire hoses. The fire hoses were turned on the demonstrators and newly deputized city employees clubbed anyone who tried to escape. Of the 65 demonstrators, 48 were wounded and 50 were arrested. Two were severely injured and many were hospitalized.

The next day, June 11, a group of 200 activists marched to City Hall calling for equality in public hiring and protesting police brutality. Again, Mayor Stinson refused to see them. On June 13, the Rev. Lendell W. Chase, pastor of the High Street Baptist Church and president of the Danville Christian Progressive Association—the local organization behind the Danville campaign—led a procession of 250 citizens to see the mayor. No luck! The doors of City Hall were barred. Sandwiches and soft drinks were served, courtesy of the High Street Church. Then the fire trucks rolled in and police in riot gear appeared. The crowd dispersed.

That night, the regular mass meeting was held at the Baptist church. It was an unusual church meeting. Police with submachine guns were stationed at roadblocks near the church. Nearby was a riot tank with four mounted machine guns. Nothing violent happened.

On July 9, 1963, the blacks extended their boycott to include the products of the Dan River Mills and to push for fair employment at the mills. Each day pickets marched at the main entrance. The picket lines were manned by local people, SNCC workers and some out-of-town volunteers. On July 17, the International Ladies Garment Workers Union (ILGWU) staged a sympathy demonstration in New York.

The Danville Establishment followed a "game plan" of five parts: (1) no negotiations, (2) fire hoses and clubbings for demonstrators, (3) wholesale arrests and sentences of 45 days in jail, (4) minimization of the opportunity for the media to photograph any police violence, and (5) incarcerate or scare all "outsiders" out of town. By August 28, over 600 protestors had been arrested and charged. A total of 236 court cases grew out of the confrontation. All were appealed. Less than one percent were overturned. Three white "outsiders" who were assisting the blacks were forced to leave town quickly before a grand jury convicted them of "inciting blacks to riot."

Throughout the summer confrontation, the blacks' tactics stood in contrast to those of the whites'. Instead of water hoses, billy clubs and a racist incarceration system they relied on prayer, mass community meetings and mutual support through singing. They held mass meetings several times a week for news updates, mutual encouragement and expression of their feelings in song. The songs expressed their suffering, their struggle, their religious values and their hopes. The meetings always ended with clasped hands and a singing of *We Shall Overcome*.

The Danville confrontation was a standoff. Neither side won but both sides were pleased with their performance. The Virginia attorney general, Mayor Stinson and the Danville Establishment leaders were satisfied with their management of the episode. They had effectively discouraged "outsiders," and they had taught the local blacks to keep their place. Their equipment—fire hoses, billy clubs, tanks and jail—worked well and the media was kept from photographing police violence.

The blacks felt that while they lost a skirmish they looked forward to winning the war. They had tested the psychological/spiritual/political tactic of nonviolence. They found that they had the physical and spiritual force to implement it. They learned that their method required more coverage by the media than they had obtained. They had tested the power and togetherness of their community and found it to be strong and supportive. They saw Danville as one episode in a long struggle that they were now sure that they would eventually win.

March on Washington, DC, 1963

A. Philip Randolph was president of the Brotherhood of Sleeping Car Porters and a vice president of the AFL-CIO. He had been a civil rights activist since World War I. In 1963, he told his fellow leaders of black organizations that the way to persuade the Washington Establishment that blacks were serious in their demand for freedom was to march on Washington. His colleagues debated the proposal and then decided to do it. The sponsors of the project were the "Big Six" of black activist organizations. They were Roy Wilkins of the NAACP; Dr. King of the SCLC; James Farmer of CORE; John Lewis of the SNCC; Whitney Young of the Urban League; and A. Philip Randolph of the BSCP. The "Big Six" provided financing, personnel and a supervising committee. Randolph was named the march director and his deputy, Bayard Rustin, did all of the detailed planning.

On August 28, 1960, an estimated 250,000 activists converged on the nation's capital to demonstrate for freedom. Twenty-one chartered "freedom trains" and 200 chartered "freedom buses" brought marchers to Washington from nearly every state. There were whites and Negroes, representatives of all major religions, economic classes, professions and political parties. Rustin obtained support from a broad range of organizations. The march was endorsed by the National Council of Churches of Christ, the American Baptist Convention, the Brethren Church, the United Presbyterian Church and by congregations and ministers of the Lutheran and Methodist churches. All major Jewish organizations endorsed the march and were represented. The Catholic archdiocese was officially represented and a large number of local and international unions participated. Initially, President Kennedy was opposed to the march and tried to stop it; but when he talked with the leaders and saw their determination he supported it.

The goal of the march was to demonstrate for jobs and freedom and to lobby Congress and the president for passage of a civil rights bill that President Kennedy was in the process of developing.

While waiting for the speeches the quarter of a million marchers on the Mall in front of the Lincoln Memorial were well entertained. The entertainers included Harry Belafonte, Clarence Jones, Marlon Brando, Joan Baez, Odetta, Josh White, Peter, Paul and Mary, Bob Dylan, the SNCC Freedom Singers, Josephine Baker, Marian Anderson and Mahalia Jackson. A. Philip Randolph opened the speaking program by saying, "We are the advance guard of a massive moral revolution for jobs and freedom!" In a tribute to women leaders of the movement, Randolph introduced Rosa Parks, Daisy Bates, Diane Bevel Nash and Gloria Richardson.

The speakers that followed included Fred Shuttlesworth, John Lewis, the Rev. Eugene Carson Blake, Rabbi Joachim Prinz and Walter Reuther. The Lewis speech was the most pointed. He said, "My friends, let us not forget that we are involved in a serious social revolution. By and large, American politics is dominated by politicians who build their careers on immoral compromises and ally themselves with open forms of political, economic and social exploitation." After an afternoon of singing and oratory, Randolph introduced Dr. King as "the moral leader of our nation." The crowd applauded and the band played *The Battle Hymn of the Republic*. With the Lincoln Memorial behind him, Dr. King delivered a speech that is compared with Lincoln's Gettysburg Address as one of the greatest in American history.

King's speech included many stirring paragraphs that are frequently quoted today, such as:

> I have a dream that one day this nation will rise up and live out the true meaning of its creed: "We hold these truths to be self-evident, that all men are created equal."
>
> I have a dream that one day, on the red hills of Georgia, sons of former slaves and the sons of former slave owners will be able to sit down together at the table of brotherhood.
>
> I have a dream that my four little children will one day live in a nation where they will not be judged by the color of their skin but by the content of their character.
>
> I have a dream that one day, down in Alabama, with its vicious racists, with its governor having his lips dripping with the words of interposition and nullification, one day right there in Alabama, little black boys and black girls will be able to join hands with little white boys and white girls and walk together as sisters and brothers.

Immediately after King's speech, the march leaders and Walter Reuther went to the White House at the invitation of President Kennedy. The president and his guests had a discussion of the civil rights bill that Kennedy was attempting to get through Congress. The black leaders and Reuther suggested a stronger bill and the president detailed the legislative process and his political difficulties in getting it passed.

At the end of the day the national media reported the march to America. Reports featured the unprecedented numbers of marchers (250,000), the complete nonviolence of the demonstration and the brilliance of the singers and speakers. The *New York Times* had a front-page story headlined: "I Have a Dream"—Peroration by Dr. King Sums Up a Day the Capitol Will Remember," by James Reston. Both white and black papers featured the dream section of the speech.

Considering the march several decades later, historians observe that it was significant on four counts. It consolidated and solidified the northern pro-desegregation sentiment of churches and nonracist citizens. It provided for an exchange of views between black leaders and the president that helped to move his administration to support civil rights. It informed the U.S. Congress that the time had come for civil rights legislation. Finally, the march and Dr. King's speech was a morale booster for the thousands of blacks who had demonstrated and been abused throughout the South. In fact the March on Washington is frequently cited as a climax and turning point in the revolution.

Paradoxically, it was also a turning point for J. Edgar Hoover, director of the FBI. While millions of Americans saw the march as evidence that desegregation was an acceptable mainstream concept, Mr. Hoover saw it as evidence of a major threat to national security necessitating increased vigilance on black leaders to prove their connection to the Communist Party.

Tallahassee Theater Desegregation, FL, 1963

In early 1963, the CORE chapter of Florida Agricultural and Mechanical University (FAMU) decided to desegregate movie theaters. CORE followed its usual three-step procedure: (1) ascertain the facts, (2) attempt negotiations and (3) when negotiations fail, take nonviolent action. For step one, two students, Patricia Stephens and Julian Hamilton, tried to enter the Florida Theater with tickets purchased for them by a white co-conspirator. The students were refused entrance. The theater manager called the police. The police arrested them and took them to jail. Their case was dropped a few days later. Tobias Simon, the students' ACLU lawyer, filed a $1 million suit against Tallahassee city officials for unlawful discrimination. Simon then offered to drop the suit if the city would desegregate the courtroom. Judge Ben C. Willis agreed. Simon withdrew the suit but Judge Willis reneged on his part of the agreement and did not desegregate the courtroom.

The second step was negotiations. The theater owners refused to discuss desegregation.

The third step—nonviolent demonstrations—was begun. The CORE sent student pickets to the theater. The number of pickets grew continuously until there were 400 on May 29. The pickets, mostly FAMU and high school students, sang, clapped and chanted while a large crowd of white onlookers watched. The police kept the two groups apart. Coincidentally, the movie advertised on the theater marquee was *The Ugly American*. As the crowds of black picketers and angry white hecklers increased, Mayor Sam Teague decided to shut the demonstration down. He obtained a court order from Judge Willis that (1) restrained CORE members from demonstrating and (2) narrowly restricted the activities of the other demonstrators.

The students, excited by their collective action, chose to ignore the judge's restraining order. But instead of picketing they decided on a protest march from the FAMU campus to the State Theater near the Capitol. The marchers walked a short distance down the boulevard before they were stopped by a line of police. The police arrested 220 marchers and then guided their continued march down to the jailhouse. As they marched the students kept cadence by shouting "Free-dom, Freedom."

The mass arrests were reported back to the FAMU campus and a follow-up march was organized. Again, about 200 students started marching toward the Capitol. Mayor Teague acted quickly. This time the line of police stopped the march, sprayed them with tear gas and arrested 37 and took them to jail.

The mass arrests and tear-gassing made national headlines. The *New York Times*, *Time Magazine* and the *Miami Herald* reported it. Accompanying stories said that Secretary of State Dean Rusk complained that the civil rights problem was putting our nation's leg in a cast in the race against communism and that President John F. Kennedy was planning new civil rights legislation.

The next day, Judge Willis held a hearing on the charge of contempt of court against the 257 students who had defied his injunction. The judge was in a judicial mood. He told the assembled students that he didn't think that most of them had purposely ignored his instructions. He said that their signs such as "Segregation is Unconstitutional," "Are you An Ugly American" and "Freedom" were not defamatory. He announced a set of rules that would govern future demonstrations: no more than 18 picketers could protest at one time at the Florida Theater and only ten at a time at the State Theater. And then Judge Willis dropped all charges against the 257 students.

Protests continued under the judge's new guidelines but they lost their luster. They lacked spontaneity, impressive numbers and media appeal. At the time it appeared that the theater desegregation campaign had failed. The students' lawyer, Tobias Simon, had a different impression. He said that Judge Willis' ruling was a tremendous victory. It was the first time that the right of Negroes to picket a white business had been recognized by a court order. He predicted the desegregation would come to Tallahassee theaters shortly. His prediction was accurate. The judge's decision was the entrance of the nose of the camel of desegregation under the tent of apartheid.

Tallahassee Two-Way Pool Desegregation, FL, 1963

On May 30, 1963, three white Florida State University (FSU) students tried to purchase tickets to swim at the Tallahassee "Negro-Only" swimming pool. The students, Anne Hamilton, James Walker and John Parrott were arrested. They told the police and a reporter that they were not associated with CORE and that they assumed that the pools were open to everyone and they wanted to go swimming. They received the "white" treatment; they were fingerprinted and released.

A couple of weeks later, in June, two FAMU students, Priscilla Stephens and Rubin Kenon decided to desegregate the "Whites-Only" pool. They tried for three days to gain admission but were unsuccessful. On the third day, Priscilla, wearing a swimsuit, managed to slip through the gate and walk toward the water. A white policeman stopped and arrested her. He put handcuffs on her wrists and led her toward his police cruiser. He kicked her and shoved her roughly into the back seat. Priscilla was stunned by the handcuffing and rough treatment.

At her trial, Priscilla was not allowed to speak in her own behalf. In prison she was put into an isolated cell. She tried to keep up her spirits by singing *Oh Freedom* and other freedom songs. After her release, Priscilla and Patricia Stephens and Rubin Kenon went to a meeting of the city commission to file a complaint of police brutality. Before they could speak, however, two city commissioners left the meeting and so adjourned it while the mayor was praising the police department. The city commission then closed the pool rather than face additional protests. It was closed for five years.

This pool desegregation effort was a failure in the short run. In the long run, i.e., five years, it was a success. During the five intervening years a transformation of cultural values occurred. The Establishment leaders—the mayor, commissioners, judge, police and prominent businessmen—moved from a belief in enforcing apartheid to one of accepting racial equality in the use of public facilities. This move was pushed by the collective weight of pressures from many sources—the U.S. Supreme Court, the president, the media and the group's own members who began to see the contradictions between the values expressed in the Constitution and those expressed in apartheid laws.

North Florida Citizen Education Project, 1963–1964

One of the principal tactics of the nonviolent black revolution—along with integrated bus rides, bus boycotts and lunch counter sit-ins—was voter registration campaigns. The North Florida Citizens Education Project (NFCEP) was typical of similar efforts in several states. The NFCEP began in January 1963 and climaxed in the 1964 presidential election. It was sponsored by CORE and led by Patricia Due and then by Spiver Gordon.

By July 1963, Due had a staff of fifteen volunteer college students. Half were white; half were black. They were paid $25 per week. The director received $70 per week. Although most of the students had some previous civil rights experience, they all participated in orientation classes. They learned the history of CORE and the basics of the philosophy of nonviolent action. They were told that they came to work, not to "socialize," and speeding and marijuana were not allowed. They worked in same-sex interracial pairs with one pair per county. CORE lawyers told them that if arrested they should not resist but they should let the police know that there was a new law that an attorney should be present during questioning. Each worker was given the telephone numbers of lawyers with CORE, the NAACP and the Lawyers Constitutional Defense Committee in St. Augustine. At all times workers were to keep headquarters advised of their whereabouts. They also had the numbers of FBI offices. Two lawyers were stationed at the NFCEP office in Quincy.

Many of the new student workers were scared by the emphasis on safety in the training sessions. Those who were not soon learned to be. In mid–July, there was a drive-by shooting that shattered the windows in the NFCEP headquarters, the "Freedom House." Another time, nightriders came by and beat up one of the white male workers. The people in the house immediately called the police, the FBI and the mayor. None of them came but an hour later someone drove by and shot at the house again.

Finding rooms for the workers was a major task. It was necessary to find people who would share their very modest accommodations with both black and white civil rights workers in spite of the pressures from the white Establishment. The actual fieldwork was equally challenging. Many rural blacks were afraid to get involved in the voting process. They knew that it was not allowed by the Establishment. Many of the rural blacks were illiterate. Education deprivation was a hallmark of the apartheid system. If they did decide to register, transportation had to be provided. This was a problem. Car rental agencies stopped renting to CORE because of vandalism to the cars. Registration offices would often be open only one day a week. One county tried to close its registration books rather than register additional blacks.

In spite of the difficulties the numbers of registered voters grew continuously. On July 27, the fieldwork of several months bore fruit in Gadsden County. When the registrar's office opened at 9:00 A.M. there were 20 Negroes waiting to register. The registering continued all day. At closing time there were still 75 would-be registrants in line. The total number registered that day was 350, making the NFCEP total to that date 1,900.

Voter registration was not the only concern of the NFCEP. Self-help and self-determination was stimulated throughout Gadsden and other counties. Area churches hosted meetings and workshops on community involvement and direct action protests. Freedom schools were started to teach reading, writing, speaking, typing and other skills. Led by the Rev. James Crutcher, Gadsden County organized a Citizens Interest Group (CIG) which continued to work for community betterment.

The presidential election in the fall of 1964 provided a test for the NFCEP. While Goldwater won Gadsden County by a slim margin, President Johnson won Florida with a significant and noted amount of help from new black voters.

Saint Augustine Campaign, FL, 1963–1964

In 1963, St. Augustine, Florida, was very much like many other southern cities; it was viciously racist. Elementary legal rights and protection did not exist for Negroes. The sheriff, L.O. Davis, was a burly thug who employed one hundred deputies, many of them prominent Klansmen. His objective, he said, was to "keep the niggers in line." St. Augustine was also the home of barrel-chested Halsted "Hoss" Manucy, who wore cowboy clothes and led a bunch of Klan-style racists who called themselves the "Ancient City Gun Club." They patrolled the county in radio-equipped cars with Confederate flags on their antennas and harassed Negroes. Manucy boasted that he had no vices; he didn't smoke, drink or chase women. All he did was "beat and kill niggers."

In 1963, Robert B. Hayling, an Air Force veteran, inspired by Dr. King's Birmingham campaign, decided it was time to end the reign of terror in St. Augustine. He wrote to President Kennedy and Vice President Johnson to inform them of the racial violence that plagued the city and to ask for their help in enforcing civil rights. He also commenced to organize a local movement to desegregate public facilities and to assure uninhibited Negro voter registration.

For his efforts, Hayling and his accomplices received the full southern apartheid treatment. The police beat and jailed the demonstrators and stood by while the Klan bombed and shot up Negro homes and fired shotguns into Negro nightclubs. In September, Klansmen abducted Hayling and three of his colleagues. They were taken to an open field where a crowd was assembled. They beat them to unconsciousness with brass knuckles and ax handles. The crowd was about to douse them with kerosene and incinerate them when the sheriff arrived. He saved them so that his city would not receive the bad publicity that goes with a burning/lynching. In February 1964, Hayling's home was shaken by a shotgun blast and the homes of two Negro families whose children had been admitted to an all-white school were burned. The Klan also threatened violence against any business that desegregated.

Hayling's letter to Kennedy and Johnson went unanswered while the White House pledged $350,000 to help the white St. Augustine Establishment celebrate the city's four hundredth birthday in 1965.

Temporarily defeated but still determined, Hayling appealed to Martin L. King for help. He told King that the St. Augustine Freedom Movement was finished unless the Southern Christian Leadership Conferences (SCLC) could come down and help them. Only King could get the tired-out demonstrators to march again. Only King could draw the national media attention necessary to lift the iron yoke of apartheid. King agreed to help and sent Hosea Williams and Andrew Young and other staff members to St. Augustine. With permission from King, Hosea Williams inaugurated night marches. They were very dangerous but they permitted day workers to participate.

On May 28, 1963, Young led a night march downtown to the old Slave Market. At the Slave Market lights from television and newspaper cameramen suddenly shattered the darkness. Klansmen poured out of the market and set upon the marchers swinging bicycle chains and iron pipes. The police watched. One of the racist thugs knocked Young unconscious. As he lay in the street others kicked and beat him. After the agreed-on interval, the cops moved in and stopped the violence and the marchers were allowed to drag themselves, bleeding and crying, back to St. Paul's church in the Negro district for first aid. The same night white marauders shot up a beach cottage that Dr. King had rented for his headquarters. It was empty at the time. The next day Dr. King wired the White House that "all semblance of law and order has broken down in St. Augustine, and the President must provide federal protection for Negroes there." However, the administration refused to help. It felt that state and local authorities could handle the problem. The administration also assured Dr. King that the FBI would "stay on top of the situation."

On May 31, 1963, Dr. King arrived in St. Augustine to take command of the campaign only to learn that Sheriff Davis had obtained a court injunction that banned night marches. The sheriff held a press conference in which he announced that the FBI was in town to protect Martin Luther King. He also announced that, "The FBI insists that Dr. King is a Communist." On June 1, Dr. King and several lawyers went to the U.S. District Court in Jacksonville and asked Judge Bryan Simpson to overrule the St. Augustine court injunction and permit night marches to continue. Judge Simpson held a hearing on the petition. He learned that one of Sheriff Davis' special deputies was Hoss Manucy, a convicted felon. He learned from Dr. Hayling how the Klan had beaten and almost cremated him and his friends. Judge Simpson asked

Dr. King and Hayling to suspend demonstrations while he studied the case. They agreed.

To get negotiations started, Dr. King invited Harold De Wolf and four Boston University colleagues to St. Augustine. King gave De Wolf a copy of their modest demands: (1) desegregation of public accommodations in St. Augustine, (2) hiring of Negroes as policemen and firemen, and (3) appointment of a biracial committee to work out harmonious race relations. De Wolf took these demands to the city officials. The city officials rejected them. But there was good news from Jacksonville. On June 9, Judge Simpson enjoined Sheriff Davis and the City of St. Augustine from interfering with night marchers and prohibited the sheriff from committing any further "cruel and unusual punishment." In his court order the judge cited instances in which Sheriff Davis had crowded ten demonstrators into a small concrete sweatbox and had crammed 21 women into a circular padded cell ten feet in diameter.

Dr. King and Hayling were overjoyed that a southern judge had found in favor of the marchers. King decided that it was time for him and Abernathy to generate some "creative tension" by going to jail. They marched to Monson Motor Lodge, which overlooks Matanzas Bay, and demanded service in the restaurant until the police came and arrested them.

That night, while King and Abernathy were in jail, a white mob assaulted a line of 400 marchers as they walked through the plaza. After the usual delay, the police dispersed the attackers with tear gas. From jail, Dr. King telephoned President Johnson and told him that St. Augustine had experienced the "most complete breakdown of law and order since Oxford, Mississippi" and that he must send federal marshals to protect black citizens. In Washington, in the meantime, the U.S. Senate defeated a southern filibuster and the civil rights bill moved a step toward adoption.

King and Abernathy bailed out of jail but the demonstrations continued. In addition to marches there were swim-ins at white-only public beaches. At some beaches, gangs of racists wielding chains attacked the swimmers. C.T. Vivian was nearly drowned in one attack. A racist politician, J.B. Stoner, visited St. Augustine to help the Establishment. He harangued a crowd of whites at the Slave Market and led a parade of 170 followers through the Negro section. A few days later, Stoner and Hoss Manucy assembled a crowd of whites and talked them into a frenzy of anti–Negro hatred.

On June 25, 800 club-wielding Klansmen attacked a column of Negro marchers at the square. They clubbed Negroes to the pavement, ripping the clothes off a 13 year-old girl and mauling a *Newsweek* reporter.

For King and Hayling and their followers, the St. Augustine campaign had become a nightmare. The Johnson administration refused to send federal marshals. Florida governor Farris Bryant ignored Judge Simpson's injunction and barred any more night marches. With the opposition of the governor, the KKK, the St. Augustine Establishment, and no help from Washington, it seemed impossible to continue the civil rights campaign. But Judge Simpson was still at work. He persuaded Governor Bryant to name an emergency biracial committee to talk to both sides and seek a settlement. King called this move "a significant first step" and offered to call off the marches to give the negotiators a chance.

On July 2, King and other Negro leaders went to Washington and witnessed President Johnson signing the Civil Rights Act of 1964. Now the blacks had new legislation to support their struggle for freedom. At that time, the confrontation in St. Augustine, the SCLC's most violent and bloody campaign, appeared to be a great deal of work and suffering for very little gain. With several decades of hindsight, it appears that it helped to keep pressure on Washington to pass the Civil Rights Act.

Mississippi Freedom Schools, 1964

Freedom Schools were organized by the Student Nonviolent Coordinating Committee (SNCC) and the Congress of Racial Equality (CORE) under the umbrella of the Council of Federated Organizations (COFO). Staughton Lynd, a Yale historian who had taught at Spelman College in Atlanta, was program director.

The COFO leaders believed that Freedom Schools were necessary to compensate for a deficiency in the state school system. Education deprivation for blacks was a component of U.S. apartheid. Black schools were grossly inferior and headed in the wrong direction. They did not prepare students to be good citizens but to be poor second-class citizens. In 1960, black students in Mississippi averaged six years of attendance at poorly equipped schools. White students averaged eleven years at well-equipped schools. The state spent four times as much per student for whites as it did for blacks. Black people in Mississippi did not know about and so could not benefit from Social Security, the Agricultural Extension Service, the Soil Conservation Service or the Farmers Home Administration.

Teachers for Freedom Schools were recruited from colleges and universities in the North and California. A total of 650 volunteers went south to participate in the projects. Nearly half were female. Nearly half were trained teachers. Ninety percent were white and 26 were from the South.

The reason for inviting northern whites to teach in the schools was generally understood. If a black Mississippian was unconstitutionally arrested, beaten or killed, America would yawn. If, however, a white volunteer from Harvard, Yale or Berkeley were so treated there would be a nationwide outcry.

The budget of the schools was $1,900 per month, per school. Classes were frequently held in churches. To provide supplies, the teachers were asked to bring any educational material they could lay hands on—typewriters, stencils, magazines, comic books, chalk, plus 25 pens and pencils and a first-aid kit. Each Freedom School had a "library" which was a collection of all of the books and reading material and games that they could collect. The educational model at the Freedom Schools was cooperative. Students participated in shaping the curriculum. Students and teachers addressed each other by their first names. Class seating was often in a circle. Prospective teachers were told that the purpose of the Freedom Schools was "to provide an educational experience for students which will make it possible for them to challenge the myths of our society, to perceive more clearly its realities and to find alternative and, ultimately, new direction for action."

An immediate objective of the Freedom Schools was to develop black leadership. The textbook was the "Curriculum Guide for Freedom Schools" by Noel Day. This book informed the reader and also raised questions about (1) the Negro in the North, (2) the "better lives" that whites live, (3) the Mississippi Establishment structure, (4) the poor Negro and the poor white, (5) materialism versus soul values and (6) the philosophy of the civil rights movement. This course required extensive reading of Negro history. The end product of this course was a deeper understanding of both the white and black cultures and a strong motivation to work for freedom in a nonviolent way.

In mid–June 1964, the COFO volunteers assembled at Western College for Women at Oxford, Ohio, for a week of orientation and training. The volunteers learned the rules of survival for white activists in the South. Always drive five miles under the speed limit. Don't sleep near a window. Don't endanger your hosts by giving their address. Don't go anywhere alone—especially at night. The volunteers were informed about the racist climate of Mississippi. They were told about Bill No. 1969 that was passed by the Mississippi legislature. It specifically outlawed Freedom Schools, required anyone conducting a school to get a license from the county superintendent of education and set fines and jail time for anyone who failed to do so.

After the training, the volunteers were sent to towns and cities throughout Mississippi to organize and run summer Freedom Schools. Students age eight to twelve took courses in language (reading, writing and spelling), black history and mathematics. Students age 13 and over could choose three courses from the following five subjects: (1) language arts, which included public speaking and creative writing, (2) American history, which included Mississippi and black history, (3) social studies, which included geography and the constitutions of Mississippi and the U.S.A., (4) science and (5) mathematics. Typing was also offered. Students read poems by Langston Hughes and used a text published by the SNCC called *Negroes in American History—A Freedom Primer*. The Freedom Schools were entertained and informed by actors and singers. A touring group called "Free Southern Theatre" performed a play called *In White America*. A group of folk singers, including Pete Seeger and the Chad Mitchell Trio, also played the schools.

By July 9, 1964, there were 1,500 students of all ages attending 25 Freedom Schools in Mississippi. One-third of the students were over 35 years of age. By the end of summer, nearly 3,000 students had studied in over 40 schools.

The Freedom Schools were supplemented by Community Freedom Centers. Thirteen of these centers were established throughout the state. The centers had classes for the very old, for mothers with children and for preschoolers. Subjects of instruction included literacy, art, music, dance, recreation, day care and health. The director of the community centers was Annell Ponder, an SCLC field secretary.

The Freedom Schools and the Mississippi Student Union (MSU) held a joint conference in Meridian from August 1964. The purpose of the conference was to celebrate their learning experience and to state their collective judgment on major issues. They stated that action was needed to achieve racial fairness in public accommodations, housing, education, health, federal aid, jobs, foreign affairs, the plantation system, civil liberties, law enforcement, city maintenance, voting and direct action. They declared their support for the Civil Rights Act of 1964 and condemned apartheid in South Africa.

As was predicted and feared, the Freedom Schools triggered an excess of violence from the Mississippi Establishment. According to one estimate, the incidents of violence related to the schools included six murders, 35 shootings in which three people were injured, 30 bombings of homes and businesses, 80 beatings and 35 bombings and burnings of churches.

The Freedom Schools had an immediate and long-term effect. Immediately, they supported the voter registration drive. In the long run, the students learned a new self-respect and educators throughout the nation were provided with examples of student participation, hands-on learning, the study of black history and the benefits of community activism.

Mississippi Freedom Democratic Party, 1964

On February 1, 1964, the Student Nonviolent Coordinating Committee (SNCC) held a meeting in Atlanta, Georgia. The purpose of the meeting was to devise a way to get national media exposure for the Mississippi Freedom Summer project. A proposal was made to challenge the national Democratic Party to open its ranks to blacks at the presidential nominating convention in August. The proposal was adopted and George Ballis, a labor leader from California, gave the project its name: the "Mississippi Freedom Democratic Party" (MFDP).

The MFDP had two jobs: (1) to organize itself in Mississippi to select delegates to go to the national convention and (2) to persuade Democrats in other states to support their project. On April 24, 1964, the MFDP opened an office in Washington, DC. Ella Baker was the office manager. The SNCC leaders promoted their cause by attending state Democratic conventions and lobbying congressmen for support. On April 26, the MFDP held a kick-off rally in Jackson, Mississippi. Attendance was 200. By May, four MFDP candidates had qualified to run in the June 2 Democratic primary: Mrs. Victoria Gray, the Rev. John Cameron, Janes Monroe Houston and Mrs. Fannie Lou Hamer.

Progress was also made in obtaining support from Democratic groups throughout the country. On February 23, 1964, the Democratic Council in Long Beach, California, adopted a resolution that called for the seating of the MFDP delegates at the Atlantic City convention. In Washington, DC, the MFDP challenge won support from the Americans for Democratic Action and the Commission on Religion and Race of the National Council of Churches. On May 21, the Young Democratic Club of the University of Virginia passed a resolution calling for seating the MFDP nominees. On June 13, the Americans for Democratic Action (ADA) passed a resolution calling for "rejection of the racist Mississippi Democratic Delegation" and the seating of the "integrated Freedom Democratic Party." On June 14, the Democratic convention in Lansing, Michigan, adopted a resolution calling for the seating of the Freedom Democrats. On June 15, the New York delegation to the national Democratic convention went on record as favoring the seating of the MFDP. On July 5, the Oregon Democratic Party pledged support for the MFDP Democrats. On July 6, the Washington, DC, Democrats supported the Freedom Democrats.

On August 6, 1964, the MFDP held its state convention in the Black Masonic Temple, near the COFO headquarters, in Jackson. Three hundred delegates participated. They elected 68 delegates and alternates who would go to Atlantic City with the goal of unseating and replacing the "regular" Mississippi delegation.

According to the rules of the Democratic Party, each of the 1,884 voting precincts in Mississippi were required to hold a meeting in June to elect delegates to the 82 county conventions. These delegates, in turn, were supposed to elect delegates to the conventions in the five congressional districts. The district caucuses would then select delegates to the state convention and to the national Democratic convention. The MFDP monitored the candidate selection process of the "regular" Democrats and found that the prescribed procedure was not followed. They discovered that three-fourths of the precincts (1,413) did not bother to hold a meeting. The MFDP collected affidavits to document these nonevents for later presentation to the Credentials Committee of the National Democratic Party.

If there was any question about the position of the "regular" Mississippi Democratic Party it was dispelled on June 30, 1964, when the party released its platform. It stated that its goals were not those of the national party. It opposed civil rights, the poll tax amendment and the United Nations. It stated, "We reject and oppose the platforms of both national parties and their candidates."

When the MFDP challenge became a national media story, Dr. Martin Luther King was drawn into it. Dr. King visited Mississippi for five days, speaking to MFDP groups and encouraging their campaign. He also met with the campaign leaders, National CORE Director James Farmer, Bayard Rustin, Ella J. Baker, James Forman and Bob Moses of SNCC. Their principal concern was financial support of the program.

On the eve of the national Democratic convention, both of the Mississippi Democratic parties felt certain that they would be seated. The MFDP had meticulously followed the required procedure for selection of delegates. Democratic groups from California to Washington, DC, supported them. They had agreed to vote for President Johnson. Most important, theirs was a struggle for freedom and democracy against apartheid and oppression. The traditional Democratic Party members were equally certain that they would be seated. They were the Establishment! They had followed the customary procedures for selection of their delegation. They had President Johnson—the most powerful politician—on their side.

On August 13, the attorney general of Mississippi secured an injunction against the MFDP from the state courts. In addition, he promised to jail the delegates if they went to Atlantic City.

The Credentials Committee of the National Democratic Party commenced its hearings in Atlantic City on August 22, 1964. The media were focused on the MFDP representatives. Aaron Henry, the Rev. Edwin King, Joseph Rauh and Dr. Martin Luther King Jr. testified, and then it was the turn of Mrs. Fannie Lou Hamer. Mrs. Hamer, a former sharecropper and a hero of the movement, had a strong emotional argument. She testified about the time when she tried to vote in June 1963 and the police beat her and others sadistically. She said, "They beat me and they beat with the long flat blackjack. I screamed to God in pain. My dress worked itself up. I tried to pull it down. They beat my arms until I had no feeling in them. After a while the first man beating my arm grew numb from tiredness. The other man who was holding me, was given the blackjack. Then he began beating me. I can't … " and then "is this America? The land of the free and the home of the brave, where we have to sleep with our telephones off the hooks because our lives are threatened daily because we want to live as decent human beings?" Her picture of America was not what President Johnson wanted on TV during his convention. He called a spur-of-the-moment press conference to upstage her. He succeeded only in calling attention to her story, which was rebroadcast the next day.

The MFDP also had a strong and well-documented legal argument. They presented evidence that the "regular" delegates, who barred Negroes from participating in their deliberations, were not faithful to the ideals of the national party. Furthermore the "regular" Democrats opposed many of President Johnson's programs and were actually supporting Barry Goldwater, To help Johnson, J. Edgar Hoover installed wiretaps in the MFDP's Atlantic City phones and kept him informed of their activities.

The members of the credentials committee were strongly impressed by the MFDP testimony. However, as stalwart Democrats who followed their leader, their report included a compromise proposal. The MFDP would be allowed two at-large delegates and was promised a fairer selection process the next time in 1968. The MFDP representatives caucused to consider the proposal. Chairman Bob Moses asked the delegation if they would be willing to take the two seats offered. The MFDP voted not to accept it. Said Mrs. Hamer, "We didn't come all this way for no two seats."

President Johnson was very unhappy with the MFDP's refusal to compromise. He was running scared and feared the loss of both black and southern white votes. The entire leadership of the National Democratic Party proceeded to apply extreme pressure on the MFDP to go along with the two-delegate proposal. They persuaded several prominent civil rights leaders to help them work on the MFDP delegates. Roy Wilkins, Dr. Martin Luther King Jr., Bayard Rustin, James Farmer and attorney Joseph L. Rauh Jr. all lobbied hard in favor of the compromise. Mrs. Hamer and her colleagues held tight to their principles and their position, standing up to all the big names of national and civil rights politics.

The Johnson administration refused to go beyond the offer of two at-large seats and the MFDP delegates were not seated. The MFDP people were disappointed. They had followed Democratic Party regulations scrupulously, they were supporting President Johnson, and they were struggling for freedom for black Americans. They were especially resentful of being lobbied by leaders of other civil rights organizations— the NAACP and the SCLC.

The credentials committee had done its work. The next problem was to keep the MFDP from raising the issue of their seating on the convention floor. To accomplish this task, the Democratic leadership applied all-out pressure on key people on both sides of the issue.

Although they weren't seated, the MFDP delegates had some compensation. Mrs. Hamer and other MFDP delegates were invited to Johnson's inaugural ball. The MFDP challenge increased black voter registration. It stimulated the Democratic Party to reform its rules in 1964, 1968 and 1972. Mrs. Hamer became a folk hero as well as a footnote in presidential election history. President Johnson, once elected, turned his recognized parliamentary and political talents to getting the Congress to enact voting and civil rights legislation.

Women's Wednesdays in Mississippi, 1964–1965

In March 1964, Dorothy Height of the National Council of Negro Women (NCNW) held a three-day summit conference in Atlanta. Participants were representatives of the National Women's Committee for Civil Rights, the National Council of Catholic Women, the National Council of Jewish Women and the United Church Women. The purpose of the conference was to discuss the treatment of women and girls who were being jailed for civil rights demonstrations. The conference listened to reports on the status of the civil rights movement and to first-hand accounts of the brutality inflicted on civil rights activists. Then, Claire Harvey, the leader of the Jackson, Mississippi, delegates, stood and issued a plea. "If northern women could visit us regularly during the summer to act as a quieting influence by going into areas that are racially tense, to try to build bridges of communication between us, between our black and white communities—to be a ministry of presence among us—it would be of tremendous help to us."

The idea was seconded by Pauline Cowan who said, "I think that what we need is to have some women in the Cadillac crowd, black and white, go down to Mississippi. We could go down and call it 'Wednesdays in Mississippi.' We could prepare, go in on Tuesdays, volunteer in the Freedom Schools on Wednesdays and then come back on Thursdays." The proposal was adopted.

The Women's Wednesday s in Mississippi was a complement to Robert Moses' program of bringing northern students to Mississippi to help register voters. Pauline Cowan became the director of the program and the NCNW supported it financially. The League of Women Voters and the American Association of University Women helped to recruit participants. The nearly 100 participants included the wife of the governor of New Jersey and the wife of the president of Massachusetts Institute of Technology.

Arrangements in Mississippi—cooperation with the Freedom Schools and places to stay—were made by an interracial team consisting of Susan Goodwillie, a white NCNW staff member, and Doris Wilson, a black YMCA executive. The two leaders attended a weeklong orientation session at Western College for Women in Oxford, Ohio. In Mississippi, their project had to be secretive. They could not be seen together in public. Their cover was that they were collecting recipes for a book on Mississippi cuisine. When a planeload of a dozen volunteers arrived from the North on a Tuesday, Goodwillie and Wilson met them at the Jackson airport. Wilson picked up the black women and took them to the homes of black families. Goodwillie met the white women and took them to a hotel.

All of the women spent Wednesday visiting Freedom Schools, talking to students and teachers and delivering the supplies they had brought with them: paper, pencils, crayons, books, etc. They visited schools in Hattiesburg, Canton, Vicksburg, Ruleville and other towns.

The Freedom Schools benefited from donations of supplies and from the experience of talking to northerners who were beginning to understand and support their plight. The Wednesday Women had their eyes opened. They learned about the poverty and fear that permeated the region. They observed the bravery of black Mississippians who defied their state laws to try to get an education. They noticed that they were followed when they were driven to a school. They were shocked to witness so many elements of a police state.

On Thursday, Goodwillie and Wilson took the ladies back to the airport and sent them back to their homes in Boston, Chicago, Minneapolis, New York City, Philadelphia, Princeton, NJ, and Washington, DC. Back home, these Wednesday volunteers would report their experiences to their community and rededicate themselves to working for civil rights. The Women's Wednesdays in Mississippi was repeated in the summer of 1965. In the fall, the program evolved into "Workshops in Mississippi," which consisted of bringing representatives of federal agencies to the state to inform and assist blacks in utilizing their services.

This project is credited with giving needed moral support to the black teachers, volunteers and students they met in the Freedom Schools and with accelerating the process of the dominant culture learning about the need to extend education and voting to blacks in the former rebel states.

Selma Voter Registration Drive by SNCC, AL, 1963–1964

Selma, in Dallas County, Alabama, was a city of 29,000 people—more than half of them blacks. It was a Black Belt community on the banks of the Alabama River, fifty miles west of Montgomery. Before the Civil War it was a slave market. Whites

in Selma expected blacks to "know their place" and viewed Supreme Court decisions, the Civil Rights Act and the whole black freedom movement as part of an outside conspiracy to destroy the southern way of life. Blacks in Selma occupied the lowest rung on the economic ladder. They worked in maintenance positions for white
businesses, as domestics and as laborers in the cotton gin and other cotton-process-
ing industries. More fortunate blacks worked at Craig Air Force Base. In Dallas
County only one percent of voting-age blacks were registered to vote, in contrast to
65 percent of whites. In Selma in 1963, only 156 of Selma's 15,000 blacks were on the
voting rolls. Registration offices were open only two days a month. Registrars would
arrive late, leave early and take a long lunch break. The few blacks who succeeded in
seeing the registrar were given a "literacy test" that was designed to guarantee failure. Most failed.

In 1960, the Dallas County Voters League was formed in an effort to help blacks
to register. It had little success. In 1962, Reggie Robinson of the Student Nonviolent
Coordinating Committee (SNCC) visited Selma to assess the feasibility of an SNCC
voter registration drive. In 1963, Bernard Lafayette and his wife moved to Selma and
set up a Voter Registration Project. They tried to recruit volunteers from Selma University but the administration feared reprisals and banned them from the campus.
One night Bernard was beaten viciously by a group of whites in front of his own
home. A neighbor came out with a rifle and chased the goons away. The Lafayettes
left Selma and were replaced by another SNCC worker. Jim Bevel, an SNCC organizing specialist, came to Selma to help the Dallas County Voter League. He gave challenging speeches at rallies. After each rally volunteers marched to the Dallas County
Courthouse to register. But each time either the registrar's office was closed or Sheriff
Jim Clark and his deputies turned the marchers away with cattle prods.

In September 1963, the SNCC executive secretary, Jim Forman, and the SNCC
national chairman, John Lewis, moved to Selma to promote voter registration. They
were immediately harassed, abused, arrested and incarcerated by Sheriff Clark. In
early 1964, a city bus driver drove away when a pregnant black lady was trying to dis-
embark. The lady was dragged to her death. The SNCC organized a boycott of the
city buses in protest. The boycott achieved no notable results.

In July 1964, Lewis mounted a voter registration march to the Dallas County
Courthouse. It ended abruptly in the mass arrest of the marchers. After that march,
a state circuit judge who called himself a white supremacist issued an injunction
against the congregation of more than three blacks in public at any one time. Clark
enforced this injunction and thereby prohibited any more marches in 1964. He even
used the injunction to harass small groups of schoolchildren.

At this time—December 1964—the SNCC Voter Registration Project was mori-
bund. Law-abiding, nonviolent tactics had failed against illegal, violent tactics. The
SNCC leaders and the volunteer followers were without success and without new
plans to pursue their objectives.

There were two prominent reasons for the defeat. One was that in an effort to
appease southern Democratic politicians, President Kennedy had appointed several

judges who were ardent segregationists. These judges had no intention of helping blacks gain access to the ballot. The second reason for the defeat was the tactics used by the Selma police and Dallas County sheriff. The three key tactics, which they learned by an analysis of the Albany confrontation, were (1) mass arrests and incarceration, (2) court collusion and (3) hidden violence.

Mass arrests, day after day, put an excessive burden on the demonstrators and eventually reduced the numbers of volunteers as well as removing the leaders. A racist court system was a necessary component of the system. It supported the mass arrests and issued injunctions as necessary. Violence against marchers had to be hidden from the media and especially TV cameras. This prevented the general public from becoming aroused and so kept Washington out of the picture.

Seeing that they were making no progress in voter registration, the local Selma leadership decided to try a different approach. Amelia Boynton and the Dallas County Voters League and the citizens committee of fifteen members approached the Southern Christian Leadership Council (SCLC) and asked for help. The SCLC studied the situation carefully and decided that Selma would be a good site for an intensive SCLC campaign.

Selma Voter Registration Drive by SCLC, AL, 1965

Before King and the Southern Christian Leadership Conference (SCLC) decided to accept the invitation of the citizen's committee to help to register voters they studied the situation carefully. They decided that there was good support in the black community and that with a new approach and new tactics they could make significant progress. They also noted that the sheriff of Dallas County and the white Establishment were typical of the deep South—dedicated racists. The SCLC accepted the invitation and for the next three months—January, February and March—they conducted a campaign with more participants and at a faster pace than the SNCC, plus the strategic use of King's appeal to the white media.

On January 2, 1965, King opened the campaign with a speech in Brown's Chapel in the African Methodist Church in Selma. A crowd of 700 came to hear the recent Nobel Prize winner and they were not disappointed. King promised that there would be mass marches to the courthouse to register voters and to arouse the federal government to action. Representatives of the national media followed King to Selma. They reported what he said and reported the obstacles to black voter registration in the South. In his State of the Union address, President Johnson declared a goal of eliminating every remaining obstacle to the right to vote.

On January 18, King and the SCLC commenced their Selma confrontations. First Dr. King and a group of Selma blacks visited an all-white restaurant—without incident! Then King led a march to the courthouse, defying a court injunction against congregating. Again—no arrests! These two nonviolent confrontations were surprising but explainable. Selma had a new public safety director, Wilson Baker, who had studied Sheriff Pritchett's strategy in Albany and was trying to copy it. Pritchett had defeated the Albany campaign by refusing to commit any violence against blacks in front of the media cameras and reporters. He had thus deprived the activists of their means of communication with the public—pictures and reports of police brutality. Baker's policy of nonviolent reaction had one flaw: it wasn't shared by the Dallas County sheriff, Jim Clark. Clark was an aggressive racist like Bull Connor and was easily led into the trap of overreaction. Baker's policy lasted one day.

On January 19, 1965, the activists marched again—down to the courthouse. This time there was a photogenic confrontation before the media. Clark was lining up the marchers in an alley. Amelia Boynton, a veteran Selma activist, stepped out of line and didn't obey Clark's order to get in line. Clark lost his cool. He grabbed Boynton by the coat collar and shoved her down the street. Angered by the sheriff's rough handling of Boynton, 60 marchers pushed into the courthouse and refused to leave. They were all arrested. The next day, the *New York Times* and the *Washington Post* ran photographs of Clark roughly pushing this elegant lady. It was just the type of national exposure that the SCLC was seeking.

The accelerated schedule of marches continued. On January 20, three groups of would-be voters marched to the courthouse. Clark arrested them. On January 22, 100 black Selma schoolteachers marched to the courthouse to protest Boynton's arrest. The sheriff prodded the teachers off the courthouse steps with nightsticks. The teachers regrouped, marched back to Brown's Chapel and held a rally. Inspired by the schoolteachers who had put their jobs in jeopardy by their activism, other common interest groups marched. The undertakers marched, veterans marched, beauticians marched and schoolchildren marched.

During one of the marches, a fifty-three year old activist, Annie Lee Cooper, momentarily forgot her nonviolence training and created an incident. Cooper stepped out of the line of marchers, Clark jabbed her with his elbow and ordered her to get into line. Cooper responded by punching Clark in the face. As Clark fell she slugged him again. Two deputies tried to wrestle her to the ground, but she broke loose, ran to Clark and punched him again. Finally three deputies pinned Cooper down and the sheriff hit her in the head with his club. The next day newspapers had pictures of the sheriff raising his club to hit Cooper while the deputies held her.

On February 1, in accordance with the SCLC campaign plan, Dr. King led 250 marchers from the church to the courthouse. They walked together in violation of the city ordinance forbidding them to walk in a group. King and his marchers were arrested and incarcerated. Energized by King's arrest, 500 Selma school children marched to the courthouse, also in violation of the court order against groups. They were also arrested. On February 2, the *New York Times* carried a page one photograph of King praying before his arrest.

On February 3, one hundred additional marchers and 300 more schoolchildren marched and were arrested. Each evening, the television news showed the mass arrests and children being led off to jail. There were many stories of deprivation and brutality within the jails. U.S. Senator Jacob Javits, a New York Republican, called the mass arrests "shocking." King sent telegrams to several congressmen suggesting that voter rights legislation was needed. A congressional delegation of 15 went to Selma to see for themselves. Congressman Charles Diggs, a black member of that group, stated that voting rights laws were necessary.

On February 4, Malcolm X, the militant black Muslim minister, went to Selma at the invitation of the SNCC. He told a capacity crowd in Brown's Chapel that "the white people should thank Dr. King for holding people in check, for there are other black leaders who do not believe in nonviolent measures." On this same day, President Johnson held a press conference to make a strong statement in support of voting rights. Also on February 4, a federal judge issued an order requiring the Selma voting registrar to process at least one hundred applicants per day.

On February 5, King's last day in the Selma jail, his "Letter from Selma Jail" appeared as an advertisement in the *New York Times*.

On February 6, George Reedy, the president's press secretary, announced that President Johnson would send a proposal on voting rights to Congress.

On February 8, Dr. King met with President Johnson for 15 minutes and made his case for federal action. The SCLC was getting its message into the national media, it was influencing congressmen and the president but they believed that they couldn't relax—they must maintain and increase the pressure.

On February 16, C.T. Vivian, SCLC executive staff member, led 25 marchers through Selma to the county courthouse to protest a new local voter registration rule that did not open the registration process to blacks. At the courthouse, Sheriff Clark blocked the entrance. Vivian lectured Clark—contrasting the principles of democracy with the practices of the Nazis. Clark overreacted. He ordered the TV cameramen to turn off their lights and then he struck Vivian in the mouth knocking him down. This incident provided another shocking story in the news that evening.

On February 18, Vivian was invited to speak at a rally in the nearby town of Marion. His speech in Marion was followed by a march, a police ambush and attack and a police riot. (The next chapter tells that story.)

On February 20, James Bevel, SCLC leader, proposed that they march from Selma to Governor George Wallace in Montgomery. The idea was a hot topic of discussion among the SCLC and SNCC leaders.

On February 23, a group of Republican congressmen in Washington issued a statement: "How long will Congress and the American people be asked to wait while this administration studies and restudies Dr. King's request for new federal legislation? The need is apparent. The time is now."

On March 2, President Johnson met with Roy Wilkins and Clarence Mitchell of the NAACP and discussed federal legislation to assure voter registration for all.

On March 5, Dr. King visited with President Johnson for over an hour. King asked the president to include federal registrars in the voting rights bill and to abolish literacy tests which had been used to prevent blacks from voting.

On March 6, a surprise happened. Seventy white people who were humanists and/or nonracists marched to the Dallas County Courthouse in Selma. Their leader, the Rev. Joseph Ellwanger, was the chairman of the Concerned White Citizens of Alabama. He made a statement: "We consider it a shocking injustice that there are still counties in Alabama where there are no Negroes registered to vote and where Negroes have reason to fear hostility and harassment by public officials when they do try to register.... We are horrified at the brutal way in which police at times have attempted to break up peaceful assemblies and demonstrations by American citizens who are exercising their constitutional right to protest injustice."

As Ellwanger spoke, a group of racist segregationists began a counter rally. They commenced to sing *Dixie* in order to drown out the speech. Ellwanger responded by leading his group in singing *America the Beautiful*. A group of blacks who were watching the confrontation chimed in with a lusty rendition of *We Shall Overcome*. An objective observer might have thought that he/she was observing a casual meeting of three rival glee clubs rather than the last event in the SCLC Selma campaign before the attempts to march to Montgomery.

Police Ambush Marchers in Marion, AL, 1965

In the early 1960s, Lucy Foster, a community leader, and Albert Turner, a bricklayer, tried to get blacks to register to vote in the city of Marion in Perry County, Alabama. They worked with a black fraternal order called the Rising Star Association. The white Establishment employed its monopoly of force and little was accomplished. The blacks were happy when assistance was offered first by the SNCC and then by the SCLC.

In 1965, the SCLC was between projects and was looking for a new challenge to revitalize its campaign. They decided to expand their registration drive to include Perry County and to add night marches to their program. Night marches were dangerous but they permitted working people to participate. The new leadership and the new tactic brought out more marchers, but the Establishmenet opposition also added new tactics. On February 3, 1965, 700 schoolchildren and their managers marched downtown in a massive demonstration. They were all arrested and hauled off to jail. The marches continued and the arrests continued until half the population of Marion was incarcerated in jails throughout the county.

On February 18, 1965, the blacks met as usual at the Zion United Methodist Church. They listened to a rousing sermon by the Rev. C.T. Vivian, SCLC officer, and then Turner led the marchers out of the church. They were headed for downtown Marion. But as soon as the marchers had exited the church they were ambushed. The State Troopers, assisted by local police and KKK-type terrorists, shot out the streetlights and attacked the marchers with truncheons. They beat up anyone who was black whether they were with the marchers or not. The troopers also beat up two UPI photographers and smashed their cameras. Richard Valeriani, a correspondent for NBC, was beaten with an axe handle and hospitalized. He required six stitches to close a cut. Some marchers were arrested and taken bleeding to jail. The rest scattered as best they could. Some returned to the church. When troopers followed them and tried to enter the church, the marchers beat them back with chair legs and rungs.

One of the black casualties was 80-year-old Cager Lee. Another was Cager Lee's 26-year-old grandson, Jimmie Lee Jackson. Jackson was in Mack's Café where his mother and sister worked. He was trying to get his grandfather to a doctor. A trooper attacked his mother. Jackson tried to protect her. Troopers cornered him in the café and shot him in the stomach. He died in the Good Samaritan Hospital in Selma a few days later. The next day the story of the police brutality and murder hit the front page of the nation's newspapers. NBC reporter Valeriana appeared on TV from his hospital bed—his speech slurred and his head bandaged.

A memorial service was held for Jimmie Lee Jackson at the Marion Zion Methodist Church. Dr. King gave the eulogy. He asked, "Who murdered Jimmie Lee Jackson?" He answered, "He was murdered by the irresponsibility of every politician from the governor on down who has fed his constituents the stale bread of hatred and spoiled meat of racism." After the service (March 3, 1965), more than 700 people walked behind the hearse in the rain for the three miles to the Heard Cemetery, a slave graveyard. The section of Highway 14 that runs in front of it has been named the Martin Luther King Memorial Parkway. It runs 85 miles through the heart of the Black Belt and is one of the longest roads in the nation so named.

In a court hearing, Al Lingo, commander of the Alabama State Troopers, admitted that Jackson's assailant was a state trooper. But neither the trooper nor Lingo nor Governor George Wallace was ever prosecuted for the murder. The trooper's ambush attack brought renewed press coverage to the Alabama voter registration campaign and stimulated new calls for federal action. Even Establishment media were critical. One Alabama newspaper called the police attack "a nightmare of state police stupidity and brutality."

There were many threats on King's life during the Alabama voter registration campaign. One was telephoned in to U.S. Attorney General Nicholas Katzenbach during the Marion confrontation. Two assassination attempts were thwarted, one by King taking a back road and another by the dense crowd around King.

The SCLC arrived at the same conclusion as the SNCC which preceded them—it was not possible to negotiate civil rights with the Marion Establishment. The Marion campaign was a failure unless consideration is given to the larger picture. It produced a story and pictures of the funeral march that shocked TV viewers nationwide and it generated the plan to march from Selma to Montgomery.

Three Marches: Selma to Montgomery, AL, 1965

The final months of the Selma campaign were a roller coaster of physical and emotional ups and downs. The freedom activists suffered a police and trooper ambush, the murder of one of their members, a bloody Sunday encounter, a prayerful attempt to march and finally a triumphal march to the Capitol in Montgomery.

The first attempt to march was on March 7. More than 500 marchers assembled at Brown's chapel in Selma. After final instructions, the marchers, led by Hosea Williams of the SCLC and John Lewis and Robert Mants of the SNCC, headed toward Montgomery. Sheriff Jim Clark waited for the marchers with his deputies and state troopers on horseback at the Edmund Pettus Bridge on the outskirts of Selma. The sheriff and his men were three deep across the highway, wearing gas masks and helmets and carrying billy clubs.

When the marchers arrived, Clark ordered them to disperse within two minutes. In one minute the police attacked the marchers. They smashed the front line of marchers with billy clubs. John Lewis's skull was fractured. Then the mounted police regrouped and attacked again, firing tear gas. Simultaneously, Clark's posse attacked from a flank with rubber hoses, bullwhips and clubs. Bleeding, gasping and choking, the marchers stumbled and dragged their wounded back to Brown's Chapel. The media carried the pictures of the troopers' attack to homes throughout the country. Editorial writers, congressmen and the public expressed shock and outrage. The day went down in history as "Bloody Sunday."

The second march was the "Prayer" or "Turnaround" march on March 9. Dr. King returned to Selma and called for another march. A court order was issued to halt the march until a hearing could be held. Dr. King did not heed the court order but quietly negotiated with representatives of the White House for a modified march scenario. He would march only to the bridge and it would be a prayerful march instead of a confrontational march.

Dr. King spoke to the marchers at Brown's Chapel and then led about 2,000 over the bridge to another blockade of troopers. The troopers stood still. Dr. King and the marchers knelt and prayed for freedom and justice in America. Then Dr. King led the marchers back to Brown's Chapel. It was not, however, a peaceful day. That night, March 9, the Rev. James Reeb, a Unitarian minister from Boston, was clubbed unconscious by four white racists outside the Silver Moon Café in Selma. He died two days later in a Birmingham hospital. Again much of the nation was shocked. There was an outpouring of telegrams to the White House demanding action. The strongest voices came from labor and religious organizations—Protestant, Catholic, Greek Orthodox and Jewish. Reeb's memorial service drew thousands from across the country. The murder of a white activist greatly increased the white public's reaction.

President Lyndon B. Johnson was the final recipient of the demands for action. On Friday, March 12, he conducted his first press conference since "Bloody Sunday." With him at the press conference was Alabama's governor George Wallace. The president had invited him to Washington for a discussion of Selma. More than a thousand civil rights advocates were outside the White House fence. President Johnson spoke to the media and to the nation. The president said that the country had witnessed "a very deep and painful challenge to the unending search for American 'freedom.'" The marchers, he said, "attempted peacefully to protest the denial of the most basic political right of all—the right to vote.... Ninety-five years ago our Constitution was amended to require that no Americans be denied the right to vote because of race or color. Almost a century later, many Americans are kept from voting simply because they are Negroes." President Johnson said, "I have made it clear, whether the governor agrees or not, that law and order will prevail in Alabama, that people's rights to peaceful assembly will be preserved and that their constitutional rights will be protected." President Johnson concluded his press conference by saying that he had advised Governor Wallace to (1) declare his support for universal suffrage, (2) assure the right of peaceful assembly in Alabama and (3) hold biracial meetings with his state's citizens. Governor Wallace made no comment. Johnson was followed by Attorney General Katzenbach, who briefed the reporters on the final draft of the voting rights bill which would be delivered to Congress the following Monday.

On Monday, March 15, Dr. King preached at a memorial service for James Reeb in Salem. More than 2,000 people attended. On Monday evening, President Johnson addressed the U.S. Congress and seventy million Americans in a televised speech. His subject was Selma and voting rights. He said, "It is wrong—deadly wrong—to deny any of your fellow Americans the right to vote in this country.... The blacks' actions and protests, his courage to risk safety and even to risk his life, have awakened the conscience of this nation." He said that Selma was a milestone in the nation's development comparable to Lexington, Concord and Appomattox—an event where "history and fate met at a single time in a single place, to shape a turning point in man's unending search for freedom." He concluded his speech with the movement's slogan, declaring, "*We shall overcome* America's crippling legacy of bigotry and injustices."

President Johnson's speech confirmed a radical change that was taking place in the racial policy of the federal government. It indicated that the executive branch would join the Supreme Court in condemning apartheid. It implied that the president would continue to turn the Congress toward racial equality and persuade the FBI to protect the rights of all citizens. Dr. King and his colleagues realized the significance of the speech and were briefly overcome with a sense of massive accomplishment. They had marched, suffered insults, imprisonment and even death for ten years to hear these words from the chief executive.

Their celebratory mood was cut short. The next day, March 16, there was another violent, racist incident. A group of Montgomery County sheriff's deputies attacked a number of SNCC protestors near the Alabama state Capitol. The posse was mounted and armed with whips, canes and police truncheons. The unprovoked attack was reported nationwide. Again there was a public outcry. The next day, Dr. King led a protest march to the Montgomery County Courthouse and the sheriff made a public apology for the attack.

✶ ✶ ✶

The third effort to march from Selma to Montgomery was well planned. First the SCLC had to get court permission—often a difficult problem. In this case, the decision was in the hands of Judge Frank Johnson. On March 17, after several days of hearings, the judge handed down his decision. He said, "It seems basic to our constitutional principles that the extent of the right to assemble, demonstrate and march peaceably along the highways and streets in an orderly manner should be commensurate with the enormity of the wrongs that are being protested and petitioned against. In this case, the wrongs are enormous. The extent of the right to demonstrate against these wrongs should be determined accordingly.

Judge Johnson was in tune with President Johnson's new policy. He approved the SCLC's march proposal. The only conditions he set were for the marchers' safety. A maximum of 300 marchers were permitted on the two-lane segment of Highway 80. An unlimited number were allowed on the four-lane section. He also enjoined Alabama officials from failing to assist the procession.

Governor Wallace was angered by Judge Johnson's decision. He told a statewide TV audience and a cheering legislature that Judge Johnson was a hypocrite and the marchers were "Communist-trained anarchists" urged on by a "collectivist press." He refused to supply security for the marchers. When the president learned of this he signed an executive order placing 1,800 Alabama National Guardsmen in federal service and named Deputy Attorney General Ramsey Clark to coordinate march security for the government. The SCLC was pleased with this support. The SCLC staff carefully planned other details—food, sleeping bags, toilets, traffic control, evening camp sites and entertainment.

On Sunday, March 21, Dr. King led 3,000 marchers down Sylvan Street to Water Street and then across the Edmund Pettus Bridge and on east toward Montgomery. Dr. King was flanked and followed by the Rev. Ralph Abernathy, Ralph Bunche, U.S. representative to the U.N., Rabbi Abraham Hershel of the Jewish Theological Seminary of America, several movie stars, clergymen, nuns, college students and assorted civil rights activists.

The streets were lined with hundreds of spectators. Some hooted and threw racist epithets but most were subdued, sensing that they were witnessing a historical event. Helicopters rattled overhead and armed guardsmen patrolled at intervals along the way. There was no violence. The field director for the SCLC was Hosea Williams. He ran a smooth and orderly march. Federal officials and guardsmen guarded their front and flanks and a convoy of guard vehicles, utility trucks and ambulances brought up the rear. As they marched, they sang:

> Many good men have lived and died,
> So we could be marching side by side.
> > Old Wallace, never can jail us all.
> > Old Wallace, segregation's bound to fall.
> Pick 'em up and put 'em down
> All the way to Montgom'ry town.

At the Lowndes County line the highway became two-lane. The column was trimmed down to the 300 the judge allowed.

The column walked seven miles. Supper was pork, beans and spaghetti, courtesy of the Green Street Baptist Church in Selma. They camped on the land of David Hall, a black farmer. Students from Berkeley, California, pitched tents for men and tents for women in deference to the white culture's fear of interracial cohabitation. There were no problems.

Day 2, March 22. Oatmeal for breakfast. The 300 activists walked 15 miles. Along the way, the Rev. Abernathy introduced Dr. King to wayside Negroes as another Moses sent by God to lead his people out of the wilderness. Overnight camp was at Rosie Steele's farm where they shared a pasture with white-faced cattle.

Day 3, March 23. The demonstrators walked 11 miles in the rain to Robert Gardner's farm. Dr. King had several blisters. He overnighted in a heated motor home. Dinner was barbequed chicken, hash, peas and carrots and a candy bar for dessert.

Day 4, March 24. The nonviolent protestors walked 12 miles to the City of St. Jude, a black Catholic school. More than 10,000 people assembled for the evening jamboree. The entertainers included Harry Belafonte, Leonard Bernstein, Dick Gregory, Joan Baez, Peter, Paul and Mary, Sammy Davis Jr., Johnny Mathis and Alan King.

Day 5, March 25. Protected by 800 federal troops, some 25,000 marchers completed the largest civil rights demonstration in southern history. They marched into Montgomery like a conquering army. The 300 who had walked the whole 57 miles wore orange vests. The walking crowd flowed up Dexter Avenue—the route of Jefferson Davis' inaugural parade. The song of the hour was *We HAVE Overcome!*"

The marchers were now ready to complete the technical objective of the march—to present a petition to Governor Wallace—but there was a hitch—the governor hid in the Capitol building and refused to accept the petition. The petition demanded the right to vote and an end to police brutality.

The celebratory mood was soon overwhelmed by another apartheid incident. A few hours after the rally in Montgomery, Viola Liuzzo, a white Detroit homemaker, was shot dead by Klansmen when she was driving marchers back to Selma. The FBI quickly nabbed the assailants. The quick action was facilitated by the fact that an FBI informer was in the car with the drive-by murderers. The FBI was "observing" but not "protecting" the marchers.

Two murderers were tried before local jurors in Lowndes County and won a mistrial. They were tried again locally and were acquitted. They were tried a third time by federal prosecutors who charged them with violating Liuzzo's civil rights. On December 3, 1965, they were convicted. It was the first civil rights conviction for a racial murder in the south.

The Selma to Montgomery marches—all well reported by the media—made a major contribution to the passage, five months later, of the Voting Rights Act of 1965. In 1996, the U.S. Congress designated Interstate Highway 80 between Selma and Montgomery as a National Historic Trail.

U.S. Supreme Court v. U.S. Apartheid, 1958–1968

In 1954, the U.S. Supreme Court triggered the civil rights revolution by replacing the doctrine of "separate but equal" of *Plessey v. Ferguson*, 1896, with the new doctrine of "segregation is unconstitutional" of *Brown v. Board of Education*. For the new doctrine of racial integration to be adopted as the law of the land it was necessary for it to be accepted and internalized by the eleven apartheid states. This herculean task was accomplished by two forces—protestors in the streets and judges in their chambers. The U.S. Supreme Court did not quit the issue after *Brown* but continued to be a participant in the ongoing reversal of national racial policy. This assistance was indispensable as other units of federal government were slow to implement the new concept. The president, the Congress and the FBI did not turn to support the equality concept until several years into the revolution. Following are twelve cases illustrating how the Supreme Court enforced the new direction in the apartheid states.

September 12, 1958: Cooper v. Aaron

The Supreme Court refused a request by Little Rock, Arkansas, school officials for a delay in desegregation of their public schools. Local officials had made the request after Governor Orval Faubus called out the state national guard to block the entrance to Little Rock High School to nine black students. The court convened a special session to hear this case.

June 30, 1958: NAACP v. Alabama ex rel Patterson

The Supreme Court struck down a state court order requiring the NAACP to produce its membership lists, holding it an unconstitutional restraint on the NAACP members' rights of association.

November 4, 1960: Gomillion v. Lightfoot

The Supreme Court held unconstitutional, as a violation of the Fifteenth Amendment guarantee of the right to vote, a state legislative districting plan that excluded almost all black voters from voting in city elections in Tuskegee, Alabama.

January 14, 1963: NAACP v. Button

The Supreme Court declared unconstitutional a state law, directed against the NAACP, forbidding solicitation of clients by an agent or an organization that litigates cases in which it is not a party and has no pecuniary interest. The court held that it infringed on the First Amendment right of association.

February 25, 1963: Edwards v. South Carolina

The Supreme Court reversed the breach-of-the peace convictions of student demonstrators who had marched peacefully to protest racial discrimination. The court held that the breach-of-the-peace statute was unconstitutionally broad and had been used in this case to penalize the exercise of free speech, assembly and petition for redress of grievances "in their most pristine and classic form," a clear violation of the First Amendment.

May 25, 1964: Griffin v. County School Board of Prince Edward County

The Supreme Court declared as unconstitutional, as a violation of the Fourteenth Amendment equal protection clause, the closing of all public schools in Prince Edward County, Virginia, to avoid desegregation.

December 14, 1964: Heart of Atlanta Motel v. United States

The Supreme Court overturned the court's decision in the civil rights cases of 1883. The court sustained Title II of the Civil Rights Act of 1964. Title II prohibited discrimination on the basis of race, religion or national origins, in accommodations that catered to interstate travelers or that served food or provided entertainment, a substantial portion of which was shipped through interstate commerce.

April 27, 1965: Harman v. Forssenius

The Supreme Court held that a Virginia law that imposed special registration requirements on persons not paying the state's poll tax violated the Twenty-fourth Amendment's ban on poll taxes in federal elections.

March 7, 1966: South Carolina v. Katzenbach

The Supreme Court upheld provisions of the Voting Rights Act of 1965 as a proper exercise of Congressional power to enforce the Fifteenth Amendment ban on racial discrimination in voting.

March 24, 1966: Harper v. Virginia State Board of Elections

The Supreme Court held that state laws that make the right to vote contingent upon payment of a tax violate the equal protection clause of the Fourteenth Amendment.

June 12, 1967: Loving v. Virginia

The Supreme Court held that a state law that provides punishment for persons who enter into interracial marriages violated both the equal protection and due process clauses of the Fourteenth Amendment. The decision stated that "the freedom to marry or not marry a person of another race resides with the individual and cannot be infringed by the state."

May 27, 1968: Green v. County School Board of Kent County, Virginia

The Supreme Court struck down a "freedom-of-choice" plan that would have maintained segregated schools in the county. The court stated that local school districts have an affirmative duty to eliminate segregation from public schools.

Meredith's March Against Fear, MS, 1966

James Meredith grew up in Kosciusko, Mississippi, as one of ten children. After eight years in the air force, he enrolled at Jackson State College in 1960. In October 1962, he matriculated at the University of Mississippi with considerable difficulties described earlier. He graduated from Ole Miss in August 1963. Meredith hit the headlines again in 1966 when, on June 5, he began a one-man march from Memphis, Tennessee, to Jackson, Mississippi. The purpose of the march was to show the world that Negroes were not afraid of whites in Mississippi and to encourage blacks to register to vote.

On the second day of the march he ran into trouble. As he was walking along

Highway 51, just inside the Mississippi state line, a white man rose from the bushes beside the road and hit Meredith in the back with a shotgun blast. He was taken to a hospital where his back was depelleted. Fortunately no vital organs were hit.

Dr. King learned of the assault and felt that he must support Meredith's march. He flew to Memphis. In the hospital room he met Floyd McKessick, national director of CORE, and Stokely Carmichael, the new chairman of the SNCC. While the CORE, the SNCC and King's SCLC had some disagreements over tactics and organization, the three leaders decided that, with Meredith's approval, they would continue the march. The three leaders, with a group of aides and field workers, drove out to the spot on Highway 51 where Meredith had been shot and, with an escort of Mississippi State Police, recommenced the march to Jackson.

After a day on the road the leaders returned to Memphis for the night. After making plans for the next day, the leaders turned to a debate of their policy differences. The debaters were McKissick, Carmichael, Roy Wilkins of the NAACP, Whitney Young of the Urban League and King. The issues discussed were the continuation of nonviolent protests, the participation of whites in the black movement, and the unity of all black organizations in the movement. McKissick argued that nonviolence had outlived its usefulness and blacks must demand their rights. Carmichael argued that blacks should seize power in areas where they outnumbered the whites. McKissick and Carmichael argued that this was a black march and they didn't need any help from the whites. Wilkins and Young were determined that the movement remain open to all races and be kept nonviolent.

Another issue was introduced by Charles Evers, brother of the slain NAACP officer Medgar Evers. He said that instead of marching up and down the highways they should be registering blacks to vote. Despite the Voting Rights Act of 1965, Mississippi lagged behind the rest of the South with only 30 percent of its eligible Negroes on the voting rolls. Carmichael and McKissick were very aggressive in their arguments and Wilkins and Young withdrew from the march. However, Carmichael and McKissick agreed to keep the march nonviolent in respect for Dr. King. King also won the unity argument—temporarily. A joint press release was agreed upon and distributed that called for federal action on civil rights. Charles Evers won his argument and the group turned to greater emphasis on voter registration along the route of the march.

At Grenada, special arrangements were made to register new voters. King led 1,300 Negroes to the courthouse where newly appointed black registrars worked far into the night to add 500 names to the voting rolls.

As the marchers headed south toward Greenwood, hundreds of blacks flocked to the highway to get a glimpse of King. As the column approached someone would shout, "There he is! Martin Luther King!" They would rush up to touch his hand. King's aides would join hands to protect him from the crowd. King would appear surprised and bewildered. He'd smile and touch as many hands as he could. At each night encampment King would go to the local Negro church and speak to the parishioners. Marching through the small towns tested the marchers' composure. Bystanders were ugly. They waved Confederate flags and shouted obscenities and threw things at the marchers.

A few days into the march the issue of slogans arose. Carmichael and McKissick wanted to use "Black Power!" in place of King's "Freedom Now!" The two sides argued to an impasse. To save the march, King proposed that both slogans be dropped for the remainder of the march. It was agreed and the march against fear and for voter registration continued.

In the town of Philadelphia, where Chaney, Schwerner and Goodman had been murdered two years earlier, violence broke out. Dr. King was conducting a memorial service on Main Street. A crowd of whites watched, jeered and then charged forward, clubbing the marchers with hoe and ax handles while the police looked the other way. Then some of the Negroes started to fight back and the police drove the mob away. That night, shots were exchanged between armed marauders and armed marchers.

On June 23, the marchers arrived at Canton in a driving rain. They proceeded to set up camp in a Negro schoolyard as previously arranged. Suddenly, out of the night, a phalanx of state and local police appeared, closed in and ordered the marchers to leave. King and the other leaders refused. Their people were wet and weary, they said, and this was a Negro schoolyard. The police laid down a barrage of tear gas and then charged. They attacked the blacks with night sticks, gun butts and whips. The marchers ran, fell and cried out in pain and disarray. King and McKissick guided their people to a nearby Negro church. They tended the wounded and tried to cope with bitter despair. Veterans of Selma's Bloody Sunday said that the Canton police attack was worse. King had never witnessed anything so vicious. He telegraphed Washington and asked for U.S. marshals to protect them. There was no response from Washington. There were some federal witnesses to the attack: John Doer, a federal employee, and a few FBI agents who did nothing. The march continued.

On June 24, King led 300 nonviolent volunteers back to Philadelphia to make a statement, to wit: "We can stand before you without fear after we were beaten and brutalized at Canton!" As they approached the courthouse they were stopped by Sheriff Lawrence Rainey, the sheriff who had held Schwerner, Chaney and Goodman in jail. Facing the sheriff and surrounded by an ugly white mob, King and Abernethy knelt to pray—with their eyes open. They said amen and then withdrew with no violence.

Finally, the marchers reached Jackson. King's wife, Coretta, and two of their children, Yoki and Marty, joined him for the triumphful procession to the statehouse. A band played *When the Saints Go Marching In*. Thirteen thousand people listened to speeches by King, Carmichael and McKissick.

The evaluations of the march made by its leaders in the '60s were largely negative. For King, it was a defeat. He had tried to unify the movement in nonviolent tactics. Instead, Carmichael and McKissick had used the march to introduce the belligerent and controversial concept of "Black Power." Roy Wilkins of the NAACP said,

"The term Black Power means anti-white power. It has to mean 'going it alone.' It has to mean separatism.... We of the NAACP will have none of this."

In historical perspective, it appears that Meredith's march against fear did make a contribution to the movement's goals. It increased voter registration by an estimated 4,000 new black voters. The gas attack shocked the public, many of whom called their congressmen. The refusal of help by Washington was notable but it may have led some Washington officials to rethink federal support of civil rights. The march also demonstrated that the blacks were not afraid to march in Mississippi—Meredith's objective.

"Operation Breadbasket," Atlanta and Chicago, 1962–1971*

"Operation Breadbasket" was a tactic used by black activists to persuade businesses that benefited from black customers to hire blacks in accord with their percentage of the local population. Here is how it worked. First, a target business that did business exclusively or extensively with black customers was identified. Second, the number of blacks employed was ascertained. If it was zero or nearly zero, the activists took the next step. Third, the Breadbasket leaders visited the manager and asked how many blacks were working for them and at what levels. Then they asked to speak to the black employees to confirm the facts. They also explained their belief that if blacks supported the business then the business should hire some blacks. If the manager withheld information or refused to cooperate or asked the activists to leave (which happened frequently), then they moved to step four. Fourth, the operation leaders called for a boycott of the business. On a Sunday, the boycott was explained by ministers in the black churches and the congregation was asked to carry it out. By Sunday noon, everyone in the black community had the message. By Monday, the convenience store or drug store or restaurant or bakery would be empty. This situation led the business manager to quickly reassess his hiring practices and consider hiring some blacks. This also worked well on manufacturers.

This system of "selective patronage" or "jobs for black consumers" was developed in Philadelphia in the early '60s. Three ministers, Leon Sullivan, Alfred Dunston and Joshua Licorish, showed how organized black consumers could persuade businesses to hire and promote blacks. Leon Sullivan was so persuasive in his meetings with business leaders that he ended up on the board of directors of U.S. Steel.

In 1962, several ministers in the Atlantic local of the SCLC invited the Rev. Sullivan down to explain the procedure and help in the organization. The Rev. Fred Bennett, a former classmate of Dr. King, administered the Atlanta program. The baking industry was the first target. Within a few months, a formal agreement was made with five bakeries that provided several dozen jobs and more than forty promotions for

---

This account and those of "The Chicago Freedom Movement" and "Cleveland Mayoral Campaign" following show the attempts made by the SCLC to take the movement north.

blacks. The program was labeled "Breadbasket" because the first targets in Atlanta had been bread companies.

Operation Breadbasket was also effective in desegregating large businesses. When Ford Motor Company was building a new assembly plant in Atlanta, a team of Breadbasket ministers paid a visit to the plant manager to encourage him to hire black workers. The manager was rude and unwilling to consider the ministers' request. With a little help from Dr. King, contact was made with Henry Ford. He was told that it might be difficult to sell Fords to blacks in Atlanta unless they were employed in the plant. Ford went to Atlanta to settle the issue. Ultimately, about a third of the labor force at the plant were blacks—a big economic boost for the black community.

Dr. King and his SCLC board of directors were impressed with the success of Operation Breadbasket in Atlanta. They spent several weeks researching and discussing the feasibility of taking the operation to other venues. They also debated the expansion of their freedom movement beyond the apartheid South to the de facto segregated North. They decided to go north and Chicago was selected as the target city. The SCLC board chose Jesse Jackson as the project leader. Jesse was a ministerial student in Chicago. His first contact with the SCLC was when he was one of thousands of students who made a spring pilgrimage to participate in the Selma voter registration drive.

Jackson surveyed Chicago's black clergy and found that they favored a Breadbasket project. To inaugurate the program, Dr. King went to Chicago and addressed a meeting of more than two hundred ministers. Jackson was skilled at motivating people and getting favorable publicity from the media. The operation took off. The first "selective buying campaign" of Jackson and his associates was against "Country's Delight Dairy." After less than a week of picketing, the company announced it would hire 44 black workers within 30 days. More successes followed.

Operation Breadbasket won an agreement with the A&P Company that provided 770 new black jobs. Sizeable gains were won from soft drink firms and grocery chains. A job agreement was made with High-Low Foods, a string of 50 supermarkets. They agreed to hire 183 black workers and to open accounts at two black banks and to stock products of six black manufacturing firms. Breadbasket boycotts were successful against Pepsi and Coca-Cola. They also won 75 new jobs from two dairy firms, Borden and Hawthorn-Mellody.

The SCLC board of directors was pleased with the Chicago program and decided to replicate it throughout the country. They held a two-day conference at the Chicago Theological Seminary to launch a nationwide program. More than 100 black ministers from a score of cities attended. Dr. King and Jesse Jackson spoke. As a result, Breadbasket teams were organized in several cities with considerable success. Dr. King visited Cleveland to announce a Breadbasket agreement with Sealtest.

Jackson's salary from SCLC was $3,000 per year at first. Later it was increased to $6,000 in recognition of his good work. He continued to direct the Chicago Operation Breadbasket until 1971.

Chicago Freedom Movement, IL, 1966

In 1966, schools in Chicago were segregated and grossly unequal. Some of the black "schools" were trailers or obsolete military barracks. The Chicago school system spent three times more to educate a white child on the North Side than it did to educate a black child on the South Side. The superintendent of schools and chief architect of the system was Benjamin C. Wills, an insider in the Daley political machine. He claimed that Chicago schools were integrated and of uniform quality. Frustrated critics of the dual school system organized the Coordinating Council of Community Organizations (CCCO), a coalition of thirty-four civil rights, religious and civic groups. The CCCO leader, the Rev. Al Raby, asked Dr. King to come to Chicago and help them desegregate schools and housing.

During 1965, Dr. King and his SCLC colleagues had debated whether or not to carry their desegregation campaign to the North. There were many pros and cons. The North did not have apartheid, i.e., segregation by state statutes. Instead, it had de facto segregation and exploitation with separate and unequal schools, residential areas and all public facilities. Chicago slum conditions were probably the worst. The Land of Lincoln had been a racist society since before the Civil War. Dr. King and his SCLC board knew it would be very different from the South, very difficult to work against an urban political machine, but also very rewarding if they could make progress. After much soul searching and against the advice of many of his advisors, Dr. King decided to accept the challenge and go to Chicago.

In early January 1966, Dr. King, accompanied by Andrew Young, Ralph Abernathy and James Bevel, went to Chicago to meet with Raby and other activists to plan their campaign. They were faced with a difficult task. Chicago was similar to southern states only in the segregation and oppression of blacks. Chicago was not governed by democracy but by a political machine. Political machine is a euphemism—it was actually a municipal dictatorship run by patronage and police power under the direction of Mayor Richard J. Daley.

The SCLC and the CCCO agreed to work together as the Chicago Freedom Movement. Their first cooperative act was to draw up a program of action. The successful Operation Breadbasket would be continued. They would conduct a block-by-block canvass of black neighborhoods to generate grassroots support. They planned southern-style marches and demonstrations to get media coverage. Special projects would be developed to attack slum conditions. The aim of the movement, according to Dr. King, was to secure the blessings of America for Negroes in housing and education and social opportunities and to create the beloved community. He said that it would be accomplished by rejecting the racism, materialism and violence that has characterized Western civilization and by working toward a world brotherhood, cooperation and peace.

On January 26, 1966, Dr. King rented a third-floor walk-up apartment on the West side. The old brick building was in a dismal Negro section known as "Slumdale." King told reporters, "You can't really get close to the poor without living and being here with them." Dr. King was too busy to spend much time in his apartment but his lieutenant, Andrew Young, did. The tactic dramatized the beginning of the movement and it impressed many blacks that he was here to help them.

The first action of the SCLC was to set up a special organization: "The Movement to End Slums" (MES). People who suffered from long-standing building code violations were encouraged to pay their rent money to MES. The rent money was placed in escrow. The MES drew money from that account to make necessary repairs. It was hoped that the slum owners would go to court to get their rent and the court case would explore their dereliction and bring about changes.

The landlords raised a big fuss and charged the MES with "grabbing tenements." The black renters were enthusiastic and involved. They took a new interest in their lodging and neighborhood and began to paint, clean up, make repairs and purchase coal with the rent money. The Chicago labor unions helped to finance the MES. The renters were assisted in forming a union that could bargain collectively with landlords to ensure basic services and the correction of grievances. If the landlords refused to cooperate, they were faced with a rent strike. The landlords and the City of Chicago sued the MES, but when they realized that it would be a long and expensive fight to get rent strikes declared illegal, they dropped their case.

The MES led to the development of the Community Union Movement (CUM), a nonprofit housing corporation. The CUM obtained a grant from the U.S. Department of Housing and Urban Development (HUD). This grant permitted CUM to buy buildings from owners who were faced with strikes and renovate them. The tenants became members of low-income cooperatives. The cooperatives outfitted the buildings with new washing machines, refrigerators, stoves, plumbing and wiring. The buildings were then resold to the people who lived there. This whole process required about two years. Before the project began, people were paying $140 to $180 per month for rent. After completion they paid $85 to $120 per month. This program served as a model of what could be done when renters organized. The MES was not well publicized nationally but, along with Operation Breadbasket, it was considered a success.

Another MES project was to try to persuade the city to adopt a comprehensive open housing ordinance and to enforce open housing requirements already on the books. The MES organized activists to picket the offices of realtors who were the most flagrant violators of open housing and they led protest marches into white suburbs where restrictive covenants were the common practice. Gage Park was selected as the first target for a protest march. On a Friday night in early August 50 activists marched into Gage Park. They were met by a screaming mob and driven out of the area. The marchers felt that they had to return the next day to make their point. On Saturday, Al Raby and Jesse Jackson led the protestors back into Gage Park. Before they had walked a block into the white subdivision they were attacked again. Bottles and rocks were thrown and both Raby and Jackson were hit, as were many others. The police made a few arrests but mostly let the barrage proceed.

The marchers tried again on Sunday. This time the mob of thousands attacked with bottles and rocks and also burned several black-owned automobiles. As many as 15 cars were destroyed. The numbers and the violence of the white mobs was so overwhelming and the police protection so minimal that this tactic had to be used very sparingly—only just enough to prove that the blacks could not be dissuaded from demanding their civil rights and just enough to stimulate the city administration to action by a threat of a possible riot.

During the Chicago Freedom Movement, youth gangs were a major threatening and disruptive element. Dr. King and his lieutenants met with the gang members and tried to switch them from violence to nonviolence. James Bevel, James Orange and other staff members worked closely with such gangs as the Blackstone Ranges, the Cobras, the Vice Lords and the Roman Saints. Dr. King would meet with the gang youths, share food and listen to their stories of hassles with the police and attempts by mobsters to get them to push dope. The SCLC leaders then explained the nature and purpose of nonviolent action and asked them to put away their guns and knives and try nonviolence as an experiment. The gang members were skeptical but interested and very much impressed with the clear demonstrations of courage by the veteran activists. Workshops in nonviolence were conducted for the youths. Bevel showed them a film of the Watts riots and compared that event with the Selma experience. At Watts, 30 Negroes had died and the cops that did it were still there. In Selma, the Negroes used nonviolent action and Jim Crow was now looking for a job. Eventually, 200 gang members agreed to give nonviolence a chance and turned out to serve as marshals at marches and demonstrations.

The SCLC and CCCO declared Sunday, July 10, "Freedom Sunday" and held a massive rally at Soldiers Field. The purpose of the rally was to focus public attention on the problems of poverty and slum housing. The program was designed to entertain and inform. Mahalia Jackson sang. Dick Gregory and other nationally known entertainers performed. There was a strong message of support from Archbishop Cody and CORE director Floyd McKissick spoke. The keynoter was Dr. King. He spoke with his combination of passion, demands and optimism.

Dr. King's demands for immediate action were targeted at specific institutions: (1) real estate brokers would be asked to support the nondiscriminatory listing and showing of properties, (2) banks to halt discriminatory loan practices, (3) city government to establish a civilian review board for the police department and desegregation of the city's schools, (4) the Chicago Housing Authority to increase the supply of low-cost public housing, (5) the state legislature to enact tenant protection legislation and (6) the federal agencies to improve federal housing policies and guarantee an income for every man. Attendance at the rally was estimated to be 30,000. Media accounts of the rally announced the arrival of the Chicago Freedom Movement and the nature of their demands. Following the rally about 5,000 supporters marched to City Hall where Dr. King posted a copy of their demands on the City Hall door.

The next day, Dr. King returned to City Hall and presented his demands to Daley in person. Mayor Daley was angry and rejected the demands on the grounds that Chicago already had a "massive" anti-slum program. For Daley and his associates, Dr. King was an intolerable nuisance. He couldn't be bought off and he continued to threaten to expose racial oppression in Chicago by means of nonviolent actions.

In mid–August, the black leaders announced that they would not be deterred by the violence at Gage Park but they would hold a march in the all-white suburb of Cicero, a city that had suffered several race riots in the past. Mayor Daley feared that the large number of marchers and the large crowds of hecklers that they would attract might create a riot and be very destructive of property. Facing this possibility, he decided to take the initiative. Mayor Daley called a negotiating conference at the Palmer House. Seventy-nine representatives of key interests were invited to participate. The Chicago Conference on Religion and Race (CCRR) conducted the discussions. Among the groups represented were the SCLC, the CCCO, the CCRR, the Chicago Real Estate Board and representatives of the city's business community. Dr. King was the chief negotiator for the blacks. He was seconded by Andy Young, Al Raby, Jesse Jackson and Jim Bevel.

The first step in the negotiations was for both parties to state what they wanted. The City of Chicago asked for a discontinuation of the demonstrations while negotiations were in progress. The blacks declined this request. As long as the city was threatened with demonstrations, the mayor had some incentive to make genuine concessions. Dr. King's team was well prepared on this question and listed nine demands:

1. The enforcement of existing open housing ordinances.
2. Amendment of that ordinance to outlaw discrimination by owners as well as by brokers.
3. An agreement by the Chicago Real Estate Board to drop its court challenge to the existing ordinance.
4. An agreement to end opposition to the statewide open housing statute.
5. A demand that the Chicago Housing Authority stop building all public housing projects in slums.
6. A demand that the Public Aid Department stop discriminatory practices.
7. A demand that banks and other lending institutions stop discriminating in their lending practices.
8. A demand that local labor unions end discriminatory practices.
9. A demand that urban renewal planners stop discriminating against black neighborhoods.

Discussion of goals of both sides occupied several long meetings. As the conversations went on, it became evident that the real estate brokers would not change their basic discriminatory policies. Dr. King and his associates had a strong detailed case and were not about to retreat. Mayor Daley broke the impasse. The mayor asked if the demonstrations would be halted if he agreed to the nine demands. When told "yes" he immediately agreed to all of the demands. Few of the negotiators had confidence that the mayor would perform as promised but they felt obligated to accept the agreement.

Evaluations of the Chicago Freedom Movement vary according to the expectations of the evaluator. Blacks who hoped and expected that it would desegregate Chicago schools and housing were disappointed and felt betrayed. Blacks who were looking for progress in a viciously segregated municipal dictatorship system could cite considerable progress. Operation Breadbasket had been successful—as far as it went. Extreme racism was laid bare—a prerequisite to attacking it. The final agreement that promised a lot but didn't deliver served to confirm the validity of the demands. Evaluators from the white culture who like to use sport jargon would say that Mayor Daley won and Dr. King and CCCO lost. An objective evaluation would consist of comparing the characteristics and level of racism in Chicago today with the situation in 1966—an exercise that is outside the purview of this chapter. Academic observers conclude that the problems of slums, segregated housing, jobs and machine government in Chicago are so complex that they require strong federal, state and municipal cooperation for a solution.

Cleveland Mayoral Campaign, OH, 1967

Dr. King and his team were bogged down in Chicago—making little progress and absent an exit. Just then, Carl Stokes was running for mayor of Cleveland, Ohio. For the first time in U.S. history it appeared that a black man might be elected mayor of a major city. Stokes invited Dr. King to come to Cleveland and help him corral the black vote while Stokes focused on the white vote. Dr. King and Ralph Abernathy and their team agreed. They saw it as an opportunity to try again to attack segregation in a northern city and to utilize the organizational expertise that the team had developed in Alabama and Chicago.

The SCLC team moved into Cleveland and set up a Stokes campaign headquarters. They registered voters, prepared and distributed literature, organized blocks and precincts, recruited volunteer workers, established a phone bank and made thousands of calls. On election day, they provided transportation for anyone who needed it.

On election night, the SCLC team watched the election results. The first results were from the white precincts and the white candidate was leading. Then the voting results started coming in from the black precincts. The turnout was heavier than usual and Stokes was getting most of the votes. Soon he was the clear winner and the newscasters announced his victory. The SCLC team was elated to have participated in the political desegregation of the Cleveland City Hall but they were also upset that Stokes forgot to thank them for delivering the crucial black vote.

J. Edgar Hoover v. Dr. King, 1964–1968

The Civil Rights Revolution was a three-level process. It consisted of reversing racial policies at the local (police, mayor, sheriff, KKK), state (governor, legislature, court) and federal (administration, Congress and FBI) levels. During the '60s these changes were resisted most aggressively by the Federal Bureau of Investigation. J. Edgar Hoover, the bureau's director from 1924 to 1972 was a confirmed racist who had learned to evade the checks and balances of the federal system. By collecting "dirt" on presidents, congressmen and federal officials he could use blackmail to maintain his appropriations, his job and a racist vendetta. Hoover had a strong dislike for Dr. King and used the resources of his agency to harass, discredit and destabilize Dr. King and the SCLC. He used both legal and illegal wire taps, smear campaigns, accusations of communism, grand theft, sexual deviation, false and derogatory reports to the president and FBI spies in SCLC offices.

The charge of communism was contradicted by the FBI's own security investigation reports on King. The charge of embezzlement was investigated and it was found that Dr. King lived on a very modest minister's salary and gave his Nobel Prize purse to the civil rights movement. The charge of sexual deviance brought attention to Hoover's sexual orientation.

In 1964, Hoover had unauthorized illegal microphones put in King's hotel rooms from Washington to Honolulu. Hoover used the tapes to give credence to the unfounded accusations he made against King in secret briefings to national political and religious leaders. The bureau bugged King's hotel rooms until January 1966, when a threatened Congressional investigation forced a termination of the electronic eavesdropping. The telephone taps on SCLC's Atlanta headquarters continued until Attorney General Nicholas Katzenbach ordered them removed in June 1966. After that date, a paid informant in the SCLC office reported to Hoover.

Dr. King accused the FBI of failing to protect the lives of civil rights activists and of employing racists as FBI agents. During the campaign to desegregate Albany, Georgia, in 1961–1962, blacks filed a number of complaints about violations of their civil rights but the FBI took no action. When Viola Liuzzo was shot to death by a drive-by Klansman in March 1965, the FBI was able to grab the perpetrator quickly. An FBI informant was in the vehicle with the killer! In August 1955, Lamar Davis, a 63-year-old farmer and veteran was shot down in Brook haven, Mississippi, in front of the courthouse before a crowd of Saturday visitors. The NAACP staffers found witnesses and gathered evidence which they submitted to the FBI. Nothing was done. No one was charged. The case was not prosecuted.

Hoover also perpetrated dirty tricks. On January 5, 1965, Coretta King (Dr. King's wife) received tapes and a letter mailed anonymously from Miami, Florida. The tape was a composite recording that Hoover had authorized his deputy, William Sullivan, to compile and send to Mrs. King. It was a combination of recordings of a meeting in which Dr. King participated plus a spliced-on portion that sounded like two people in an intimate embrace. The letter reviled Dr. King and suggested that he commit suicide before he was exposed. King and his colleagues listened to the tape and recognized another dirty trick by Director Hoover. They knew that only the FBI had the facilities and motive for bugging and recording King's meetings.

The Hoover-King confrontation was the most one-sided of the one-sided revolution. Nonviolent resistance didn't work against unprincipled tactics by the director of the national police force. Hoover's campaign was eventually successful. It established the climate and conditions conducive to King's assassination and to the way it was presented to the public—as the work of a single individual.

Dr. King v. President Johnson re: Vietnam, 1967

Dr. King and his Southern Christian Leadership Conference (SCLC) worked with President Johnson for several years to get anti-apartheid legislation enacted by Congress. However, on the subject of the Vietnam War, Dr. King and the president were diametrically opposed.

For 30 years the Vietnamese fought for self-determination. First they fought the Japanese and forced them out in 1945. Then the French attempted to repossess their former colony. The Vietnamese fought them from 1946 to 1954 and defeated them at Dien Bien Fu. Then the U.S. took over. A puppet government was set up under Ngo Dinh Diem and the U.S. tried to conquer the country. Five U.S. presidents participated in the unequal struggle. President Truman helped the French by financing 80 percent of their war effort. President Eisenhower sent several thousand military advisors. President Kennedy sent more advisors—up to 16,000. President Johnson faked a Tonkin Gulf incident and escalated the U.S. involvement. President Nixon escalated the war exponentially but was finally defeated and withdrew in 1973.

For civil rights activists the Vietnam War posed a dilemma. If they criticized the war, they would incur the wrath of President Johnson—the first president to deliver civil rights legislation. If they were silent on the war, they would betray their own belief in equity and freedom for all races. Leaders of SNCC and CORE recognized the identity of the moral issues in the civil rights movement and the anti-war movement and endorsed an anti-war position. Coretta Scott King, a close advisor to Dr. King, was a pacifist. She was a member of the Women's Strike for Peace and spoke publicly for peace. Jim Bevel, another of King's advisors, was a strong peace advocate as was Andrew Young, another King colleague. In the black community there was bitter opposition to the war. Many black families saw their menfolk enlist because there were no jobs, sent to the front in disproportionate numbers as compared to whites and sent back as corpses.

Dr. King struggled with this dilemma for a year. He studied the situation in Vietnam, reasoned with his colleagues, consulted his Christian faith and then made his decision. He felt that as a Golden Rule Christian he was obliged to hold to Christian principles and oppose the war. He then proceeded to speak and demonstrate against the war.

On February 25, 1967, Dr. King gave his first speech devoted entirely to the Vietnam conflict at the Nation Institute in Los Angeles. In that speech he referred to "one of history's most cruel and senseless wars." He spoke of "our paranoid anti–Communism, our failure to feel the ache and anguish of the have-nots." He said, "I speak out against it not in anger but with anxiety and sorrow in my heart, and above all with a passionate desire to see our beloved country stand as the moral example of the world.... We must combine the fervor of the civil rights movement with the peace movement. We must demonstrate, teach and preach until the very foundations of our nation are shaken."

In March 1967, Dr. King spoke against the war in Chicago, Louisville, Kentucky, and Atlanta. In a speech at the Overseas Press Club, Dr. King called on Negroes and all white people of goodwill to boycott the war by becoming conscientious objectors to military service.

His most famous denunciation of the war was at the Riverside Church in New York City on April 4, 1967. He was invited to speak by the Clergy and Laymen Concerned About Vietnam. When he rose to speak he received a standing ovation. Following are six points he made in that oration that show his reasoning and his values:

1. He was not speaking to Hanoi but making "a passionate plea to my beloved country."

2. The expenditure for the war prevented the implementation of the War on Poverty. "America would never invest the necessary funds or energies in rehabilitation of its poor so long as adventures like Vietnam continued to draw men and skills and money like some demonical suction tube."

3. The human cost of the war fell disproportionately on the poor blacks. "We are taking the black young men who had been crippled by our society and sending them 8,000 miles away to guarantee liberties in Southeast Asia which they had not found in southwest Georgia and East Harlem."

4. He opposed the war because he was a "Christian minister."

5. If he condemned violence in American ghettoes, then he must speak against "the greatest purveyor of violence in the world today—my own government."

6. He opposed the war because he could not tolerate what it was doing to the Vietnamese people. "For nine long years we supported the French in their efforts to recolonize Vietnam. And when they moved out, we took their place, refusing to let Ho Chi Min unify his own country, refusing to let the Vietnamese people hold general elections as prescribed by the 1954 Geneva Agreement. Instead, we converted a civil war over nation unification into an American war over Communism.... We supported a ruthless dictatorship in South Vietnam which aligned itself with extortionist landlords and executed political opponents.... We poisoned their water, bombed and machine-gunned their huts, annihilated their crops and sent them wandering into the towns, where thousands of homeless children roamed the streets like animals, begging for food and selling their mothers and sisters to American sol-

diers.... We have destroyed their land and crushed their only non–Communist revolutionary political force—the Unified Buddhist Church."

Dr. King concluded his remarks by outlining four steps that the U.S. should
take: (1) halt the bombing, (2) declare a unilateral cease fire, (3) initiate peace talks
with the National Liberation Front and (4) set a date for the removal of all foreign
troops from Vietnam in accordance with the Geneva Agreement.

Democracy, with its accommodation of opposing points of view, functions im-
perfectly in time of peace. In time of war, it is seriously compromised. There is a closing of ranks in support of the government and its war and strong pressures are
brought to bear on dissenters. Dr. King, one of the first persons of national stature
to question the Vietnam War, was subject to that pressure. Dr. King's Riverside speech
was sharply criticized by *Newsweek*, *Life*, the *Washington Post*, and *New York Times*,
the *Reader's Digest*, the FBI, the Jewish War Veterans of America, Congressman Joe
D. Waggoner, Carl Rowan (a black journalist), Ralph Bunche (U.S. representative to
the United Nations), Whitney Young of the Urban League, Roy Wilkins of the NAACP,
Senator Edward Book (black) of Massachusetts and Jackie Robinson a star athlete.
On April 10, President Johnson received a special report from the FBI which de-
famed Dr. King. Johnson permitted J. Edgar Hoover to circulate the report to the
media. On April 12, the NAACP's 60-member board voted unanimously to oppose
any effort to fuse the civil rights movement with the anti-war movement. A few jour-
nals and journalists supported Dr. King's right to express his views.

Dr. King was stunned by the volume and acerbity of the criticism. However,
within a few days, he recovered his composure and answered his critics in a series of
press conferences, statements and speeches. Here are some examples of his response:

1. "I will not stand idly by when I see an unjust war taking place and fail to take
a stand against it."

2. "We initiated the buildup of this war on land, on sea and in the air and we
must take the initiative to end the war."

3. "The U.S. was practicing more violence than any other nation."

4. "No one can pretend that the existence of the war is not profoundly affect-
ing the destiny of civil rights."

5. "I challenge the NAACP and other critics of my position to take a forthright
stand on the rightness or wrongness of the war rather than going off creating a
nonexistent issue."

6. "I've fought too long and too hard now against segregated accommodations
to end up segregating my moral concerns.... But I know that justice is indivisible.
Injustice anywhere is a threat to justice everywhere."

On April 15, Dr. King participated in a massive anti-war rally at the United Nations in New York. The rally was sponsored by James Bevel's Spring Mobilization
Committee. Dr. King was asked to march as his participation would increase the

number of marchers and the media coverage. More than 100,000 people marched. Among the leaders were Dr. King, Bevel, Dr. Benjamin Spock, Harry Belafonte, Pete Seeger, Stokely Carmichael and Floyd McKissick. It was the largest anti–Vietnam demonstration the city had seen.

After the New York march, Dr. King and his retinue flew to California to participate in a rally at the University of California. Dr. King gave an eloquent speech against the war. "We have flown the air like birds and swam the sea like fishes, but we have not learned the simple act of walking the earth like brothers." The students gave him an enthusiastic reception and the world press gave his speech and the rally good coverage.

In May and June 1967, Dr. King toured the country, speaking against the war. At the same time, President Johnson was escalating the war. By 1967, the U.S. was spending billions each year to subdue the Vietnamese peasants. Some 485,000 American men were fighting there. Dr. King announced that the SCLC would depart from its past policy of political neutrality and support candidates at all levels who opposed the war.

President Johnson was very unhappy with Dr. King's anti-war campaign. The principal response from his administration, however, came from the FBI. The FBI confused King's civil rights and peace advocacy with the perpetrators of urban riots and targeted King in its COINTELPRO, a secret campaign against "black nationalist hate groups." It employed 44 field officers to try to collect incriminating evidence so it could spread pernicious and fictitious news stories that King was a violent and revolutionary threat, he was a misguided messiah, he was a Communist, an embezzler and a sex pervert.

Dr. King's opposition did not stop the war, the cost of which was high. The Vietnamese lost two million people of both sexes and all ages killed, and four million people injured. The bombing knocked out 70 percent of their industrial plants and left four million homeless. The U.S. lost 57,000 killed—all adult, male soldiers. The total cost of the war to the U.S. from 1950 to 1973 was $23.9 billion.

The Orangeburg Massacre, SC, 1960 and 1968

In the '60s, Orangeburg, South Carolina, was a town of 20,000 inhabitants— mostly white. It was the headquarters of an ultra-right-wing group, Truth About Civil Turmoil (TACT), and the location of the segregated Southern Methodist College. It was also a center of higher education for blacks in South Carolina. Claflin College, established in 1869, provided agricultural training for blacks under the auspices of the Methodist Episcopal Church. South Carolina State College, a land grant college for blacks, was close to downtown. These academic enclaves, however, were well segregated. Black students were not allowed to go to the drive-in theater and a college curfew kept them on campus all night. Most painful for the students was their exclusion from the local bowling alley.

In February 1960, news of the student sit-ins in Greensboro, North Carolina, stimulated the students to think about demonstrating for freedom. Organizers from CORE visited Claflin and State College and gave classes in nonviolent methods of demonstration. In late February 1960, a group of students decided to conduct a march to demonstrate their opposition to apartheid. They assembled at State College and then proceeded to march downtown. Stores were hurriedly closed but there was no violence and no arrests. On March 14, they marched again from the campus to the bowling alley. This time the weather was freezing and the police were prepared. They sprayed the marchers with tear gas and with water jets. Then they arrested 500 students and filled their jail. They put the overflow into a chicken coop surrounded by a seven-foot fence.

In the absence of strong or professional leadership, the students focused on their studies for several years. However, there was some forward movement from Washington. The Civil Rights Act of 1964 led to the desegregation of restaurants in Orangeburg. The bowling alley, however, which had a snack bar, remained for whites only.

In 1967, three white professors visited the campus and reawakened student interest in the apartheid system. They encouraged the students to question the anachronistic nature of their education in which they didn't study or discuss the civil rights of blacks. The visiting professors were suspended but the damage was done. A group of students demonstrated for more discussion of civil rights in front of the house of the college president. Three of the students were immediately suspended from classes. The rest of the students responded with a two-week boycott of all classes. This dispute was settled only when a representative of NAACP met with Governor Robert McNair. McNair promised to improve the quality of education. A federal court decreed that the suspension of the student protestors violated their right of free speech. It was also agreed that students could organize a chapter of the NAACP and a Black Awareness Coordinating Committee (BACC).

In early February 1968, the students began a series of marches from the college to downtown to call attention to their list of ten grievances. On February 8, students built a bonfire of scrap lumber on Watson Street at the entrance to their campus. State College students added fuel to the fire while they sang *We Shall Overcome* and *We Shall Not Be Moved*. Four squads of highway patrolmen were quickly dispatched to that corner of the campus. A fire truck arrived and extinguished the bonfire in the street. Most of the students then headed back to their dorms. Some hung around and heckled the officers who were on both sides of the path with firearms at the ready. The patrolmen had been instructed to shoot only as a last resort. One officer was knocked down by a stick of wood hurled by a student. An officer fired a "warning shot." Immediately, several other officers commenced to fire. There was a ten-second burst of crossfire aimed at the students on the lawn. The students ran or crawled for cover—except for three who had been hit.

Sophomore Henry Smith was hit by five shots in the chest, back and neck. He was taken to the still-segregated Orangeburg Hospital. He died that night in the emergency room. Samuel Hammond, a State College football player, was shot in the back and killed. Delano Middleton, a high school student whose mother worked at the college, was also shot. He died in the hospital.

The college community was stunned. Classes were suspended for two weeks at both Claflin and State College. The U.S. Department of Justice, Civil Rights Division, filed briefs to desegregate the Orangeburg Hospital and the bowling alley. A federal judge ordered the bowling alley desegregated. Martin Luther King Jr., then in the midst of promoting the Poor People's Campaign, called for a trial of the officers who shot the students. Students from the two colleges staged protests at the state Capitol in Columbia. The governor proposed some capital improvements for State College but did not admit that the highway patrol did anything wrong.

Nine white officers who participated in the shooting were tried under federal civil rights laws in Florence, South Carolina, in May 1969. They were found not guilty. Cleveland Sellers, a civil rights activist who had been wounded in the shooting, was indicted on a charge of rioting plus a long list of other "crimes." He was tried in 1970 in a barricaded Orangeburg courthouse and found guilty and sentenced to one year in prison.

AFSCME Workers Strike, Memphis, TN, 1968

Memphis was far ahead of other big cities in the South in complying with *Brown v. Board of* Education. It had dismantled legal school segregation in the late 1950s. Blacks were first admitted to Memphis State University in 1958. With prompting from the NAACP other aspects of city life—buses, parks and boat docks—had been desegregated in the early '60s. In 1961, 13 black students attended a previously all-white school under heavy police protection.

In matters of economic rights, however, Memphis was still an apartheid state. Blacks still occupied the lower rungs of the economic ladder. The sanitation workers averaged $1.60 an hour. They had no workers compensation, no written grievance procedure, no paid vacations and very few had a pension plan. They could be fired at any time for any reason or for no reason. Nearly all of the 1,100 workers were black. In 1964, the Memphis sanitation workers organized a union and affiliated with the American Federation of State, County and Municipal Employees (AFSCME) as Local No. 1733. In August 1966, the union voted to strike for better wages and working conditions. They were stopped cold by a court injunction based on a law that banned strikes by city workers.

In 1968, there were two incidents that reawakened an interest in a strike. On January 30, after a morning shower, 21 black street repairmen were sent home with only two hours of "show-up" pay while the white supervisors collected a full day's pay. Two days later in heavy rains, an old-model garbage truck with a hydraulic compacting ram short-circuited and crushed two sanitation workers to death. Neither had life insurance. In the next few days, union officers drew up a list of grievances.

They wanted recognition of the union by the city, a pay raise, paycheck deduction of union dues, overtime pay and improved safety conditions. The Memphis city officials refused to discuss their demands.

On February 12, Lincoln's birthday, the sanitation workers struck. The AFSCME national office had not approved the strike but supported the strikers. The black community supported the strike. The City of Memphis officials were non-cooperative. The city council's Committee on Public Works agreed to recognize the union but then the full council voted it down.

To call public attention to their plight, black leaders led a march on February 23 from the City Auditorium to the Masonic Temple. On Main Street the police herded the marchers to one side and then swarms of white officers attacked them with mace. The police attack escalated the local labor dispute into a major civil rights confrontation. The NAACP was drawn into the case along with local preachers and students. There were daily protest marches downtown and the blacks boycotted the two white papers in favor of the two black papers, and held mass meetings each night to keep everyone informed. To manage all the activities, an umbrella organization was set up: the Community on the Move for Equality (COME). It was led by the Rev. James Lawson, a leader in the Nashville student movement who had taken a pastorate in a Memphis church.

Lawson, who had known Dr. King since the Montgomery boycott, asked him for help. King agreed to visit Memphis and lead the strikers in a march. The march, scheduled for March 18, had to be postponed because of a 16-inch snowfall that closed the city down. It was held on March 28 and it was a disaster. King's plane was delayed. He arrived late and so dispensed with his usual exhortation to nonviolence. A lot of high school students, untrained in nonviolence, joined the march. One part of the march disintegrated into a small riot. Store windows were broken. Police wearing gas masks waded into the line of marchers. At the end of the day, 74 people were wounded and one marcher, a high school junior, Larry Payne, was shot dead by a policeman. That night, the national guard moved in to maintain order.

Lawson and King felt that they had failed to conduct a nonviolent protest. They had to do better. The next day, March 29, 400 adults marched to City Hall in good order. They passed rows of guardsmen with fixed bayonets but there was no violence. King met with the Invaders, a Black Power group that was blamed for the disruption the day before. Union officials redoubled their support for the strike and King pledged that he would lead a march again on April 8.

On April 3, King returned to Memphis and registered at the Lorraine Motel with several of his associates. The following evening, April 4, after a day of meetings he was on the balcony of the Lorraine waiting to go to dinner. A shot rang out and King fell. He was rushed to St. Joseph's Hospital where he died.

Memphis and the nation were in shock. Fires and sniper fire filled the night as 4,000 national guardsmen patrolled the streets. The next day, a massive memorial march moved into City Hall Plaza past lines of national guardsmen. Meanwhile, after nonstop negotiations at the Claridge Hotel, a strike settlement was stitched together.

On April 16, the city council approved recognition of the AFSCME union, a dues checkoff through a credit union, pay raises, a new package of benefits and a policy of rehiring the fired workers. In return, the union gave a no-strike pledge. The union members approved the settlement overwhelmingly by voice vote and the sanitation workers went back to work on April 17.

King's assassination was the most traumatic catastrophe to strike the U.S. since the death of President Kennedy four and a half years earlier. The blacks had lost their Moses and the whites had lost "the conscience of America."

The assassination of Dr. King has been explained in a number of ways. One explanation is that it was executed by James Earl Ray acting alone. Another explanation widely believed by blacks is that King's death was a conspiracy. As a representative of the latter point of view, Andrew Young makes the following points:

(1.) It is questionable that James Earl Ray possessed sufficient intelligence to escape from Memphis, acquire a passport and fly to England on his way to Rhodesia. Someone must have helped him.

(2.) The number of unexplained deaths of people who opposed the Vietnam War suggests a conspiracy by the U.S. secret agencies. The list includes Bob Spike, a church leader murdered in 1966; Bernard Fall, killed in a freak accident in Vietnam (he was the most knowledgeable critic of U.S. policy); and Thomas Merton, an influential theologian and outspoken opponent of the U.S. war in Vietnam, killed in an "accident" in Thailand in 1968.

(3.) The FBI had conducted a campaign to vilify and discredit King's freedom campaigns for many years accusing him of Communism, misappropriation of funds and sexual misconduct. The first two were not supported by any evidence and the third was probably a reflection of a fear of black sexuality that was a part of a neurotic southern racist tradition.

(4.) James Earl Ray was never given a trial that would have answered many questions even though both he and the King family asked for a trial.

Thirty years later, in 1998, an investigating journalist, Gerald Posner, writing in the *Crisis* (Sept–Oct, 1998) stated, "My extensive investigation shows that the government was not behind Ray, but while it may not have pulled the trigger, its outrageous conduct created an atmosphere where a racist like Ray thought it was safe to shoot a black leader."

The truth about the full responsibility for Dr. King's death will probably remain unknown or subject to two interpretations by two cultures.

AFSCME Workers Strikes, Atlanta and Charleston, 1968

The AFSCME strike in Memphis stimulated workers in Atlanta, Georgia, and Charleston, South Carolina, to similar action. In Atlanta, the AFSCME sanitation workers compared their wages with others and concluded that they also deserved a raise. They made a simple request for a raise but it was not granted. The members of the union, the American Federation of State, County and Municipal Employees (AFSCME), voted to strike. The Atlanta AFSCME officers had little experience in negotiating with city officials but they knew where help was available. They went to the SCLC headquarters in Atlanta and asked for assistance. The SCLC was in the process of planning the Poor Man's March on Washington but they couldn't ignore a request for help from poor workers in their own back yard. Andrew Young, an SCLC board member and longtime associate of Dr. King, agreed to work with the sanitation workers.

Young's first step was to recruit local black ministers to participate in the union struggle. The union's first move was a sit-down strike in front of the sanitation trucks. The union members and their supporters linked arms and sat in the driveway. The trucks started, moved toward the strikers and stopped. The police were called in to clear the driveway. The police arrested the protestors and took them to jail. However, they were immediately released without even being booked or charged.

The mayor of Atlanta, Ivan Allen, had been elected with significant support from the black community. He was not running for re-election but he wanted to leave office with a good record. He didn't want to sully the city's motto: "A City Too Busy to Hate" and he didn't want the strike to escalate into a TV camera-attractive confrontation.

Mayor Allen drew up a contract revision that would give the garbage workers a two-step pay increase plus back pay for the two weeks that they were on strike. The union called a meeting to consider the mayor's proposal. At the meeting, a firebrand speaker criticized the proposal and so inflamed the workers that they voted to reject the contract.

Young thought that Allen's offer was as good as the union could get. He asked the union leaders to hold a second meeting to permit him to present the pros and cons of the proposed contract. At the second AFSCME meeting the next morning, Young took the podium. On the blackboard he showed the workers their take-home pay at the old level and with the new contract and argued that it was the best deal they were likely to get. The union members voted to accept the new contract and they went back to work.

This confrontation was resolved in three weeks with a minimum police activity, no physical abuse and even, perhaps, some positive publicity for Atlanta. The workers got a raise and the city got its sanitation service operating. The reasons for this outcome were that Andrew Young was a skilled negotiator and Mayor Allen believed in freedom and equity.

✶ ✶ ✶

A similar scenario occurred in South Carolina. Workers at the Medical College in Charleston heard about the AFSCME strike in Memphis and decided that they must take the initiative to better their working conditions. In the fall of 1968 a dozen black women hospital workers got together and agreed to work to organize a union.

In March of 1969 the college administrators learned about the union project and immediately fired the twelve pro-union activists.

The firing didn't stop the union movement—it accelerated it. Four hundred and fifty hospital workers walked off their jobs in protest. A week later sixty black workers at the Charleston County Hospital also took a sympathy walk. Local 1199 of the union of Retail, Wholesale and Department Store Workers (AFL-CIO) also supported the Medical College ladies. Walter Reuther and a delegation of prominent labor leaders visited Charleston to show their support for the strike.

Following the example of the Atlanta workers, the Charleston women asked the SCLC for assistance. Again Andrew Young answered the call. He met with the workers and helped them organize the whole community to support the strike. Marches were conducted daily to inform and energize the public. A boycott of downtown Charleston stores was organized to get the attention and then support of the merchants. Strike sympathizers were urged to purchase only food and medicine until the strikers' demands were met. Young and the strike leaders wrote press releases. Strike support meetings were held nearly every night at the United Methodist Church. First a preacher spoke, then a choir sang, and then the strike leaders reported their progress and plans. The mass meetings kept everyone informed and morale high.

The strikers' demands were modest. They asked for: recognition of the union by the hospital administration; an end to racial discrimination in hiring practices and wages paid; reinstatement of the twelve workers who were fired. As the strike stretched into June, the strike leaders sought a nationwide boycott of the South Carolina textile industry. June 20 arrived, and the hospital was still unwilling to negotiate. The strikers tried a new tactic—they contacted the Charleston longshoreman, who had closed the port of Charleston on the day of Dr. King's funeral, and asked them to conduct a sympathy strike.

The boycott of downtown businesses began to hurt. After forfeiting an estimated fifteen million dollars in lost sales to tourists and blacks, the Charleston businessmen had had enough. The governer also wanted to end the strike, as it was giving the state adverse publicity. Responding to this pressure, the hospital's administrators agreed to talk.

Andrew Young and Stoney Creek, of the SCLC, met with William McCord and William Huff, of the South Carolina Medical College, and Jay Iselin, a New York attorney, to discuss a settlement. After a series of meetings involving vigorous debate, an agreement was worked out. The hospital agreed to recognize the union and provide a dues check-off system. The issues of a general raise in pay and the rehiring of the dismissed workers were discussed and resolved. Finally, on June 26, 1969, after sixteen weeks, it was announced that the strike was over, and the union was recognized.

The Charleston hospital workers AFSCME strike and the recognition it received marked the end of an era. It was the last civil rights campaign managed by the SCLC, and the last confrontation between blacks and the establishment during the nonviolent freedom revolution.

III

Leaders of the Revolution

Leaders of the black activists contrasted sharply with those of the white Establishment. The two sets of leaders were separated by membership in two very different cultures—each with its unique history, value system, social institutions and concepts of democracy and justice. Black leadership required two qualities beyond leadership skills. They had to be job-independent from the white Establishment and they had to have a passionate desire for freedom. That desire had to be sufficient to counter any fear of white violence and retribution.

There were four categories of black leaders: lawyers, ministers, students and women. Lawyers, like those in the NAACP, worked diligently and successfully both before and during the revolution to eliminate apartheid laws and protect the rights of demonstrators. Black ministers were leaders in the black community and in the black churches which emphasized hope, freedom and nonviolent action for democracy. The ministers were well educated—usually better than their adversaries. They had a keen understanding of the white culture and political system and knew how to use the white media to inform the public and influence the Washington establishment.

The student demonstrators represented a post–World War II generation that was determined to attain its constitutional rights of equal treatment under the law and the right to vote and run for elected office. The significant and critical role of women leaders was underreported. A fourth of the leaders presented in this chapter are women who excelled in managing demonstrations, challenging apartheid laws and teaching nonviolent action.

All of these leaders enjoyed strong and continuous support from three sets of institutions, the church-centered black community, the NAACP and other civil rights organizations and the black colleges. The roles of the black communities, the black churches and the NAACP are generally recognized. The role of the black college professors and administrators is less well known. They had to maintain a low profile to keep their jobs and so continue to support the student activists. The role of the civil rights organizations is addressed at the end of this chapter.

These leaders—sixty are introduced here—had a lot in common. They were all well educated both formally and by their experience in living in a segregated society. They were closely associated with the black church and religion. They all had a strong commitment to introducing more equity and democracy into the U.S. political system. For further insights into their leadership, the reader is referred to the reference books in the bibliography and to the leaders' own books on their participation and observations re the Freedom Revolution.

Abernathy, Ralph David (1926–1990)

Abernathy was born in Linden in Marengo County in the Black Belt of Alabama. He earned a bachelor's degree at Alabama State College in 1950 and a master's degree from Atlanta University in 1951. He served in the Army during World War II and then was ordained a Baptist minister. He joined the NAACP in 1951. In 1955, he was one of the main organizers of the Montgomery bus boycott. In 1957, he was co-founder of the Southern Christian Leadership Conference (SCLC), the principal management organization of the nonviolent revolution. As an activist/leader he was arrested 19 times and his house was bombed once. Throughout the civil rights/freedom revolution Abernathy was Dr. King's associate, counsel, cellmate and soul-brother. Together they planned tactics, marched, went to jail, faced tear gas, sang, prayed and led the revolution. Following Dr. King's assassination, Abernathy assumed leadership of the SCLC and directed the Poor People's March on Washington in 1968. He was the pastor of Atlanta's West Hunter Street Baptist Church and worked with the Foundation for Economic Enterprises Development. Abernathy's book, *And the Walls Came Tumbling Down*, provides an unexcelled first-hand account of the civil rights struggle.

Baker, Ella Josephine (1903–1986)

Ella Baker was born in Norfolk, Virginia. She graduated from Shaw Boarding School in Raleigh, North Carolina, in 1927 with a bachelor's degree. She was class valedictorian. In 1931, she was national director of the Young Negroes Cooperative League, a buying cooperative that bought food in bulk and distributed it to members. She worked in the Works Progress Administration literacy program.

In 1943 she was employed as field secretary for the NAACP. She traveled the South establishing NAACP chapters. In 1955, she worked with Bayard Rustin and A. Philip Randolph raising money for the Montgomery bus boycott. In 1957, she was the first executive secretary of the SCLC. In 1960, Baker noted the enthusiastic burst of sit-ins by youths throughout the country and decided to harness it. She promoted a youth conference at her alma mater, now Shaw University, on April 15 and 16. The conference led to the founding of the Student Nonviolent Coordinating Committee (SNCC).

Baker used her influence to keep the SNCC student-run and not dominated by adults. She believed that group-centered leadership was more effective than hierarchical leadership. In 1964, Baker helped to launch the Mississippi Freedom Democratic Party that challenged the all-white delegation at the 1964 Democratic presidential nomination convention. Ella Jo Baker was called the "Godmother of the Civil Rights Movement."

Barry, Marion Shepilov, Jr. (March 6, 1936–)

Barry was born to sharecroppers on a cotton plantation near Itta Bena, Mississippi. His father was murdered when he was eight years old. He grew up in poverty. After completing high school, he enrolled in LeMoyne College in Memphis, Tennessee. He was elected president of the college NAACP. In 1958, he earned a degree in chemistry. He then went to Fisk University in Nashville and got a master's degree. At Fisk, Barry led several student sit-ins against segregated facilities. In 1960, he became the first national chairman of the Student Nonviolent Coordinating Committee (SNCC). In 1960, he resigned the SNCC job and began a teaching career. In 1964, he organized campaigns against discrimination and police brutality in Washington, DC. He also raised funds for the SNCC in New York City. In 1965, Barry led protests against the Vietnam War and helped to organize the Free DC Movement which sought to put the capitol's government into the hands of its citizens. Following Dr. King's assassination, Barry went into politics. In 1974, he was elected to the Washington, DC, City Council. In 1979, he was elected mayor of Washington, DC. In 1994, he was re-elected to his fourth term.

Bates, Daisy Gaston (1920–1999)

Daisy Gaston was born in Huttig, Arkansas. Her parents tried to teach her an attitude of submissiveness toward whites but she rejected that attitude. She visited Canada and northern states and observed that in many places people of different races and cultures lived in harmony with mutual respect.

Daisy married L.C. Bates, a newspaperman, and they settled in Little Rock. In 1952, she was elected president of the Arkansas NAACP. In 1957, she participated in initiating legal action against the Little Rock Plan for school integration. That case enabled the Little Rock Nine to enter Central High School that fall. During the integration of Central High School, Mrs. Bates was the chief counselor and protector of the nine black students. She was assisted by the 101st Airborne Division of the 327th Infantry Division.

Daisy Bates suffered the usual abuses of civil rights activists under U.S. apartheid. She was arrested for denouncing judicial racism in Little Rock. On August 22, 1957, a rock crashed through her living room window with a note that said: "stone this time—dynamite next." She was arrested and convicted for refusing to reveal NAACP records on membership and financing. Her conviction was overturned upon appeal to the Supreme Court. The KKK burned crosses on her lawn. Two firebombs were tossed at her house. The *State Press* that Daisy and her husband had published for 18 years was forced to close by the whites' harassment.

When the NAACP awarded the Spingarn Award to the Little Rock Nine in 1958, the students insisted that Mrs. Bates be included in the citation. Mrs. Bates was awarded honorary degrees by the University of Arkansas and Washington University. In 1996, she carried the Olympic torch through Little Rock. She also wrote a book, *The Long Shadow of Little Rock*.

Belafonte, Harold George, "Harry" (March 1927–)

Belafonte was born in New York City, the son of a Jamaican mother and a Martinique father. He attended public school in Jamaica and high school in New York City. He served in the Navy during World War II. He attended Irwin Piscator's dramatic workshop in New York City. From 1949 to 1984, Belafonte had a remarkably successful career in acting, singing, directing and film and TV production. His album *Calypso* in 1956 was the first solo album in history to sell a million copies.

Like his idol, Paul Robeson, Belafonte was an assiduous civil rights activist as well as an artist. He was partially blacklisted in the '50s. (This was in the McCarthy era when artists who were not right wing were discriminated against.) He, in turn, blacklisted segregated theaters and would not perform in them from 1954 to 1966. He was a major fund-raiser, financial supporter, strategist and diplomatic spokesperson for the civil rights movement. In 1956, he helped to raise money to support the Montgomery bus boycott. He also helped to raise funds to support the Freedom Rides and voter registration campaigns. In 1963, he helped establish the Southern Free Theatre in Jackson, Mississippi. He frequently served as a liaison between the SCLC and the Kennedy administration. He was a close friend of Dr. King.

In 1982, he was awarded the Martin Luther King Jr. Nonviolent Peace Prize. In the 1980s and 1990s, Belafonte became an international humanitarian with his aid to victims of famine in Africa. In 1986, he was awarded the title of Goodwill Ambassador for UNICEF. Mayor Mario Cuomo of New York City appointed him to lead the Martin Luther King Jr. Commission to Promote Knowledge of Nonviolence.

Bevel, James Luther (October 19, 1936–)

James Bevel was born in Itta Bena, Mississippi. In 1958, he attended the Highland Folk School in Tennessee where he was introduced to theories of nonviolent social change. In 1959, he became an ordained Baptist minister. In 1961, he earned a B.A. at the American Baptist Theological Seminary in Nashville. Bevel also attended a workshop for student activists at Vanderbilt University that was sponsored by the Fellowship of Reconciliation. In 1960, he married Diane Nash, chairman of the Nashville Student Movement, and led sit-ins that forced Nashville businessmen to desegregate their stores. In 1961, Bevel was a founding member of the Student Nonviolent Coordinating Committee (SNCC). In 1962, he joined the SCLC as the director of student training. He was one of the co-leaders of the Albany Campaign, the Chicago Freedom Movement and the March on Washington. Bevel composed several freedom songs. In 1967, he left the SCLC to become executive director of the Spring Mobilization Committee to End the War in Vietnam. In 1980, he founded the Students for Education and Economic Development. In 1989, he organized the National Committee Against Religious Bigotry and Racism. In the 1990s, he worked to eliminate capital punishment.

Bond, Julian (January 14, 1940–)

Bond was born in Nashville, Tennessee. His father, Horace Mann Bond, was president of Lincoln University in Lincoln, Pennsylvania, and then of Atlanta University. When he was attending Morehouse College in 1960–61, Julian participated in the student campaign to desegregate Atlanta. In 1962, he took charge of communications for the SNCC. He directed the information campaign that supported the sit-in movement that led to the desegregation of the lunch counters of many of the nation's largest chain stores.

In 1964, he visited Africa. Upon his return he became a feature writer for the *Atlantic Inquirer* and later its managing editor. Also in 1964, Bond was elected to the Georgia House of Representatives. The Georgia legislature refused to seat him because of his opposition to the Vietnam War. In 1965, the Supreme Court ordered him seated and he served until 1975. In 1968, Bond led a black delegation to the Democratic National Convention in Chicago in opposition to the white delegation led by the racist governor, Lester Maddox. He became nationally recognized as a spokesman for civil rights, for peace in Vietnam and against police brutality. In 1975 he was elected to the Georgia State Senate, where he served for 12 years.

Bond received honorary degrees from the University of Bridgeport, Wesleyan University, Lincoln University and Tuskegee University. He served as a visiting professor at Drexell University, Harvard University and the University of Virginia. He was a Pappas Fellow at the University of Pennsylvania. In 1972, he published *A Time To Speak—A Time To Act*. In 1998, he was named chairman of the NAACP.

Carter, Robert L. (March 11, 1917–)

Carter was born in 1917 in Careyville, Florida. His father died in 1918 and his mother moved to New Jersey where she worked as a laundress. Carter grew up in extreme poverty. He won a scholarship to Lincoln University in Pennsylvania where he earned a degree in political science. He studied law at Howard University Law School and then received a Rosenwald Scholarship to study at Columbia University. In 1941, Carter was drafted into the Army Air Force where he served as a lieutenant. In 1944, he left the Air Force and went to work with Thurgood Marshall, the chief counsel for the NAACP Legal Defense Fund. He ran the day-to-day operation of that fund. In 1950, Carter argued the first of 22 cases before the Supreme Court. Included were three of the five cases that were combined into *Brown v. Board of Education*. Carter initiated the use of behavioral science as an argument for social equality. He cited studies with dolls that demonstrated the unfavorable effect of segregation on the psyche of young children. Chief Justice Earl Warren cited the doll study as a key reason for the Supreme Court's decision. Commencing in 1956, Carter worked as the NAACP in-house lawyer for more than a decade. In 1958, Carter represented Daisy Bates in the Little Rock desegregation struggle. After the revolution, Carter ran a private law practice in New York. In 1972, President Nixon appointed him to the federal bench for the New York Southern District. In 2004, the NAACP honored Robert L. Carter as a major architect of *Brown v. Board* in a 50th anniversary celebration of that decision.

Clark, Septima Poinsette (1898–1987)

Septima Poinsette was born on May 3, 1898, in Charleston, South Carolina. Her father was born a slave on the Joel Poinsette farm near Georgetown. After the Civil War, her father worked as a caterer and her mother took in laundry. Septima completed the twelfth grade at Avery Normal Institute in Charleston and passed the state teachers' exam in 1916. Her first teaching position was at John's Island in a two-teacher black school. As the teacher-principal with 132 students, she was paid $35 per month while across the road in a white school with three pupils the white teacher was paid $85 per month. In 1919, Septima returned to Charleston to teach the sixth grade at Avery Normal Institute. She joined the NAACP and became a civil rights activist. She worked in an NAACP campaign that won the right of blacks to teach in public schools. In 1937, Septima studied at Atlanta University where she took a course from W.E.B. Du Bois.

Septima married in 1920 and bore two children. She lived in Columbia, South Carolina, from 1929 to 1947. During that time she received a B.A. from Benedict College and an M.A. from Hampton Institute. She also worked with Thurgood Marshall and others in developing a court case to require equalization of teachers' salaries. In 1945, Federal District Judge J. Waring ruled that black teachers should receive equal pay if they had equal education. The case was won and Septima's salary was tripled.

From 1947 to 1956, Septima worked in Charleston public schools. She was a member of the Charleston NAACP and attended workshops on desegregation protests at Highland Folk School in Monteagle, Tennessee. In 1956, she was accused of holding membership in a civil rights organization in violation of state law. She lost her teaching job and retirement benefits—after teaching for 40 years. She went to Tennessee as director of workshops at the Highland Folk School. The school taught human brotherhood and emphasized a cooperative rather than a competitive use of learning. She and Ella Baker taught techniques of school desegregation, voter registration and leadership. In 1961, Septima joined the staff of the SCLC as director of education. She was the first female SCLC board member. At age 63 she traveled through 11 southern states, organizing SCLC workshops to teach nonviolent tactics and psychology and promote literacy and voter registration. Her work was dangerous. Thirty persons were killed in the SCLC voter registration campaigns.

After leaving the SCLC, she conducted workshops for the American Field Service Committee. In 1978, she was awarded an honorary doctorate of human letters by Charleston College. In 1979, President Jimmy Carter gave her the Living Legacy Award. Dr. Martin Luther King called her "the Mother of the Movement." Ms. Clark published two autobiographies; *Echo in My Soul* (1962) and *Ready from Within; Septima Clark and the Civil Rights Movement* (1986).

Conyers, John, Jr. (May 16, 1929–)

Conyers was born in Detroit, Michigan. He earned a B.A. at Wayne University in 1957 and a J.D. from Wayne State Law School in 1958. He made a career of law and politics. In 1964, he was elected to represent Detroit in the U.S. Congress. He was re-elected to Congress 15 times by ever-increasing pluralities reaching 84 percent in 1992. He was a founding member of the Congressional Black Caucus and a major supporter of President Johnson's Voting Rights Act of 1965 and other civil rights legislation. In April 1968, Conyers submitted a bill to Congress to create a national holiday on Dr. King's birthday. The bill was passed and signed by President Reagan on November 22, 1983. Conyers authored several books on the U.S. military and its campaigns in the twentieth century.

Cotton, Dorothy Foreman (1931–)

Dorothy Lee Foreman was born in Goldsboro, North Carolina, in 1931. Her father was a tobacco factory worker. Dorothy went to Shaw University in Raleigh, supporting herself by working as a housekeeper for the university president. She attended Virginia State College in Petersburg and earned a degree in English and library science. She married a college acquaintance, George Cotton. Mrs. Cotton then attended Boston University and earned a master's degree in speech therapy in 1960.

Dorothy Cotton had a long and distinguished career in the center of the civil rights struggle. It began when she joined the Gillfield Baptist Church in Petersburg and became a protégé of Wyatt T. Walker, chairman of the local NAACP. She helped Walker protest segregation at the library and at a lunch counter and she taught direct-action tactics to students. In 1960, Cotton and Walker moved to Atlanta to join Dr. King's SCLC team. Cotton worked closely with Dr. King, Abernathy, Walker and Andrew Young on projects such as Freedom Rides, voter registration and the Poor People's Campaign. In 1963, she became director of the SCLC's Citizen Education Program. The program taught southern blacks citizenship and the tactics of nonviolent action using the U.S. Constitution, the Bill of Rights and the Fourteenth Amendment. Cotton toured the South with Andrew Young and Septima Clark, recruiting candidates for the program. From 1961 to 1966, more than 6,000 people were trained at the Citizenship Schools. Cotton was a gifted singer and often led programs featuring freedom songs.

After Dr. King's assassination, Cotton had a second career in administration and academia. She was director of the Child Development/Head Start program in Jefferson County, Alabama. She worked at the Bureau of Human Services of the City of Atlanta. She was the Southeastern Regional Director of ACTION, a federal volunteer program. In 1982, Cotton went to Cornell University as director of student activities. In 1991, she conducted seminars on leadership development and social change.

Du Bois, William Edward Burghardt (1868–1963)

On August 27, 1868, W.E.B. Du Bois was born in Great Barrington, Massachusetts, a small, mostly white New England town. He attended Fisk University, a black institution in Nashville, Tennessee. He then studied at the University of Berlin and Harvard University, where he earned a doctorate.

He made contributions of national significance in the fields of history, sociology and freedom activism. His book *Black Reconstruction in America 1860–1880*, published in 1935, radically changed the general concept of the cause of the Civil War and the nature of Reconstruction. He argued that the Civil War was not a contest between northern industrialists and southern planters but a war over the continuation of slavery. He presented evidence to show that the Reconstruction was not about abuse of southerners by northern carpetbaggers and southern scalawags but an unprecedented experiment in democracy which focused on education and enfranchisement. He noted that in 1866 the Freedmen's Bureau reported that in 11 former slave states and the District of Columbia there were 740 schools, 1,314 teachers and 90,489 Negro pupils. In July 1870, there were 4,239 schools with 9,307 teachers serving

247,333 pupils. He found that the public school system in most southern states began with the enfranchisement of the Negro during Reconstruction.

In his book *The Souls of Black Folk*, published in 1903, Du Bois argued against Booker T. Washington's education policies and advocated equality for blacks in voting, educational and economic opportunities.

In the field of civil rights, Du Bois is one of the "founding fathers." He organized the Niagara Movement in 1905 to challenge racial segregation and oppression. In 1909, Du Bois, in collaboration with John Dewey and others, founded the National Association for the Advancement of Colored People (NAACP)—the single most influential agency in the struggle for freedom in the U.S. during the twentieth century. From 1910 to 1934, Du Bois was the editor of the *Crisis*, the NAACP magazine. The *Crisis* was instrumental in fomenting the Harlem Renaissance in the 1920s and an advocate of the decolonization of Africa.

From 1934 to 1944, he taught, researched and wrote at Atlanta University. He then returned to work for the NAACP on international policy. Du Bois sought to draft a petition to bring U.S. human rights violations against African Americans before the United Nations. Mrs. Eleanor Roosevelt and other members of the NAACP board objected and he was fired. After leaving the NAACP in 1948, Du Bois helped to found the Peace Information Center, which distributed the Stockholm Antinuclear Peace Appeal and campaigned against the Korean War.

During the Cold War, Du Bois was a peace activist and so incurred the wrath of the federal government. He was denied a passport and he was indicted as an agent of an unnamed foreign country. He won his case and so the U.S. government did not put this octogenarian into prison. After a long career of fighting for human rights and justice he became disillusioned with living in a country that denied civil rights to blacks and emigrated to Ghana, where he died in 1963. He authored more than a dozen scholarly books.

Due, Patricia Stephens (1939–)

Patricia Stephens was born in 1939 to Lottie Powell and Horace W. Stephens in St. Hebron, near Quincy, Florida. She attended high school in Belle Glade in Palm Beach County where her stepfather was an instructor. She graduated in 1957. Patricia enrolled at Florida Agricultural & Mechanical University (FAMU) with a music scholarship and graduated in 1965. Patricia married John Due, a civil rights lawyer, and they had three daughters, Tananarive, Johnita and Lydia.

Patricia began working for CORE as a civil rights activist while at FAMU in Tallahassee. She was involved as a leader/participant in the three Tallahassee civil rights actions: attempts to desegregate lunch counters, swimming pools and movie theaters. On one of their nonviolent demonstrations police hit her in the face with tear gas, damaging her eyesight. Patricia became a CORE field secretary and directed a successful CORE voter registration drive in north Florida. After 1968, she continued to be active in local, regional and state civil rights organizations and actions. On March 7, 2000, she participated in the largest protest in Florida history when an estimated 50,000 people descended on Tallahassee to object to Governor Bush's turning back the clock on affirmative action. In 2003, Patricia Due published her memoir, *Freedom in the Family* (co-authored by her daughter, Tananarive), one of the best firsthand accounts of the civil rights movement.

Edelman, Marian Wright (June 6, 1939–)

Marian Wright was born in Bennetsville, South Carolina. Her father was a Baptist minister. In 1960, she graduated from Spelman College as valedictorian. She participated in a sit-in at the City Hall in Atlanta and was arrested. In 1963, she graduated from Yale Law School. She also studied at the Sorbonne University in Paris and at the University of Geneva, Switzerland.

From 1964 to 1968, she headed the NAACP Legal Defense Fund in Mississippi where she pioneered legal representation for blacks. She endured imprisonment, threats and discrimination such as denial of entrance to a state courthouse. She was the SCLC Congressional liason for the Poor People's Campaign in 1968.

After the revolution, she was appointed director of the Harvard University Center for Law and Education. In 1973, she founded the Children's Defense Fund. In 1980, she chaired the board of trustees of Spelman College. She was awarded honorary degrees by several universities. In 1985, she was given a McArthur Foundation Fellowship. In 1988, she received the Albert Schweitzer Humanitarian Award.

Evers, Medgar Wylie (July 2, 1925–June 12, 1963)

Evers was born in Decatur, Mississippi. After serving in the army during World War II, he and his brother, Charles, enrolled at Alcorn A&M College. On election day in 1946, the two brothers, accompanied by several armed friends, went to the polling place with the intention of voting. They were met by 200 whites who were opposed to blacks voting. They decided not to vote. A year later they returned and succeeded in voting. Medger applied to the University of Mississippi Law School but was rejected because of his race.

In 1954, Evers was named the first field secretary of the NAACP in Mississippi. In that capacity, he led voter registration drives, fought segregation, organized a boycott to integrate Leake County schools and the Mississippi State Fair, played a major role in getting James Meredith admitted to the University of Mississippi and won a lawsuit that integrated Jackson's privately owned buses. He filed a similar lawsuit to integrate Jackson's public parks. He helped to organize the Jackson Movement, an NAACP-led coalition of black organizations that sponsored mass meetings, demonstrations and boycotts to challenge apartheid in Mississippi. He also investigated racially inspired crimes, including the murders of Emmett Till and the Rev. George Lee.

On May 28, 1963, a Molotov cocktail was thrown at Evers's house. On June 12, 1963, he was fatally shot in the back as he walked to the door of his house. Evers was buried at Arlington National Cemetery with full military honors. He was posthumously awarded the NAACP Spingarn Medal. His assailant was convicted of the murder on February 5, 1994.

Farmer, James Leonard (January 12, 1920–)

Farmer was born in Holly Springs, Mississippi. His father was a Methodist minister and professor at Wiley College in Marshall, Texas. Farmer attended Wiley College and then Howard University in Washington, DC. At Howard he studied Mahatma Gandhi's philosophy of nonviolent resistance. In 1941, he earned a bachelor of divinity degree but he refused ordination in the Methodist Church because it was segregated.

In 1942, Farmer founded the Congress of Racial Equality (CORE) in Chicago. Its goal was to seek an end to apartheid. By 1963, CORE had 70,000 members, a paid staff of 35 and an annual budget of $700,000. Farmer led CORE in making major contributions to the Freedom Revolution. They supported the student sit-ins, they sponsored the Freedom Rides that challenged and defeated segregated transportation in the South and they cooperated with the SCNC on several campaigns. From 1960 to 1966, Farmer worked for the pacifist organization The Fellowship of Reconciliation. He also worked as a union organizer and campaign manager for the NAACP. Farmer pushed the idea of "compensatory action" by employers—an idea that was later picked up and enacted as affirmative action. Farmer was jailed many times. In 1965 he published a book, *Freedom When?*

In 1966, when the CORE leaders turned away from their original emphasis on nonviolent action and embraced Black Power, Farmer left the organization. He taught at Lincoln University, worked as assistant secretary of Health, Education and Welfare and then from 1982 to the early 1990s he taught at Mary Washington College in Fredericksburg, VA. He continued to be a prominent spokesman for human rights and nonviolent solutions to sociopolitical problems.

Fauntroy, Walter (February 6, 1933–)

Fauntroy was born in Washington, DC. He graduated cum laude from Virginia Union University in 1955. In 1958 he earned a bachelor of divinity degree at Yale University Divinity School. He was ordained a Baptist minister and became the pastor of Bethel Baptist Church in Washington, DC. In 1960, he was named director of the Washington chapter of the SCLC. He was the local coordinator of the March on

Washington in 1963. In 1965, he helped to organize the Selma to Montgomery march. Fauntroy was vice chairman of a White House conference on civil rights. In 1967, President Johnson appointed him vice chairman of the Washington, DC, City Council. In 1971, he was elected to represent Washington in the U.S. House of Representatives—a position he held until 1990. He chaired the Congressional Black Caucus from 1981 to 1983. Fauntroy received honorary degrees from Georgetown University Law School, Yale University and Virginia Union University. In 1989, he was given the National Urban Coalition's Hubert Humphrey Humanitarian Award.

Forman, James (October 4, 1928–)

Forman was born in Chicago but spent his early childhood with his grandmother in Marshall County, Mississippi. He attended Wilson Junior College in Chicago and then served in the air force from 1947 to 1951. From 1953 to 1957, he studied at Roosevelt University in Chicago, earning a degree in public administration. He also studied at Brown University.

In 1960, Forman worked with the CORE Emergency Relief Committee. He assisted black Tennessee farmers who were evicted for registering to vote. He also participated in a CORE Freedom Ride in an effort to desegregate interstate bus travel. He was arrested and badly beaten. In 1960–61, he assisted students in their sit-in campaigns. During 1962–63, he helped to organize protests in Atlanta, Savannah and Rome, Georgia, Greenwood, Mississippi, Danville, Virginia, Cambridge, Maryland, and Selma, Alabama.

In 1964, Forman joined the SNCC and quickly became its executive secretary. Under his leadership, the SNCC was an effective civil rights organization. He worked in the Alabama campaign. In 1966, SNCC had a divisive internal debate over tactics. Robert Moses believed that the SNCC's role was to serve as a catalyst while the local people provided the leadership. Forman believed the SNCC should provide leadership. Another issue was the insistence of the Black Panthers to talk more about violence and exclusiveness than about nonviolence and cooperation. By 1969, the SNCC was fractured over these issues and suffering from government harassment and Forman left.

In 1969, Forman organized the Black Economic Development Conference in Detroit. The conference produced the Black Manifesto which demanded that white churches and synagogues give African Americans $500 million in reparations for slavery. More than $1 million was received from white organizations in response to this manifesto. It was used to support publications. Forman published several books, including *The Making of Black Revolutionaries: A Personal Account* (1972). Forman is considered one of the premier leaders of the Freedom Revolution.

Gray, Fred David

Gray was born in Montgomery, Alabama. He earned a diploma at Nashville Christian Institute and in 1951 received a B.S. from Alabama State University. In 1954, he earned a law degree at Case Western Reserve University. He was a cooperating attorney with the NAACP Legal Defense Fund. He attained national prominence in the late 1950s by defending Dr. King and Rosa Parks in the Montgomery bus boycott case. In 1973, Gray filed a $1.8 billion class-action suit on behalf of 623 black men who unwittingly participated in a U.S. Public Health Service study of syphilis in Tuskegee from 1932 to 1972. He won an out-of-court settlement of more than $10 million in 1975. Gray received a number of awards, including the Man in the News *New York Times* award in 1966, the Equal Justice Award of the National Bar Association in 1977 and the Charles Hamilton Houston Medallion of Merit in 1986.

Green, Ernest G. (September 22, 1941–)

Green was born in Little Rock, Arkansas. He attended Horace Mann High School for three years. At the beginning of his senior year in 1957, he was one of the nine students selected to desegregate Little Rock Central High School. To attend classes, the nine met at Daisy Bates's house and then were taken to school in a station wagon escorted by machine-gun mounted jeeps.

Green endured the harassment of the white students, did well in his classes and was the first black to graduate from Little Rock Central High in 1958. At graduation, one of the guests was Dr. King who sat in the audience with Ernest's mother, Mrs. Bates and friends. Green continued his education at Mississippi State University earning a B.A. in 1962 and an M.A. in 1964. He had a successful career in administration and banking. From 1968 to 1976, he was director of the A. Philip Randolph Education Fund. From 1977 to 1981, he was an assistant secretary of Labor. He was a member of the National Board of the NAACP, a board member of the Winthrop Rockefeller Foundation and the National Board of the African Development Foundation. Green and his eight co-desegregators were awarded the Congressional Medal of Honor and the NAACP Spingarn Medal for their accomplishments.

Gregory, Richard Claxon, "Dick" (October 12, 1932–)

Gregory was born and grew up in a St. Louis slum. During the Great Depression, Gregory's mother, Lucille Gregory, worked as a domestic in a St. Louis suburb for $2 a day and car fare. Before he entered the first grade, Dick started working to help support the family by hauling groceries. He attended Southern Illinois University at Carbondale from 1951 to 1956 with two years out for a hitch in the army. He was a track star and a budding comedian. In 1959, he married Lillian Smith. They settled in Chicago and raised ten children. By 1962, Gregory was a national celebrity and the first black superstar entertainer. Throughout the '60s he supported the civil rights movement with his wit, his money and his person. He participated in voter registration drives throughout the South. From 1962 to 1974, he was jailed 20 times for demonstrating peacefully. In 1968, Gregory was the presidential candidate of the Freedom and Peace Party with a platform of pro-civil rights and anti-war. Gregory advocated vegetarianism and was a historian of the King assassination. In 1978, *Ebony* gave him its Heritage and Freedom Award for his contribution to the civil rights movement. Gregory published several books, including *From the Back of the Bus* (1962), *An Autobiography* (1964) and *The Murder of Martin Luther King Jr.* (1977 with Mark Lane).

Hamer, Fannie Lou Townsend (1917–1977)

Fannie Lou Townsend was born October 6, 1917, in Ruleville, Mississippi. She was the youngest of 20 children. She began picking cotton at age six. Her father's three mules were poisoned by racist whites. In 1962, Mrs. Hamer and 17 other African Americans tried to register to vote. They were rejected and their bus driver was arrested. Mrs. Hamer was ordered to leave the plantation where she had worked for 18 years. In 1963, she attended a voter registration training session. Mrs. Hamer and others were arrested in Winona, jailed and beaten. Mrs. Hamer sustained permanent eye and liver damage. In 1962, she began to work for the SNCC for $10 a week. She participated in the Selma march. In 1968, she was a co-founder of the Mississippi Freedom Democratic Party.

In 1969, Mrs. Hamer founded a 680-acre agricultural cooperative called Freedom Farm. She worked with the Delta Ministry and the National Council of Negro Women to develop housing and a day-care center in Ruleville. Mrs. Hamer was a gifted singer and orator. In 1969, Morehouse College in Atlanta awarded honorary degrees to Mrs. Hamer, the Rev. M. L. King Sr. and Vice President Hubert Humphrey. In 1970, she was awarded a doctor of humane letters by Columbia College. In 1977, she died of cancer. The inscription on her headstone reads, "I'm sick and tired of being sick and tired." A few weeks later, the Mississippi legislature unanimously adopted a resolution praising Mrs. Hamer for her service to the state.

Height, Dorothy Irene (March 24, 1912–)

Height was born in Richmond, Virginia. She applied for entrance to Barnard College but was not accepted as the school already had two black students. She went to New York University and the New York School of Social Work and earned bachelors and masters degrees. She was a civil rights activist from the 1930s to the 1990s. She worked for the YWCA for 20 years and helped to desegregate it. She became a

New York City Welfare Department case worker in 1934 and served on several special commissions. From 1952 to 1955, she was a member of the Defense Advisory Committee on Women in the Service. In 1958, she became president of the National Council of Negro Women (NCNW), a civil rights organization with about four million members. She served as its president into the 1990s. As council president she led voter education drives and mentored students who worked in the civil rights movement. In 1964, she participated in the Wednesdays in Mississippi project. She was a contributor and consultant to the U.S. Agency for International Development and the U.S. secretary of State. In 1978, the National Newspaper Publishers Association gave her its Distinguished Service Award. She received honorary degrees from Tuskegee University, Coppin State College in Maryland, Harvard University and Pace College in New York. On her birthday, March 24, 2004, Ms. Height was awarded the Congressional Gold Medal at a nationally televised celebration of her lifetime contributions to freedom and equality. She has recently published her memoirs, *Open Wide the Freedom Gates.*

Henry, Aaron (1922–1997)

Henry was a drug store owner in Clarksdale, Mississippi. He was a member of the NAACP and joined the revolution in the 1950s. "Doc" Henry participated in numerous civil rights actions, leading demonstrations, boycotts and voter registration drives. Henry was president of the Mississippi NAACP from 1960 to 1993. He was the founding chairman of the Mississippi Freedom Democratic Party in 1964. After the revolution, he became a powerful force in the regular Democratic organization and in 1992, he was elected to the Mississippi state legislature.

Houston, Charles Hamilton (September 3, 1895–April 22, 1950)

Houston was born in Washington, DC. He graduated Phi Beta Kappa from Amherst College, taught English, then entered the army. After the army, he attended Harvard Law School and then practiced law in Washington. In 1929, he became the dean of Howard Law School. At Howard, he hired new faculty and made the school into a laboratory for devising strategies to win civil rights for blacks. He taught his students that all Negro lawyers should be social engineers. In 1935, he became the first full-time legal counsel to the NAACP. He argued many civil rights cases before the Supreme Court. Houston is credited with planning the 20-year legal assault on cases of U.S. apartheid that led to the *Brown v. Board of Education* decision. His most famous student was Thurgood Marshall. Houston was awarded the NAACP's Spingarn Medal in 1958. Howard University named its new law school in his honor. Houston died five years before the beginning of the nonviolent revolution but no one made a greater contribution to turning the Supreme Court 180 degrees from *Plessy v. Ferguson* to *Brown v. Board of Education.*

Hunter-Gault, Charlayne (February 27, 1942–)

Charlayne Hunter was born in Due West, South Carolina. In 1961, she matriculated at the University of Georgia—desegregating the university in the process. After graduation, she won a Russell Sage Fellowship for graduate work at Washington University. Charlayne then pursued a career in journalism and news broadcasting. Her career included work with the *New Yorker* magazine, NBC News in Washington, DC, PBS's *MacNeil/Leherer Newshour* and teaching at the Columbia University School of Journalism. She won many awards, including the Journalist of the Year award from the National Association of Black Journalists and two Emmy Awards. In 1977, she became chief of National Public Radio's African Bureau. In 1992, she published her autobiography, *In My Place*.

Jackson, Jesse Louis (October 8, 1941–)

Jesse Jackson was born in Greenville, South Carolina, in 1941. In 1959, he graduated from Greenville's Sterling High School. He won a football scholarship from the University of Illinois. However, when he learned that African Americans were not permitted to play quarterback he enrolled at North Carolina A&T College in Greensboro. At A&T he was a star athlete, an excellent student and a participant in student sit-ins. In 1964, he earned a B.S. in sociology. He was hired by CORE as director of southern operations. He attended Chicago Theological Seminary and was ordained to the ministry.

In 1963, he was a leader in the desegregation of Greensboro, N.C. In 1965, he was one of the leaders in the Selma to Montgomery march and was appointed to the SCLC staff. He was sent to Chicago to lead Operation Breadbasket where he recruited more than 200 ministers to work in Chicago. The campaign was a great success and in 1967 he became the national director of Operation Breadbasket.

In 1971, Jackson left the SCLC and founded Operation PUSH (People United to Save Humanity). In 1984, he founded the Rainbow Coalition and ran for president of the U.S. His platform was (1) a freeze on defense spending, (2) a program for full employment, (3) self-determination for the Palestinians and (4) political empowerment of African Americans through voter registration. In the primaries, Jackson won 3.2 million votes out of 18 million cast. In 1988, he ran again and won nearly seven million votes out of 23 million cast.

By 1979, Jackson had become an unofficial international diplomat for the U.S. He went to South Africa, with the approval of President Carter, and spoke against apartheid. He lobbied for peace between Israel and the Palestinians. He negotiated for the release of hostages held by terrorists. In 1973, he was co-author of a book, *Blacks in America; A Fight for Freedom*. In 1993, he was awarded the Martin Luther King Jr. Nonviolent Peace Prize.

Jordan, Vernon Eulion, Jr. (August 15, 1935–)

Jordan was born and raised in Atlanta, Georgia. He majored in political science at De Pauw University in Indiana, graduating in 1957. In 1960, he earned a law degree at Howard University in Washington, DC. Jordan worked on the 1961 desegregation suit that forced the University of Georgia to admit black students.

From 1961 to 1963, he was the NAACP Georgia field secretary. From 1964 to 1968, he headed the Voter Education Project of the Southern Regional Council and succeeded in registering about two million black voters throughout the South.

In 1969, Jordan was appointed a Fellow of the Institute of Politics at Harvard University's Kennedy School of Government. In 1970, he became the executive director of the United Negro Fund. In 1972, he was appointed executive director of the National Urban League. In 1980, he was shot in the back by a sniper. He recovered fully. In 1992, he was a close advisor to Bill Clinton in his campaign for the presidency. Jordan received honorary degrees from more than 50 U.S. colleges and universities.

King, Martin Luther, Jr. (January 15, 1929–April 4, 1968)

King was born in Atlanta, Georgia. He was the son and grandson of Baptist ministers. In 1948, he received a B.A. in sociology from Morehouse College in Atlanta. In 1951, he graduated first in his class from Crozier Theological Seminary in Chester, Pennsylvania. In 1955, he earned a doctorate in systematic theology at Boston University. In 1954, he became the pastor of the Dexter Avenue Baptist Church in Montgomery, Alabama. In 1955, he led the Montgomery bus boycott. King combined New Testament and Gandhian concepts to develop nonviolent tactics which he employed to replace apartheid laws with pro-freedom laws.

In 1957, he was the co-founder of the Southern Christian Leadership Conference (SCLC). King was an exceptional orator. In 1963, he delivered his "I Have a Dream" speech to 250,000 people assembled at the Lincoln Memorial in Washington. His oratory, his negotiations with Washington and his leadership of the civil rights movement contributed directly to the passage of the civil rights acts of the 1960s.

King, like all other black leaders, suffered from the resistance to change of the white Establishment. His house was shotgun blasted and bombed three times. He was arrested and incarcerated many times. The FBI harassed King and his family throughout the 1960s with wiretaps, dirty tricks and attempts to discredit him. J. Edgar Hoover tried to prove that the SCLC was infiltrated by Communists but he found no evidence.

King led civil rights campaigns in Selma, Alabama, Chicago and St. Augustine, Florida, and the Selma to Montgomery march. King's contributions to the freedom of blacks were recognized internationally. He was awarded a Nobel Peace Prize in

1964. Streets were renamed for him throughout the land. He was awarded numerous honorary degrees. He published several books that defined the logic and philosophy of the Freedom Revolution.

On April 4, 1968, Dr. King was assassinated in Memphis, Tennessee. One hundred and fifty thousand mourners attended his funeral. Riots broke out in 63 U.S. cities. On November 2, 1986, President Reagan proclaimed a national holiday in King's memory. President Reagan said: "The majesty of his message, the dignity of his bearing and the righteousness of his cause are a lasting legacy. In a few short years he changed America for all time. He made it possible for our nation to move closer to the ideals set forth in our Declaration of Independence: that all people are created equal and are endowed with inalienable rights that government has the duty to respect and protect. Dr. King's activism was rooted in the *true patriotism* that cherishes America's ideals and strives to narrow the gap between those ideals and reality."

Dr. King is remembered in a variety of ways. To the blacks, he was a Moses. He led them out of the wilderness of U.S. apartheid toward the promised land of democracy. The white Establishment in apartheid states considered him a rabble-rouser. The FBI thought that he was a Communist. Theologians and philosophers praise him for rediscovering the practicing pacifist Christianity. Historians say he continued the struggle for freedom of the Civil War and finally liberated the formerly enslaved people. For President Johnson, he was first a collaborator on civil rights legislation and then his severest critic on the Vietnam War. To people around the world he represented the potential of nonviolent civil action to achieve justice and freedom. In 1986, the U.S. Congress declared January 17 a national holiday in his honor.

King, Coretta Scott (April 27, 1927–)

Coretta Scott was born on a farm in Marion, Alabama, on April 27, 1927. Her father was a successful trucker and farmer, so successful that resentful whites set fire to their family home and destroyed it in 1942. Coretta Scott graduated from Lincoln High School, a private black institution with an integrated faculty. She then attended Antioch College and earned a B.A. in music and education. In 1951, she enrolled at the New England Conservatory of Music in Boston and eventually earned a Mus.B. in voice. She also met and dated a young doctoral candidate at Boston University, Martin L. King Jr.

They were married June 18, 1953. They were blessed with four children, Yolanda Denise, b. November 17, 1955; Martin Luther III, b. October 23, 1957; Dexter Scott, b. January 30, 1961; and Bernice Albertine, b. March 28, 1963.

Coretta King supported and complemented her husband's work for civil rights. When the Kings visited India in 1959, Coretta sang spirituals at events where her husband spoke. She got her husband released from a Georgia prison by a call to presidential candidate John F. Kennedy in 1960. In 1962, Coretta King was a delegate to the Women's Strike for Peace Seventeenth Disarmament Conference in Geneva, Switzerland. She accompanied her husband to the Nobel Peace Prize award program in Oslo, Norway, in 1964. In the mid–1960s, she sang in freedom concerts which raised funds for the SCLC. In the late '60s she filled her husband's speaking engagements when he was unable to meet them. After Dr. King's assassination, Coretta kept his speaking appointment at an anti–Vietnam war rally in New York and helped to launch the People's March to Washington.

In 1969, Mrs. King published her memoirs, *My Life With Martin Luther King Jr.* In 1970, she established the Martin Luther King Jr. Center for Nonviolent Social Change in Atlanta. In the '70s and beyond, Mrs. King became a nationally known advocate for peace. She participated in the campaign to establish a national holiday in honor of Dr. King and helped to plan the annual celebration of his work which began in 1986. Coretta Scott King received a large number of awards, including honorary degrees from Boston University, Brandeis College, Morehouse College, Princeton University, Northeastern University and Bates College.

King, Martin Luther, Sr. (1899–1984)

M.L. King Sr. was born in Stockbridge, Georgia. His father was a sharecropper. He became a licensed Baptist minister at age 18. He earned a B.A. in theology at Morehouse College in Atlanta in 1939 and succeeded his father-in-law as pastor of the Ebenezer Baptist Church in Atlanta. He was a community leader and a member of the NAACP. He was a proud parent and supporter of M.L. King Jr. After Dr. King's death, he continued to speak out for faith and freedom. He addressed the Alabama state legislature and delivered the benediction at the Democratic National Convention in 1980.

Lawson, James Morris (September 22, 1928–)

Lawson grew up in Massillon, Ohio, as the son of a Republican AME Zion minister who preached the gospel of love but also wore a .38 on his hip to prevent harassment by white people. Lawson graduated from Baldwin Wallace College and studied at Oberlin Theological Seminary and Vanderbilt University Divinity School. In 1951, while he was national president of the United Methodist Youth Fellowship, he refused induction into the army for the Korean War on pacifist grounds and served more than a year in a federal prison. His church sent him to India where he did missionary work and studied Gandhi's philosophy of nonviolence. In 1958, he met a group of young black preachers in the Capers Memorial CME Church in Nashville, Tennessee. They organized the Nashville Christian Leadership Council (NCLC) and affiliated with the SCLC. At Vanderbilt, Lawson ran workshops on nonviolent action under the sponsorship of the Fellowship of Reconciliation (FOR). A large number of the movement's leaders went through his workshops. In 1960, the businessmen in downtown Nashville suffered losses because of the waves of student trainees practicing nonviolent sit-ins. Lawson was held responsible and expelled from Vanderbilt. This led 10 of the 16 divinity faculty members to quit in protest. In 1961, he rode the buses with the Freedom Riders. Lawson worked at the SCLC in Albany, Georgia, and in the Mississippi Delta. Throughout the civil rights movement, he was one of the principal interpreters and teachers of Gandhi's philosophy of satyagraha—nonviolent civil action.

Lewis, John (February 21, 1940–)

Lewis was born near Troy, Alabama. He grew up on a small farm as one of ten children in a poor sharecropping family. In 1957, he matriculated at the American Baptist Theological Seminary in Nashville, Tennessee. He earned a B.A. in 1961. As a student, he participated in workshops on nonviolent action taught by James Lawson of the FOR. Lewis became an FOR field secretary. He attended the Highland Folk School where he was influenced by Septima Clark. He was active in the Nashville student movement and in the Nashville desegregation campaign of 1960. He was a founding member of the Student Nonviolent Coordinating Committee (SNCC) in 1960. He led Freedom Rides in South Carolina and Alabama and was severely beaten. From 1963 to 1966, he was the SNCC's national chairman. In 1963, he spoke at the March on Washington and criticized the federal government's failure to protect civil rights activists. He also called on African Americans to participate in the civil rights protests until "the unfinished revolution of 1776 is complete." Lewis marched with Dr. King in Selma and he was beaten on Bloody Sunday. In 1966, the SNCC turned from nonviolence to non-nonviolence and Lewis left. In 1970, he became the director of the Voter Education Project of the Southern Regional Council. In 1975, Lewis was awarded the Martin Luther King Jr. Nonviolent Peace Prize. He served on the Atlanta City Council from 1981 to 1986. In 1986, he won a seat in the U.S. Congress and was re-elected four times. He is the author of *Walking With the Wind*: *A Memoir of the Movement*.

Lowery, Joseph E. (1924–)

Lowery was born in Huntsville, Alabama. He attended Clark College, the Chicago Ecumenical Institute, Garnett Theological Seminary and Morehouse University. He earned a degree of doctor of divinity. He was ordained and commenced his ministry at the Warren Street Church in Birmingham, where he served until 1961. Lowery was a co-founder of the SCLC and served as one of the first vice presidents. In 1957, he succeeded the Rev. Ralph Abernathy as SCLC president and reactivated Operation Breadbasket—a program to encourage businesses that profited from black customers to hire blacks. He worked at helping Haitian refugees who were jailed by the government. He also co-planned a march from Selma to Washington, DC, to support renewal of the Voting Rights Act in 1982.

Marshall, Thurgood (July 2, 1908–January 24, 1993)

Thurgood Marshall was born in Baltimore, Maryland. His mother was a teacher and his father a head waiter and steward. He graduated cum laude from Lincoln University with a B.A. He graduated magna cum laude from Howard University Law School in 1933. He passed the Maryland bar in 1933. In 1935, he participated in a case that desegregated the University of Maryland Law School where he had been denied admission because of his race. In 1938, he was admitted to practice before the U.S. Supreme Court.

In 1939, Marshall became the director of the NAACP Legal Defense and Education Fund. Under Marshall's leadership, the fund was the principal agent in turning the U.S. Supreme Court 180 degrees from support of segregation to finding segregation unconstitutional. He and his colleagues won civil rights cases which they argued before the court. Some of the points of law that they established were: (1) blacks could not be excluded from primary elections, (2) segregation in interstate commerce was unconstitutional, (3) blacks could not be excluded from juries, (4) state courts could not enforce exclusive real estate covenants, (5) a state could not hurriedly construct a Negro law school to avoid accepting blacks at the white law school and (6) a state university could not assign blacks to a segregated desk in a classroom or table in a cafeteria. Marshall culminated his career with the NAACP by successfully arguing the revolutionary case of *Brown v. Board of Education.*

President Kennedy nominated Marshall for judge of the Second Court of Appeals in 1961. In 1964, President Johnson appointed him solicitor general. In 1967, President Johnson nominated Marshall to the U.S. Supreme Court, where he served for 24 years. Throughout those 24 years on the supreme court bench, Marshall's opinions constituted a standard of the liberal position. He opposed laws that prohibited women from exercising their discretion over their pregnancies. He opposed all laws that permitted the imposition of the death penalty. He had a consistent concern for the rights of labor, the rights of women and the struggles of minorities and the poor. Marshall received many honors, including 20 honorary degrees and having the University of Maryland Law School named in his honor. When Marshall's achievements are considered with historical perspective, it appears that he was the outstanding human rights attorney of the twentieth century.

Mays, Benjamin Elijah (August 1, 1894–March 28, 1984)

Mays was born in Ninety-six, South Carolina, the youngest of eight children.

His father was a sharecropper. Mays attended Virginia Union University in Richmond and then Bates College in Lewiston, Maine, where he graduated with honors in 1920. In 1925, he earned an M.A. at the University of Chicago School of Divinity. In 1935, he earned his PhD. He taught at Morehouse College in Atlanta and at South Carolina College in Orangeburg. In 1934, he was appointed dean of the School of Religion at Howard University in Washington, DC. He visited India and talked with Mahatma Gandhi. In 1941, he co-authored a civil rights manifesto. From 1940 to 1967, he served as president of Morehouse College. In 1944, he was elected vice president of the Federal Council of Churches of Christ and in 1948 he helped to organize the World Council of Churches in Amsterdam, Holland. Mays was a distinguished scholar of the black church and the blacks' religion. He authored several books, including *The Negro Church* (1933) and *The Negro's God as Reflected in His Literature* (1938). Mays was a central figure in the NAACP and was awarded the NAACP's Spingarn Award.

Dr. Mays introduced M.L. King Jr. to Gandhi's philosophy of nonviolent resistance and was his senior advisor throughout his career. He was also an advisor to President Jimmy Carter. He received numerous awards and honorary degrees. He delivered the benediction at the March on Washington and the eulogy at Dr. King's funeral. In 1977, he was awarded the Martin Luther King Jr. Nonviolent Peace Prize.

McCain, James

A native of South Carolina, McCain earned a bachelor's degree at Morris College in Sumter. He did graduate work at Temple University in Philadelphia. He then joined the faculty at Morris College where he lectured for 11 years and served as dean for seven of those years. He joined the NAACP and became president of the Sumter chapter.

McCain then accepted a position as principal of a school district in Marion, South Carolina. After five years in that position, he was fired for being a member of the NAACP. He was then hired as a high school principal in Clarendon County, South Carolina. After one year, he was fired for being a member of the NAACP. His next job was assistant director for the South Carolina Council of Human Relations. Two years later in October 1957, he became the first full-time secretary for CORE. Within a year, he had established seven CORE groups across South Carolina. In February and March 1960, McCain organized sit-ins at Claflin College in Orangeburg, Morris College in Sumter and Friendship College in Rock Hill.

McKissick, Floyd B. (March 9, 1922–April 28, 1991)

McKissick was born in Asheville, North Carolina. His father was a bellhop. He served in the army during World War II and then attended Morehouse College and

North Carolina College. He earned a B.A. in 1951. With the help of a desegregation suit filed by Thurgood Marshall, he attended the University of North Carolina Law School at Chapel Hill. McKissick filed his own lawsuit to get his five children admitted to all-white schools. In 1947, he participated in the Journey of Reconciliation—an effort by the Fellowship of Reconciliation to integrate interstate travel in the upper South. In 1962, he became the head of the Durham Chapter of CORE. In 1966, he participated in Meredith's March Against Fear in Mississippi. The same year, he became executive director of CORE. He then moved CORE to an emphasis on Black Power instead of nonviolence. In 1968, he left CORE but continued to be a promoter of black economic development. In 1969, he authored *Three-Fifths of a Man* and in 1974, he founded Soul City in Warren County, North Carolina. In 1990, he was appointed to a district judgeship in North Carolina.

Meredith, James H. (June 25, 1933–)

Meredith was the seventh of 13 children born on his parents' 84-acre farm in Kosciusko, Mississippi. He served in the U.S. Air Force from 1951–1960. He attended Jackson State University and then sought to enroll at the University of Mississippi to obtain his bachelor's degree. He was stopped by Governor Barnett in a dramatic physical confrontation. Meredith then filed a class-action lawsuit alleging that the University of Mississippi requirement that applicants submit recommendations from alumni (a regulation adopted after *Brown v. Board of Education*) was discriminatory and unconstitutional. The U.S. District Court supported the university. The U.S. Fifth Circuit Court of Appeals, however, supported Meredith. With that court decision, plus assistance from Constance Baker Motley of the NAACP Legal Defense Fund and U.S. marshals sent by President Kennedy, Meredith matriculated at Ole Miss.

In 1964–65, Meredith did graduate work at the Univesity of Ibadan, Nigeria. In 1966, he initiated a march from Memphis, Tennessee, to Jackson, Mississippi, to demonstrate that blacks had no fear of racists. On the march, large numbers of blacks were registered to vote and Meredith won a reputation of having no fear. He published a book, *Three Years in Mississippi* (1966). He attended the Columbia University Law School and earned a degree in 1968. In 1984 and 1985, he taught a course, Blacks and the Law, at the University of Mississippi. In 1989, he joined the staff of U.S. Senator Jesse Helms, a North Carolina racist, as his domestic policy advisor.

Mitchell, Clarence M., Jr. (1911–1984)

Mitchell was born March 8, 1911, in Baltimore, Maryland. He was the eldest of six children. His father was a chef. He attended Lincoln University in Pennsylvania where he was captain of the debating team. He graduated in 1932. He earned a law degree from the University of Maryland Law School and did graduate work at Atlanta University and the University of Minnesota. He was the executive secretary of the Urban League in St. Paul. In 1942 he became a member of the Fair Employment Practices Committee, which was established by President Roosevelt by Executive Order 8802. In 1945, Mitchell became the director of the Washington office of the NAACP. In 1956, Mitchell was arrested for attempting to use a whites-only railroad terminal waiting room in Florence, South Carolina.

During his 28 years as the NAACP's chief Washington lobbyist, Mitchell developed a close working relationship with both Democrats and Republicans and enjoyed many successes. In 1957, Congress passed the first civil rights legislation since Reconstruction. He witnessed President Johnson signing both the Civil Rights Act of 1964 and the Voting Rights Act of 1965. He also lobbied for the Fair Housing Act of 1968. Mitchell was an advisor to President Truman and President Carter. He received many awards, including the NAACP's Spingarn Medal and the Medal of Freedom—the nations highest civilian honor—presented by President Carter in 1980.

Moses, Robert Parris (January 23, 1935–)

Moses was born in Harlem in New York City. His father was a janitor and his grandfather was a Baptist circuit preacher in Tennessee, South Carolina and Virginia. He graduated from Hamilton College and then earned a master of philosophy degree at Harvard in 1957. He taught mathematics in a high school in New York until 1960 when he read about the Greensboro sit-ins.

Moses was strongly influenced by the French philosopher Albert Camus, who held that people should work for change, should refuse to be "victims" of violence and should avoid violence themselves. He believed that local people must develop their own leadership and not depend on civil rights workers.

In 1960, Moses went to Atlanta as an SNCC volunteer. In 1961, he joined the SNCC and was sent to Mississippi to work on voter registration. He worked on the Freedom Election in 1963. He directed the Freedom Summer of 1964 when nearly a thousand northerners—mostly white college students—joined African American activists in Mississippi to help blacks register to vote. He helped to organize the Mississippi Freedom Democratic Party. He organized Freedom Schools as he believed that education was a primary weapon in the battle against segregation.

Moses experienced beatings, trials bristling with hostile spectators and a five-week incarceration in the Magnolia Jail. Five people who worked closely with Moses on voting rights were killed. In 1966, he went to Canada as a conscientious objector to war. In 1969, he went to Tanzania to teach math. In 1982, he received a MacArthur Genius Grant which he used to create The Algebra Project—a program for improving the math skills of inner-city students.

Motley, Constance Baker (September 14, 1921–)

Constance Baker Motley was born in New Haven, Connecticut. Her father and mother were natives of Nevis in the Lesser Antilles. The family lived in an integrated neighborhood and Constance attended integrated schools. After high school, Motley attended Fisk University in Nashville for a year and a half and then transferred to New York University. In 1946 she earned a law degree at Columbia University. From 1945 to 1965, she was one of the skillful lawyers of the NAACP Legal Defense and Education Fund. She argued ten cases before the U.S. Supreme Court and won nine of them. In 1960–61, she helped Charlayne Hunter and Hamilton Holmes gain admission to the University of Georgia. In 1962, she managed the legal campaign that eventually required the University of Mississippi to admit James Meredith. In 1964, Motley was elected to the New York State Senate. In 1965, she was elected president of the Borough of Manhattan. In 1966, President Johnson appointed her to a federal judgeship. Motley received a great many honorary degrees from universities.

Nash, Diane Judith (May 15, 1938–)

Diane Nash was born in Chicago. She was raised a Roman Catholic. In her late teens she was a runner-up in the Chicago "Miss America" contest. She attended Howard University in Washington, DC, and transferred to Fisk University in Nashville, Tennessee, in 1959. At Fisk, Diane attended workshops on Mahatma Gandhi's theory of nonviolent resistance led by James Lawson. Diane was elected chairperson of the Student Central Committee and was a leader in the student sit-ins in February 1960. She was a co-founder of the Student Nonviolent Coordinating Committee (SNCC) in Raleigh, North Carolina, in April 1960. She was arrested and imprisoned in Rock Hill, South Carolina, for civil rights activism. Beginning in 1961, Diane was a leader of the SNCC Freedom Rides and the SNCC head of Direct Action. She married James Bevel, another civil rights activist. (She took his name as her middle name.) In 1962, Diane Nash and James Bevel moved to Georgia to work with the SCLC. She bore a child during the Albany campaign and spent ten days in jail in Mississippi for contempt of court. In 1964–65, they participated in the Selma voting registration campaign.

During the 1980s and 1990s Nash (now divorced) lived and taught in Chicago and continued to be a civil rights and political activist.

Nixon, Edgar Daniel (July 12, 1899–February 27, 1987)

Nixon was born in Robinson Springs, Alabama, the son of a tenant farmer. At age 13 he began to work full-time, first in a meat-packing plant, then on construction jobs and finally as a Pullman car porter. He held the porter job until his retirement in 1964. Nixon supported the drive by A. Philip Randolph to unionize the Pullman porters in the '20s and '30s. In 1938, he was elected president of the Montgomery local of the Brotherhood of Sleeping Car Porters. He was president of the Montgomery branch of the NAACP from 1939 to 1951. In 1943, he organized the Alabama Voters League to promote black voter registration. Nixon achieved his own registration in 1945. When Rosa Parks was arrested on December 1, 1955, she called her friend Ed Nixon for help. He bailed her out and proposed a boycott of the buses on the day of Park's trial. Nixon continued to be an activist for poor blacks until his death.

Parks, Rosa Louise McCauley (February 4, 1913–)

Rosa McCauley was born February 4, 1913, in Tuskegee, Alabama. Her father was a carpenter and her mother a schoolteacher. At age six, she went to a one-teacher black school in Pine Level. The school was built and heated by blacks with no help from the town, county or state. It was open five months of the year. The windows had no glass and the children walked to school. Nearby was a white school. It was built and maintained with public funds, including taxes from blacks. It was open nine months. The windows had glass and the children were bused to school.

Rosa lived on a small farm. They had fruit, pecan and walnut trees, a garden, chickens and cows. Their income came from her mother's teaching, sale of eggs, chickens and calves and their work as farm laborers on other people's land. Rosa picked cotton when she was six.

Rosa attended the school at Alabama State Normal and then Spring Hill School eight miles from her home. Rosa and her little brother walked to and from school each day. Rosa attended the Booker T. Washington Junior High in Birmingham for the ninth grade. She attended Alabama Normal School for the tenth and eleventh grades. At age 16, Rosa quit school to take care of her mother and run the farm. In 1933 she finished high school and received her diploma. Rosa married Raymond Parks, who worked as a barber by day and as a civil rights activist by night.

In 1943, Rosa tried to register to vote. She was prevented by the customary ploys—switched registration days, denials that she passed the exam, etc. She persisted and succeeded in registering in 1945 when she was 32 years old. To qualify to vote she had to pay a yearly poll tax of $1.50 per year *retroactively* back to when she was 21.

In 1943, Rosa Parks joined the Montgomery chapter of the NAACP and served as secretary for 13 years. She also managed the office of Edgar Daniel Nixon, the state NAACP president, and the regional officer of the Brotherhood of Sleeping Car Porters. She also joined the Montgomery Voters League. In the summer of 1955, Rosa attended the Highlands Folk School in Monteagle, Tennessee.

On December 1, 1955, Rosa Parks refused to obey a racist bus driver. It was not because she was a seamstress with tired legs as reported in the white media. It was because she was a tough, well-educated, civil rights advocate who was tired of receiving abuse, hate and discrimination from the whites every day.

NAACP President Edgar Nixon was sad to see the apartheid system work so predictably but excited to get a suitable plaintiff for a court case. A plaintiff had to be committed, tough, knowledgeable and without character blemishes that the Establishment lawyers could pounce upon. Rosa satisfied those requirements. Her case was pursued to the U.S. Supreme Court. On November 13, 1956, the court rendered its opinion that segregation on the Montgomery buses was unconstitutional.

In 1979, Parks was awarded the NAACP Spingarn Medal. In 1980, she received the Martin Luther King Jr. Nonviolent Peace Prize. In 1981, she was given an honorary degree by Mount Holyoke College. In 1987, she founded the Rosa and Raymond Parks Institute for Self-Development. In February 1991, a bust of Rosa Parks was unveiled at the Smithsonian Institution. In 1992, she published *Rosa Parks—My Story*.

Randolph, Asa Philip (1889–1979)

Randolph was born in Crescent City, Florida, the younger son of a minister of the African Methodist Episcopal Church. In 1911, he graduated from Cookman Institute in Jacksonville, Florida, and migrated to New York City and Harlem. He worked at odd jobs and attended City College of New York where he studied history, philosophy, economics and political science. Between 1914 and 1925, Randolph belonged to a group of African Americans known as the Harlem Radicals. Other eminent members were Marcus Garvey and W.E.B. Du Bois. Asa joined the Socialist Party, whose leader was his hero, Eugene V. Debs. In 1917, Asa and his friend Chandler Owen founded and co-edited a monthly journal, *The Messenger*. In it they opposed America's participation in World War I, counseled African Americans to resist the military draft and proposed economic solutions to the "Negro problem."

In 1925, he began his career as a labor organizer and civil rights activist. At one time the Pullman Car Company offered Randolph a blank check and invited him to fill in any amount up to $1 million if he would quit the union. He rejected the offer. He continued his work and in 1937 the Pullman Company recognized the Brotherhood of Sleeping Car Porters. In 1955, Randolph became a vice president of the merged AFL-CIO. He campaigned relentlessly and often successfully to get unions to desegregate. When he retired from his vice presidency, the AFL-CIO was the most integrated institution in America.

In June 1941, Randolph won a major civil rights victory. By planning a protest march on Washington, he persuaded President Franklin D. Roosevelt to issue Executive Order No. 8802 banning the exclusion of blacks from employment in defense plants. In 1948, Randolph accomplished a second civil rights coup. He persuaded President Harry S. Truman to outlaw segregation in the armed services by issuing Executive Order No. 9981. In 1963, Randolph enjoyed a third major civil rights victory. He conceived and directed the March on Washington that marked a turning point in the civil rights revolution.

The leaders of the SCLC and CORE regarded Randolph as the elder statesman of the civil rights movement. In 1964, President Lyndon B. Johnson awarded Randolph the Presidential Medal of Freedom, the nation's highest civil honor. In 1965, Randolph founded the A. Philip Randolph Institute which worked to persuade African Americans to join the labor movement. Randolph spent his last years as vice president of the AFL-CIO.

Robinson, Jo Ann Gibson (April 17, 1912–)

Jo Ann Gibson was born near Culloden, Georgia, on April 17, 1912. She was the youngest of 12 children. She was the valedictorian of her high school class in Macon. She graduated from Fort Valley State College and then earned a master's degree in English at Atlanta University. She studied at Columbia University for one year. In 1949, she accepted a position as professor of English at Alabama State College in Montgomery. Upon arriving in Montgomery, she joined the Dexter Avenue Baptist Church and the Women's Political Council (WPC).

Like other blacks, she received discourteous and disrespectful treatment from Montgomery bus drivers and decided that a bus boycott was needed. When the Supreme Court ruled that segregation was unconstitutional, Robinson, now president of the WPC, threatened a bus boycott unless the abuse of blacks was stopped. There was no reply to her threat. When Rosa Parks was arrested for not relinquishing her seat to a white man, Jo Ann Robinson moved. She and Fred Gray, a local attorney and assistant pastor of the Holt Street Church of Christ, called for a bus boycott for the following Monday, December 5, 1955. Working far into the night, Robinson, John Cannon, chairman of the Business Department at Alabama State, and two seniors mimeographed 52,500 copies of a boycott announcement that she wrote. (Robinson had to pay for 35 reams of paper out of her own pocket.) The leaflets were distributed throughout the city by volunteers and the boycott began as planned. Monday night, 6,000 people attended the rally at the Holt Street Church. The Montgomery Improvement Association (MIA) was organized and M.L. King was chosen its president. Robinson could not accept a position in the MIA as she worked for the state and would be fired. The officers had to be ministers, or self-employed lawyers or doctors. Robinson was a member of the MIA executive board because of her position as president of WPC.

The Establishment identified Robinson as a boycott leader and she was harassed by police. One night a policeman threw a large stone through her picture window. She reported the policeman's squad car number but her complaint was ignored. Two weeks later, two men in police uniforms poured acid over her car.

After the boycott was successful, Robinson accepted teaching positions in Louisiana and then California. She retired from teaching in 1976. In 1987, she published an autobiography titled *The Montgomery Bus Boycott and the Women Who Started It.*

Rustin, Bayard (1910–1987)

Rustin was born in West Chester, Pennsylvania. In high school he was a football player. When his team visited a restaurant and he was denied service because he was black, he sat until he was thrown out. Rustin attended Cheyney and Wilberforce colleges. In 1936, he joined the Young Communist League, attracted by their humanistic objectives. Five years later, he quit that organization and became a democratic socialist. In 1941, he became an organizer for the Fellowship of Reconciliation. He helped to found CORE. In 1942, Rustin was brutally beaten by police in Tennessee when he refused to move to the back of the bus.

In 1947, he was arrested in North Carolina for participating in a Freedom Ride. He was convicted and spent 22 days on a chain gang. In 1949, he published an account of that experience and it led to the abolition of chain gangs in North Carolina.

Rustin helped to persuade President Truman to desegregate the armed forces. In 1952, Rustin became the executive Secretary of the War Resisters League. January 10–11, 1957, he participated in the conference that organized the Southern Christian Leadership Conference (SCLC) in Atlanta. At the conference, Rustin provided a key working paper on direct action. He advocated nonviolence, dividing the white community between their economic and political interests and recognizing the churches as the most stable institution in the black culture and the necessary basis of their campaigns.

In 1957, he managed the Prayer Pilgrimage to Washington. In 1963, Rustin helped to plan and direct the March on Washington for Jobs and Freedom. He planned the march in detail. Rustin was an advisor to Dr. King and, like King, he received special scrutiny from the FBI. The FBI tapped his phones and kept him under surveillance. J. Edgar Hoover, FBI chief, believed that he was a Communist and all Communists were planning a violent overthrow of the U.S. government. Hoover did not know that Rustin was a prominent advocate of nonviolence—a non–Communist concept. After the revolution, Rustin headed the A. Philip Randolph Institute.

Shuttlesworth, Fred Lee (March 18, 1922–)

Shuttlesworth was born in Mugler, Alabama. He earned a B.A. from Selma University and a B.S. from Alabama State Teachers College. He became a Baptist minister and served several churches, including the First Baptist Church in Birmingham, Alabama. In 1955, he participated in an unsuccessful attempt to put African Americans on the police force. When the NAACP was banned in Alabama, he co-founded the Alabama Christian Movement for Human Rights (ACMHR). In 1957, he co-founded the SCLC and served as its secretary from 1958 to 1970. In 1963, Shuttlesworth led a major anti-segregation campaign in Birmingham which hastened the passage of the 1964 Civil Rights Act. He led numerous nonviolent demonstrations and suffered several beatings, arrests and firebomb attacks on his home. He had a reputation as a man who knew no fear.

In 1963, he gave the invocation at the March on Washington and the SCLC gave him the Rosa Parks Award. He was an advisor to Dr. King and also active in CORE. He was president of the Southern Conference Educational Fund, a 17-state interracial civil rights organization that promoted integration. After the revolution, he became the pastor of a church in Cincinnati and director of the Shuttlesworth Housing Fund, which assisted poor people to purchase homes.

Smith, Kelly Miller

Smith was born in the all-black delta town of Mound Bayou, Mississippi. He obtained degrees from Morehouse and Howard. He was the pastor for 34 years at the First Baptist Church in Nashville, Tennessee. Smith was a founding member of both SCLC and its Nashville affiliate, NCLC. He pursued civil rights projects with great energy. He volunteered his children for desegregation suits. He published a collection of essays entitled *Social Crisis Preaching*.

Steele, Charles Kenzie (February 7, 1914–1980)

Charles Steel was born in Gary, West Virginia, just 15 miles from the site of the infamous Hatfield-McCoy feud. Charles was the only child of Henry L. and Lyde Bailor Steele. Steele's father worked in the dangerous profession of bituminous coal mining. Charles studied at Morehouse College, earned a degree and became a minister. He led the Tallahassee bus boycott in 1956–1958. In 1957, he was a co-founder of the Southern Christian Leadership Conference. He was an exceptionally gifted speaker, organizer, inspirer and leader. He received his share of abuse from the white Establishment. He is honored in the black culture as one of the principal leaders of their revolution.

Thurman, Howard (November 18, 1900–April 10, 1981)

Thurman was born in Daytona Beach, Florida. In 1923, he earned a B.A. at Morehouse College. In 1926, he earned a M.Div. at Colgate-Rochester Divinity School. From 1929 to 1932, he was professor of religion at Morehouse and Spelman Colleges in Atlanta. From 1932–1934, he was professor of theology at Howard University. In 1944, he co-founded the Church for the Fellowship of All Peoples in San Francisco.

In 1953, he became Boston University's first full-time black professor. In 1965, he retired from teaching and directed the Howard Thurman Educational Trust.

Thurman published more than 20 books and hundreds of journal articles. A major theme in his philosophy was a striving for an inclusive community and a search for common ground among all people. His lectures on social theology influenced Dr. King and many other clergymen-leaders. Thurman held many guest lectureships and received 14 honorary doctorates from Ivy League colleges and universities. His most famous book was *Jesus and the Dispossessed*.

Vivian, Cordy Tindell (July 30, 1924–)

Vivian was from Boonville, Missouri. He earned a B.A. at Western Illinois University in 1948 and a B.D. from the American Baptist Theological Seminary in 1958. He was a member of the SCLC cabinet as vice president in charge of direct action. Later he became the director of SCLC affiliates. He was beaten up during a prison term following a Freedom Ride. He confronted Sheriff Jim Clark on the courthouse steps in Selma in 1965.

After the revolution, he formed his own tutoring organization called Visions. He authored a book on Black Power. He earned a doctorate at the new School for Social Research in 1984.

Walker, Wyatt Tee (August 16, 1929–)

Walker was born in Brockton, Massachusetts. He attended Virginia Union University in Richmond, earning a B.S. in 1950 and a masters in divinity in 1953. In 1975, he received a D.Min. from Colgate Richester Bexley Hall/Crozer. He was the minister of the Gillfield Baptist Church in Petersburg, VA, from 1953 to 1960. He organized the Petersburg Improvement Association and led his parishioners in a Prayer Pilgrimage to protest the closing of schools to avoid desegregation.

In 1960, Dr. King hired Walker as executive director of the SCLC, a post he held for four years. He worked hard. He expanded the SCLC chapters in several states. He increased the SCLC staff. He organized Project C, the detailed plan for desegregating Birmingham in 1963. He directed the marches and sit-ins by walkie talkie. He managed Dr. King's speaking engagements. He was a creative thinker and made significant contributions to the SCLC's strategies for influencing the white culture. He was a productive money raiser. By 1963, the SCLC had an operating budget of $900,000. Walker's salary was $10,000 per year.

In the spring of 1964, Walker left the SCLC and joined the newly organized Educational Heritage Book Service. Later he became the pastor of the Canaan Baptist Church in New York City's Harlem. He enjoyed a long career in promoting civil rights and services for blacks by working with state and regional organizations. He was an expert on black gospel music. Walker authored several books, including *Somebody's Calling My Name, Black Sacred Music and Social Change* (1979) and *Road to Damascus* (1985).

White, Walter Frances (July 1, 1893–March 28, 1955)

Walter White was born in Atlanta, Georgia. His father was a mailman and his mother a teacher. In 1912, he enrolled at Atlanta University where he played football, won awards for debating and was elected president of his class. He graduated in 1916. At that time the city tried to limit black children to a sixth-grade education. White and other educated blacks organized a chapter of a new civil rights organization, the NAACP, and defeated the proposal.

In 1918, White moved to New York City and was hired as assistant secretary of the NAACP. He was immediately involved in a variety of NAACP projects—attempting to desegregate schools, hospitals and neighborhoods and eliminate lynchings.

White was a superior investigator. He could interview blacks and then, because of his white complexion, he could pose as a northern newspaper reporter and interview whites. In 1919, he investigated race riots in Chicago. Then he visited Phillips County, Arkansas, and investigated the massacre of 200 sharecroppers by white mobs. During his career he investigated 41 lynchings and eight race riots.

In 1930, he successfully opposed a presidential nomination to the Supreme Court. President Herbert Hoover nominated John J. Parker from North Carolina to fill a vacancy on the high court. White discovered that Parker, when running for governor, had proposed to end voting rights for blacks. The NAACP conducted an intensive campaign against the nomination. The Senate voted 41–39 to deny Parker a seat on the Supreme Court.

In 1931, White followed James Weldon Johnson as the CEO of the NAACP. In that position, he was the premier spokesman for African Americans for nearly a quarter century (1931–1955). He persuaded President Roosevelt to support anti-lynching legislation. He worked with President Truman to establish the Committee on Civil Rights. He also urged Truman to desegregate the armed forces and to require all federal agencies to adopt fair employment practices.

In 1948, White published his autobiography, *A Man Called White*. White established a relationship between the African American community and the office of the president that was indispensable to the execution and success of the civil rights revolution. White died on March 28,1955, after witnessing the NAACP's greatest legal victory, the Supreme Court's decision in *Brown v. Board of Education*.

Wilkins, Roy Otaway (August 30, 1901–September 8, 1981)

Wilkins was born in St. Louis, Missouri. He graduated from the University of Minnesota in 1923. He was night editor of the college paper and editor of a black weekly, *The St. Paul Appeal*. He moved to Kansas City, where he was the managing editor of the Kansas City Call for eight years. He was also active in the NAACP. In 1931, Wilkins went to New York City to become an assistant to Walter White, executive secretary of the NAACP. He was the editor of the NAACP organ, *The Crisis*, from 1934 to 1949. In 1934, he was arrested for the first time when he demonstrated to protest the refusal by Attorney General Homer Cummings to include the issue of lynching on the agenda of a major conference on crime. In 1955, he became the executive secretary of the NAACP—a position he held for 22 years.

Wilkins was widely regarded as "Mr. Civil Rights." He earned this sobriquet because he used the NAACP's national membership of 400,000 and its network of lawyers to support the direct action of the SCLC and the CORE and his own talents to negotiate civil rights legislation. The NAACP supplied money and members support for the March on Washington in 1963. Wilkins advised presidents from Roosevelt to Carter and was a friend of President Johnson. The civil rights legislation that Wilkins helped to obtain included the Civil Rights Act of 1964, the Voting Rights Act of 1965 and the Fair Housing Act of 1968. Wilkins was awarded the NAACP's Spingarn Medal in 1964. He received over 50 honorary degrees. He retired in 1977 after 46 years with the NAACP.

Williams, Hosea Lorenzo (January 5, 1926–)

Williams was born and grew up in Attapalgus, Georgia. He served in the military from 1944 to 1946. In 1951, he earned a B.A. in chemistry at Morris Brown College in Atlanta. He earned an M.S. at Atlanta University. He then got a job as a research chemist with the U.S. Department of Agriculture in Savannah, Georgia. In the 1950s, he participated in NAACP desegregation drives. In 1960, he founded the Southeastern Georgia Crusade for Voters and directed a successful voter registration drive. In 1962, his crusade affiliated with the SCLC.

In 1963, Williams moved to Atlanta to work for the SCLC as project director. He was an advisor to Dr. King and organized grassroots voter registration drives. In 1965, he led the "Bloody Sunday" march in Selma. Williams was a vigorous leader in marches, demonstrations, sit-ins and strikes and was arrested more than a hundred times.

From 1969 to 1971, he served as executive director of the SCLC under President Ralph Abernathy. In 1971, he resigned that position and organized an SCLC chapter in Atlanta to focus on grassroots action. In 1972, Williams founded and pastored the Martin Luther King Jr. Church of Love in Atlanta. In 1974, he was elected to the Georgia General Assembly as the Atlanta representative. From 1976 on, he ran his own business, the Southeast Chemical Manufacturing and Distributing Corporation. From 1977 to 1979, he again was executive director of the SCLC.

Williams continued his interest in assisting the poor though nonviolent action. In 1985, he was elected to the Atlanta City Council. In 1987, he led a march to protest segregation in Forsyth County, a white suburb of Atlanta, and was attacked by the Ku Klux Klan.

Young, Andrew Jackson (March 12, 1932–)

Young was born in New Orleans. He grew up in a racially mixed, middle-class neighborhood. His father was a dentist. When Andrew and his brother were taunted as "niggers," their father hired a professional boxer to teach them how to fight. As a result, Young had no fear of the white community and could not be intimidated. He earned a B.S. degree from Howard University in 1951 and a bachelor of divinity from Hartford Theological Seminary in Connecticut in 1955. He was ordained by the United Church of Christ. From 1955 to 1959, he served churches in Alabama and Georgia. He became a civil rights activist and launched the first voter registration drive in Thomasville, Georgia. In 1957 he was employed by the National Council of Churches. In 1959, he went to New York to become an assistant director of the council. In 1961, he joined the SCLC to coordinate funding and administer the SCLC Citizen Education Program. He did a lot of negotiating for the SCLC and was known for his coolness, rationality and effectiveness. In 1964, he became the executive director of the SCLC and in 1967 its executive vice president. Young played a major leadership role in the SCLC and was involved in the Birmingham, Selma and Chicago confrontations, anti–Vietnam War protests and other civil rights campaigns.

After Dr. King's assassination, Young followed a political and diplomatic career. He was elected to the U.S. House of Representatives from Georgia in 1972. In 1977, he left Congress to become the U.S. ambassador to the United Nations. In 1981, he was elected mayor of Atlanta and re-elected in 1985. He chaired the committee that hosted the 1996 Olympic Games in Atlanta.

Young received more than 30 honorary degrees. He was awarded the Presidential Medal of Freedom, the NAACP's Spingarn Medal, the Legion of Honor from France and in 1989 he was named Municipal Leader of the Year by *American City and Country* magazine. In the 1990s, Young preached every Sunday while continuing his career as a civil rights leader. In 1994, he published *A Way Out of No Way* and in 1996 *An Easy Burden*—one of the best accounts of the nonviolent Freedom Revolution.

Young, Jean Childs (1933–1994)

Jean Childs was born on July 1, 1933, in Marion, Alabama. Her father owned a grocery and candy store. She attended Lincoln High School and then matriculated at Manchester College in North Manchester, Indiana. She graduated in 1954. Jean Childs married Andrew Young in June 1954. She was not the woman behind the man but the woman beside the man. The Youngs' Atlanta home was a meeting place for civil rights workers. Jean participated in a number of civil rights demonstrations such as marches in Birmingham, Alabama, and St. Augustine, Florida, the 1963 March on Washington, the 1965 march from Selma to Montgomery, the 1966 march in Mississippi and the 1968 Poor People's Campaign.

After Dr. King's assassination, Jean Young became a prominent advocate of childrens' welfare. She was awarded an honorary doctorate by Loyola University in Chicago and New York City Technical College. She received the NAACP Distinguished Leadership award in 1989 and the YWCA Woman of Achievement Award in 1993.

Young, Whitney Moore, Jr. (July 31, 1921–March 11, 1971)

Young was born in Lincoln Ridge, Kentucky. He grew up on the campus of Lincoln Institute where his father was on the faculty and later the president. From 1933 to 1937, he attended the institute. From 1937 to 1941, he attended Kentucky State Industrial College in Frankfort, Kentucky. He served in the military during World War II. In 1946 and 1947, he earned a master's degree in social work at the University of Minnesota. Upon graduation, he went to work for the St. Paul Urban League as industrial relations secretary. In 1949, he was appointed executive secretary of the Omaha, Nebraska, chapter of the National Urban League (NUL). In 1954, Young was named dean of the Atlanta University School of Social Work. He studied at Harvard as a Rockefeller Foundation scholar. He was the executive director of the Urban League from 1961 to 1971. He opened Urban League branches in the South and participated in voter registration and economic development programs.

The Urban League was a nonprofit organization and so its members could not lobby the government. This meant that Young could not march, demonstrate and sit-in. However, he was very effective in working behind the scenes. He was a frequent advisor to the leaders of the civil rights movement and to President Johnson. Young helped to plan and implement the 1963 March on Washington. He also participated in the Council for United Civil Rights Leadership CUCRL), a consortium founded in 1963 to facilitate fund-raising and information sharing among several civil rights organizations.

Young split with Dr. King over the war in Vietnam. Young believed that Communism must be stopped in Southeast Asia. He did not speak against the war until Richard M. Nixon was president. In 1969, President Johnson awarded Young the Medal of Freedom. In March 1971, Young went to Lagos, Nigeria, to participate in a conference with African leaders and he died there while swimming. Young published several books, including *To Be Equal* in 1964 and *Beyond Racism—Building an Open Society* in 1969.

Nonviolent Civil Rights Organizations

The nonviolent civil rights leaders were members of local, state and national nonviolent activist organizations that constituted an interstate network similar, with reference to communications and cooperation, to the network of the white Establishment in the 11 apartheid states. At the national level there were six nonviolent activist organizations, the NAACP, the NUL, the NCNW, the CORE, the SCLC and the SNCC. All had local chapters. Also at the national level were five special-purpose organizations that made significant contributions to the struggle. They were the FOR, the BSCP, the LDEF, the SRC and the VEP.

At the local level there were a large number of ad hoc freedom activist groups— all closely tied to the black churches and to the regional and national organizations. A brief review of these organizations will round out the picture of the leadership of the African American nonviolent civil rights revolution.

The "Big Six"

National Association for the Advancement of Colored People (NAACP). The NAACP was founded in 1910. Its goal is "to achieve through peaceful and lawful means, equal citizenship for all American citizens by eliminating segregation and discrimination in housing, employment, voting, schools, the courts, transportation and recreation. The first president was a white Boston lawyer, Moorfield Stacey. By 1919, the NAACP was primarily a black southern organization. The NAACP and its offshoot, the Legal Defense and Education Fund, conducted an intensive court action campaign from 1915 to 1955 that persuaded the Supreme Court to outlaw apartheid and paved the way for the Freedom Revolution. During the revolution, it supplied legal support to activists and worked for civil rights legislation in Washington. It was also very active in demonstrations and voter education. In 1914, the NAACP instituted the Spingarn Medal to honor outstanding achievements of African Americans.

National Urban League (NUL). The NUL was founded in 1911 by the merger of three agencies with similar goals. Its objectives were to help African Americans who had recently migrated to northern cities and to end discrimination in labor unions, federal programs and the armed forces. Under the leadership of Whitney Young in the 1960s, it opened branches in southern cities and participated in voter registration projects. Young also supported the March on Washington in 1963 and was an advisor to both Dr. King and President Johnson.

National Council of Negro Women (NCNW). The NCNW was founded by Mary McLeod Bethune and 35 African American women leaders on December 5, 1935, in New York City. The NCNW was dedicated to improving the economic, social, cultural and educational conditions of African American women. Mary Bethune was president from 1935 to 1949. Dorothy Height was president from 1958 to the 1990s. In addition to many other activities, the NCNW held voter education drives in both the North and the South and worked with the SNCC in raising funds to hire students to work on voter registration.

Congress of Racial Equality (CORE). The CORE was founded in Chicago in 1942 by members of the Fellowship of Reconciliation. Its purpose was to conduct nonviolent, direct-action protests to promote social justice and racial equality. CORE leaders James Farmer and Bayard Rustin participated in CORE's first restaurant sit-in in Chicago in 1942. In 1947, CORE organized the first Freedom Ride to integrate interstate travel in the upper South. It also conducted sit-ins in St. Louis in 1949, in Baltimore in 1953 and it tried to integrate an Esso station in Marion, South Carolina, in 1959.

In the 1960s, CORE was one of the most active civil rights organizations. It helped to organize Freedom Summer in Mississippi, the Mississippi Freedom Democratic Party, the wave of lunch counter sit-ins and the continuation of Meredith's March Against Fear. In 1966, CORE had a change in leadership and its philosophy of nonviolence was replaced by the concept of Black Power.

Southern Christian Leadership Conference (SCLC). The SCLC was founded in January 1957 at Ebenezer Baptist Church in Atlanta, Georgia, by 60 African American ministers and NAACP members. Their purpose was to employ nonviolent tactics to support the Montgomery bus boycott and other direct actions to eliminate racial segregation. The founders included Dr. King, the Rev. Abernathy, the Rev. T.J. Jemison, the Rev. Shuttlesworth and the Rev. Steele. Dr. King was elected president. The SCLC supported sit-ins and Freedom Rides and encouraged the organization of the SNCC. In 1962–1963, it had 50 full-time staff members and 85 chapters throughout the South and it organized civil rights campaigns in Alabama, Virginia and Florida. After Dr. King's assassination, the SCLC was led by the Rev. Abernathy (1968–1977), the Rev. Lowrey (1977–1997) and Martin Luther King III in 1997.

Student Nonviolent Coordinating Committee (SNCC). The SNCC was founded April 15, 1960, by student leaders from 60 colleges at Shaw University in Raleigh, N.C. Marion Barry was the first chairman. In 1961, James Forman became the executive secretary. The SNCC objective was to foster nonviolent direct action to eliminate racial segregation. The SNCC was a prominent participant in sit-ins as well as in the March on Washington, the Mississippi Freedom Democratic Party and the Selma to Montgomery march. In 1966, Stokely Carmichael became the SNCC chairman and its basic policy was reversed. The goal of nonviolent integration was replaced by the concept of Black Power. In 1967, the name was changed to the Student *National* Coordinating Committee. Soon after Dr. King's death the SNCC declined and then disappeared.

Special Purpose Organizations

The work of the "Big Six" nonviolent civil rights organizations was supported, supplemented and facilitated by five ancillary organizations—each with its special contribution. These were the FOR, the BSCP, the LDEF, the SRC and the VEP.

Fellowship of Reconciliation (FOR). The FOR was founded in 1914 by Henry Hodkins, an English Quaker, and Friedrich Siegmund Schultze, a pacifist chaplain to the kaiser of Germany at Cambridge (England) University. Its aim was to promote pacifism and international understanding. The first U.S. chapter was organized in

1915. Most of the FOR members were students, ministers and professors. The FOR sponsored the first Freedom Ride in 1947. The FOR supplied two advisors to help direct the Montgomery bus boycott, the Rev. Glenn Smiley and Bayard Rustin. In the civil rights revolution, the FOR played the role of experts and instructors in nonviolent tactics.

FOR members helped to establish several public interest organizations such as the American Civil Liberties Union, the National Conference of Christian and Jews, the Workers Defense League and the Congress of Racial Equality. The FOR has more than 30,000 members worldwide.

Brotherhood of Sleeping Car Porters (BSCP). The BSCP was founded in 1925 by A. Philip Randolph. The goals of the union were to improve pay and working conditions for African American porters and maids employed by the Pullman Company and to reduce racism in the larger society. Randolph and the BSCP were successful in both. In 1937, the BSCP won an agreement with the Pullman Company for improved wages and working conditions. In 1941, Randolph's threatened march on Washington persuaded President Roosevelt to issue Executive Order 8802 prohibiting discrimination in defense industries and government agencies. In 1955, when the AFL merged with the CIO, the BSCP was instrumental in getting the new agency to include civil rights as its agenda. In 1963, Randolph was the chief architect and the BSCP a major supporter of the climactic March on Washington. During the '60s Randolph and the BSCP constituted a unifying force among the sometimes-contentious civil rights leaders.

Legal Defense and Education Fund (LDEF). The LDEF was established by the NAACP on October 11, 1939. Its purpose was stated in the charter: "To render free legal aid to Negroes who suffer legal injustice because of their race or color and cannot afford to employ legal assistance; To seek and promote educational opportunities denied to Negroes because of their race or color; To conduct research and publish information on educational facilities and inequalities furnished for Negroes out of public funds and on the status of the Negro in American life."

The LDEF was the agency primarily responsible for the Supreme Courts turn from supporting apartheid to finding it unconstitutional.

Southern Regional Council (SRC). The SRC was founded in 1944. It was a biracial research and information group located in Atlanta, Georgia. Its objective was to report on social conditions and improve race relations and reduce poverty in the South. Two of its major contributions were accurate reporting of segregated conditions and the establishment of the Voter Education Project.

Voter Education Project (VEP). The VEP was founded in 1961. Its objective was to provide financial and technical assistance to voter registration projects conducted by civil rights organizations. It was initiated by Harold Fleming, director of the Southern Regional Council. It was supported by President Kennedy and by the Big Six civil rights organizations. It was financed by grants from the Taconic, Field and Stern Foundations. It was located in Atlanta under the wing of the tax-exempt, nonpartisan Southern Regional Council. The VEP, working through its recipients, succeeded in enfranchising two million black voters.

Local Organizations

In the cities and counties where freedom seekers were active, it was usually necessary to form a special civil rights organization. The purpose of this organization was to facilitate the training of volunteers, to justify and receive professional assistance from the SCLC, the CORE, the SNCC, the VEP or the NAACP and to establish a position for negotiating with the white Establishment. These local groups were the principal force that ran the revolution

Alabama Christian Movement for Human Rights. The Alabama Christian Movement for Human Rights (ACMHR) was representative of this level of organization and leadership. It was organized in the late '50s by the Rev. Fred Shuttlesworth and other Birmingham ministers. It replaced a chapter of the NAACP that had been banned by a court injunction. It brought all the freedom activists together and focused their energies on their goal of defeating apartheid.

Following is a list of 28 other grassroots organizations.

Twenty-eight Local Civil Rights Action Organizations

1. AM—Albany Movement
2. AVL—Alabama Voters League
3. BACC—Black Awareness Coordinating Committee
4. CC—Coordinating Council, Greensboro, NC
5. CUCRL—Council for United Civil Rights Leadership
6. CCCV—Chatham County Crusade for Voting
7. CCCO—Coordinating Council of Community Organizations, Chicago
8. CCRR—Chicago Conference on Religion and Race
9. COFO—Council of Federated Organizations, Mississippi
10. CUM—Community Union Movement, Chicago
11. COME—Community on the Move for Equity, Memphis, TN
12. DCVL—Dallas County Voters League
13. DCPA—Danville Christian Progressive Association, VA
14. GCF—Greensboro Community Fellowship, NC
15. ICC—Inter-City Council, Tallahassee, FL
16. LCFO—Lowndes County Freedom Organization, AL
17. LCCMHR—Lowndes County Christian Movement for Human Rights
18. MIA—Montgomery Improvement Association, AL
19. MES—Movement to End Slums, Chicago
20. MVL—Montgomery Voters League, AL
21. NCLC—Nashville Christian Leadership Council, TN
22. NAG—Nonviolent Action Group, Howard University
23. PIA—Petersburg Improvement Association, VA
24. SGCV—Southern Georgia Crusade for Voters
25. SECJ—Student Executive Committee for Justice, Greensboro, NC

26. UDL—United Defense League, Baton Rouge, LA
27. WPC—Womens' Political Council, Montgomery, AL
28. UJAMMA Familyhood (in Swahili), Howard University

Historians discover, sort, select and interpret data to support theses about what happened—when, where, why, how and by whom. In the case of the blacks' civil rights revolution, some historians logically focus on Dr. King and present a credible account of how he led a 12-year, nonviolent campaign that led to a desegregated and freer society. It is the thesis of this book that our freer society was achieved in two stages. First, the NAACP-LDEF persuaded the Supreme Court to stand for integration. Then Dr. King, assisted by 50 fellow ministers, working with the SCLC and the Big-6 and supported by scores of local groups and a few hundred thousand brave volunteers, attacked the entrenched apartheid system in 11 states. They gained the support of the public and of President Johnson and obtained from the U.S. Congress a series of statutes that provide a basis for a freer and a more democratic society.

IV

Accomplishments

One of the two major objectives of the Civil War was to extend full rights to formerly enslaved people. The Fifteenth Amendment to the Constitution, ratified on February 3, 1870, was a step in that direction.

Amendment XV

Section 1. The right of citizens of the United States to vote shall not be denied or abridged by the United States or by any State on account of race, color or previous condition of servitude.

Section 2. The Congress shall have power to enforce this article by appropriate legislation.

The nonviolent revolution awakened Congress to its obligation to implement the Fifteenth Amendment. With the president leading and public opinion pushing, Congress proceeded to enact a series of laws—the Civil Rights Acts of 1957, 1960, 1964, 1965 and 1968. The Twenty-Fourth Amendment to the Constitution completed the series.

Civil Rights Act of 1957

The Civil Rights Act of 1957 was the first civil rights bill passed by Congress in 82 years. It was produced by Senate Majority Leader Lyndon B. Johnson. He used his considerable political skills to push it through Congress. At that time, Senator Johnson was planning to run for president and wanted credit for passing a civil rights bill to attract votes from blacks and northern liberals. But he also needed to reassure the southern racist Democrats that he was one of them. First he whittled the bill down to what he thought was a minimal content that represented the political center. Then he argued with southerners that it was the weakest bill that could be passed and he argued with northerners that it was the strongest bill that could be passed. Opposition was tenacious. Senator Strom Thurmond of South Carolina filibustered against the bill for 24 hours—but in vain. The watered-down bill was finally passed with a vote of 60 to 15.

The 1957 bill had four points: (1) interference with the voting rights of a person was a federal offense, (2) the president would appoint a bipartisan commission on civil rights, (3) a civil rights division would be established in the Department of Justice and (4) the Department of Justice was authorized to sue violaters of the Fifteenth Amendment. The *New York Times* called the bill "incomparably the most significant domestic action of any Congress in this century." The *New York Times* exaggerated. The bill was generally regarded as weak and it lacked adequate enforcement provisions. Black leaders hesitated to applaud its passage.

The 1957 bill did not achieve the goal of guaranteeing voting rights. While the U.S. Department of Justice was able to enforce it on a case-by-case basis, the apartheid states refused to enforce it. The Department of Justice brought voting rights suits in Alabama, Georgia and Louisiana. The department won each case. They were then appealed to the Supreme Court which upheld the Justice Department. However, the local municipalities continued to withhold voting rights. A common practice was to drop blacks from the voter rolls and for such things as a misspelling on a voter application. Local juries were usually white and racist. Registration clerks refused to release voting records. In large areas, white lawyers would not represent black voters and there were no black lawyers. The Southern Regional Council reported that the number of black citizens registered to vote in 11 southern states grew only from 1,238,100 in 1956 to 1,266,488 in 1958. The council also reported that there were 28 counties in the southern states in 1958 where the black population ranged up to 82 percent of the total population and there was not one African American registered to vote. This bill was very weak but it carried a strong message. It announced that the U.S. Congress could pass a civil rights bill and it offered the hope that a more effective bill could be passed by the next Congress.

Civil Rights Act of 1960

In May 1960, Congress passed a second civil rights bill. It was an improvement over the 1957 bill. The Department of Justice was given the right to examine local voting records on demand. It could sue individuals who practiced discrimination in the voting process. Federal courts were given the authority to enroll rejected voter applicants. It forbade economic as well as physical retaliation for exercising the right to vote.

The act of 1960, however, was not effective for several reasons. The compromises required to get the bill approved by the Senate engendered loopholes that were exploited by racist voting registrars. The Justice Department was not assiduous in enforcing voting rights. Many southern courts were presided over by racist judges who did not enforce the new law. Dr. King and A. Philip Randolph made a joint statement about the 1960 act. They said that the bill "does not meet the needs of abolishing second-class citizenship."

Twenty-fourth Amendment to the Constitution

On January 23, 1964, the Twenty-fourth Amendment to the U.S. Constitution was ratified. It prohibited apartheid states from using poll taxes as a tactic to keep blacks disenfranchised. Most of the debate on this amendment occurred in the '40s during the build-up to revolution. Its final ratification in 1964 was appropriate as it coincided with the revolution-inspired drive to open the vote to all citizens. The Amendment follows:

Amendment XXIV

Section 1. The right of citizens of the United States to vote in any primary or other election for President or Vice President, for electors for President or Vice President, or for Senator or Representative in Congress, shall not be denied or abridged by the United States or any State by reason of failure to pay any poll tax or other tax.

Section 2. The Congress shall have power to enforce this article by appropriate legislation.

Civil Rights Act of 1964

John F. Kennedy was elected president in 1961 with the help of many southern racists. At the beginning of his administration, he was poorly informed about the civil rights movement and even appointed some racists to judgeships. However, he learned fast. The Battle of Birmingham—with scenes of fire hoses, abused children, attack dogs, billy clubs and bombs—made him keenly aware of the issues in dispute and gave him a new perspective.

In June 1963, President Kennedy spoke to the nation on TV and expressed his newly evolved belief in freedom for all. He said: "We preach freedom around the world, and we mean it, and we cherish our freedom at home. But are we to say to the world, and much more importantly to each other, that this is a land of the free except for the Negroes; that we have no class or caste system, no ghettos, no master race, except with respect to Negroes?" He followed this speech the following week by sending a bill to Congress that outlawed discrimination on grounds of race in all public accommodations in the U.S.

For five months, the apartheid senators prevented Kennedy's bill from being considered by the Senate. Then he was murdered and a new president took the reins.

President Lyndon B. Johnson had also been deeply affected by Birmingham and he had been elected with the help of racist politicians. Moreover, he had a natural affinity for the underdog. Less than a week after Kennedy's death, he went before the Congress and asked them to pass Kennedy's bill as a "monument" to the fallen leader.

President Johnson strengthened Kennedy's bill and then buttonholed and jawboned congressmen to get it passed. Opposition was strong. Senator Richard Russell of Georgia called the bill a "vicious assault on property rights and on the Constitution." Southern senators mounted a filibuster that lasted 82 days. The entire congressional delegations of Alabama, Arkansas, Georgia, Louisiana, Mississippi, North Carolina, South Carolina and Virginia voted against it. Finally the Senate passed the bill by a vote of 73 to 27 and president Johnson signed it on July 2, 1964. At the signing ceremony, the observers included Dr. King, Whitney Young, Roy Wilkins, Attorney General Robert Kennedy, Burk Marshall, Nicholas Katzenbach, cabinet members and J. Edgar Hoover.

In announcing the bill to a national TV and radio audience, President Johnson said: "Those who are equal before God shall now be equal in the polling booths, in the classrooms, in the factories and in the hotels, restaurants, movie theaters and other places that provide services to the public." In conclusion he said, "Let's lay aside irrelevant differences and make our nation whole...."

The Civil Rights Act of 1964 was challenged in the courts and the Supreme Court upheld it. The 1964 act addressed omissions and weaknesses in the previous acts. It stated that every American was entitled to the "full and equal enjoyment of goods, services, privileges, advantages and accommodations of any place of public accommodation ... without discrimination or segregation on the grounds of race, color, religion or national origin." The law forbade racial discrimination in transportation. It prohibited discrimination related to voter registration. It created an Equal Opportunity Commission to help ensure job opportunities for African Americans. It specified that literacy tests must be written and uniformly administered. The act prohibited discrimination in large businesses and in labor unions. It authorized a three-judge federal court to expedite voting rights cases.

The 1964 law was much more effective than the 1957 and 1960 civil rights laws. "Whites Only" signs were taken down and hundreds of public facilities were opened to blacks. There were two reasons for this change: 1) Failure to comply with the law could lead to fines and even imprisonment and 2) Strong leadership from two presidents—Kennedy and Johnson—had the effect of turning the white culture away from racism and toward racial tolerance.

Evaluations of the 1964 act tended to divide along cultural lines. Blacks compared it with their dream of a classless society; whites compared it with previous civil rights acts. Blacks noted the omissions. There was no unambiguous section proclaiming Negro voting rights. The bill ignored the problem of segregated housing and Negro poverty. Nor did it do anything to acknowledge or stop the excessive violence still being committed against blacks by the police and "justice" systems in the South from St. Augustine to Jackson, Mississippi.

In the white culture the act was generally praised and questions were raised: "What more does the Negro want? What will it take to make the demonstrations end?" This attitude by white Americans vexed Dr. King. His response was: "Why do white people seem to find it so difficult to understand the Negro is sick and tired of having reluctantly parceled out to him those rights and privileges which all others received upon birth or entry in America? I never cease to wonder at the amazing presumption of much of white society, assuming that they have the right to bargain with the Negro for his freedom. This continued arrogant ladeling out of pieces of rights of citizenship has begun to generate a fury in the Negro."

While the 1964 act was a great leap forward, it still failed to provide blacks with equal rights. Enforcement continued to depend on time-consuming and costly lawsuits which were not even a possibility for poor Negroes or those living in regions with no black lawyers.

Voting Rights Act of 1965

Events in Selma, Alabama, during 1965 constituted a final showdown between an irresistible force and an immoveable object. The blacks, struggling nonviolently for freedom after centuries of oppression, refused to stop marching, praying, demonstrating and singing. The apartheid Establishment, protecting its traditional way of life, would not be moved. The result was a violent confrontation that was shocking the nation. It was not only a legal fight, it was a struggle of wills, values and determination. At Selma, the contest was stalemated. A new, outside force was necessary to tip the balance one way or the other and resolve the issue. Just at that historical moment, a new and powerful outside force appeared, broke the deadlock and changed the basic ideology of America. That new force was the president of the United States, Lyndon B. Johnson. President Johnson watched the Selma spectacle on TV with the rest of the nation and then proceeded to use his considerable power and talents to replace rule by apartheid laws with civil rights based on the U.S. Constitution.

Friday afternoon, March 4, 1965, Dr. King flew to Washington and had a meeting with President Johnson. For 75 minutes they talked about a voting rights act. In the past, President Johnson had been doubtful about getting one through Congress. On this day he was optimistic and determined.

The following Saturday, President Johnson had a meeting with Governor George Wallace of Alabama. Wallace told the president that the real problem was King's demonstrators—not their complaints about the right to vote. President Johnson told Wallace that he was wrong. The protestors were being denied one of America's most fundamental rights, and Wallace and his state troopers should protect, not attack, peaceful demonstrators seeking to draw attention to their plight.

President Johnson advised Governor Wallace to do three things: declare his support for universal suffrage, assure the right of peaceful assembly in Alabama and hold biracial meetings with the state's citizens. President Johnson then escorted Governor Wallace to the Rose Garden to conduct his first press conference since Alabama's "Bloody Sunday." Johnson spoke to reporters while more than a thousand civil rights enthusiasts marched outside the White House fence. He said that the Selma marchers had "attempted to peacefully protest the denial of the most basic political right of all—the right to vote." But they "were attacked and some were brutally beaten." This revealed "a deep and very unjust flaw in American democracy…. Ninety-five years ago our Constitution was amended to require that no American be denied the right to vote because of race or color. Almost a century later, many Americans are kept from voting simply because they are Negroes."

On March 11, President Johnson spoke to the nation on TV. He said that he was submitting legislation to Congress that would clear the way for blacks to exercise their constitutional right to vote. He said, "At times, history and fate meet in a single place to stage a turning point in man's unending search for freedom. So it was in Lexington and Concord. So it was a century ago at Appamattox. So it was last week in Selma, Alabama."

A few months later, on August 6, 1965, the U.S. Congress passed the Civil Rights or Voting Rights Act and the president signed it into law. This law was a breakthrough in extending civil rights to blacks. It prohibited the use of literacy tests to screen voter applicants. It made the sole requirement for voting a proof of age and residency. It banned all the tricky and misused devices previously employed to keep blacks from voting—poll taxes, literacy tests and knowledge of government tests. It authorized federal examiners to process voter applications in communities where the black applicants had been turned down by local officials. It shifted enforcement responsibilities from the executive to the judiciary. It required "preclearance" by the Department of Justice or a special court for a change in voting procedures or for gerrymandering voting districts in order to exclude black voters from a municipal election.

This bill was immediately effective. Even before the bill was passed some southern congressmen switched from opposition to support when it became evident that the bill would pass. Within two months of passage, more than 56,000 blacks registered to vote in 20 counties in which federal examiners were working. In Mississippi, the number of registered voters increased from 22,000 to 150,000 within a few months. In Georgia, Julian Bond was elected to the Georgia House of Representatives in the first election after the bill was adopted.

The 1965 act was a success because the federal government proceeded to enforce it seriously. Its enforcement throughout the South was the first clear indication that the federal government was no longer an accessory to apartheid but an enforcer of democratic voting procedures.

The Fair Housing Act of 1968

Title VIII of Public Law 90–284 is known as the Fair Housing Act of 1968. President Lyndon B. Johnson signed it into law on April 11, 1968. This act created a national housing policy. It made discrimination in the sale, rental or financing of housing illegal. It empowered the U.S. attorney general to take action to enforce the law. Also in 1968, the Congress passed the Indian Civil Rights Act. This law extended some of the Constitution's Bill of Rights to Native Americans. It gave them the rights of free speech and the free exercise of religion.

Conclusion

The civil rights revolution was a compound sociopolitical, legal and ethical phenomenon. It involved the Supreme Court, three presidents, the Congress, the FBI, a dozen governors, the white Establishment and hundreds of thousands of African American activist in 11 states for 12 years. It resulted in several significant and permanent changes in our society. There are valid reasons why some historians say that it was one of the six most determining events in the history of our nation.

Its principal accomplishment was to uproot the legal basis of the U.S. system of apartheid and replace it with a cluster of civil rights laws and supreme court decisions based on democratic principles. The NAACP established the precondition for revolution with court challenges of apartheid laws from 1915 to 1955. The Supreme Court struck the fatal blow with its *Brown v. Board of Education* decision that outlawed school segregation. Thousands of African American demonstrators persuaded the public and then the president and the Congress that new laws were needed. Presidents Eisenhower and Kennedy wrestled with the problem and President Johnson guided civil rights bills through Congress and signed them into law. The Freedom Revolution eliminated apartheid laws in Virginia, North Carolina, South Carolina, Georgia, Florida, Alabama, Mississippi, Louisiana, Texas, Arkansas and Tennessee. School segregation laws were eliminated in six border states: Delaware, Kentucky, Maryland, Missouri, Oklahoma and West Virginia. De facto segregation was reduced in other states.

This replacement of apartheid laws with civil rights laws signaled a fundamental shift in the ideology that governed racial relations in our society. Before the revolution, the ideology of racism governed political decisions regarding race. After the revolution, the concept of equal treatment under the law became the operating ideology. This shift in political ideologies was similar to the shift from slavery to nonslavery during the Civil War.

According to historians, the Freedom Revolution had several spin-off effects in addition to terminating apartheid. The successes of the movement encouraged women throughout the country to reassert their demands for equal pay and equal opportunities. Some of the revolution's nonviolent tactics were borrowed by Native

Americans in their attempts to get the U.S. to honor its treaty obligations in regard to their land. Dr. King was the first person of national stature to propose that the non-violent principles of Golden Rule Christianity be applied to Vietnam. The Poor People's March on Washington, planned by Dr. King but implemented after his death, was followed by President Johnson's War on Poverty that reduced poverty in America by ten million people.

A unique product of the revolution was the elevation of its leader to the status of honored citizen. Dr. King is honored by a national holiday and street names throughout the land. The reasons for this homage are that Dr. King was the chief tactician, negotiator, spiritual leader and spokesman for a successful civil rights revolution and that he rediscovered nonviolence—taught it, demonstrated it and incorporated it into the theology of Golden Rule Christianity.

Bibliography

Abernathy, Ralph David. *And the Walls Came Tumbling Down*. New York: Harper & Row, 1989.

Appiah, Kwame Anthony, and Henry Lewis Gates, Jr., eds. *Africana: The Encyclopedia of the African and African-American Experience*. New York: Basic Civitas Books, 1999.

Ayers, Alex, ed. *The Wisdom of Martin Luther King, Jr.* New York: Meridian Books, 1993.

Blaustein, Albert P., and Robert L. Zangrando. *Civil Rights and the Black American*. New York: Washington Square Press, 1968.

Bailey, Thomas A., and David M. Kennedy. *The American Pageant*. Boston: D.C. Heath, 1983.

Bond, Julian. *A Time to Speak, a Time to Act— The Movement in Politics*. New York: Simon and Schuster, 1972.

Branch, Taylor. *Parting the Waters: America in the King Years, 1954–63*. New York: Simon and Schuster, 1988.

_____. *Pillar of Fire: America in the King Years, 1963–65*. New York: Simon and Schuster, 1998.

Bullard, Sara. *Free at Last: A History of the Civil Rights Movement and Those Who Died in the Struggle*. New York: Oxford University Press, 1993.

Carroll, Peter N., and David W. Noble. *The Free and the Unfree*. New York: Penguin Books, 1977.

Chafe, William H. *Civilities and Civil Rights*. New York: Oxford University Press, 1980.

Collier-Thomas, Bettye, and V.P. Franklin. *My Soul Is a Witness: A Chronology of the Civil Rights Era, 1954–1965*. New York: Henry Holt, 1999.

Cords, Nicholas, and Patrick Gerster. *Myth and the American Experience*. Volume II. Encino, CA: Glencoe Press, 1973.

Davies, Peter, ed. *Human Rights*. New York: Routledge, 1988.

Davis, Townsend. *Weary Feet, Rested Souls: A Guided History of the Civil Rights Movement*. New York: W.W. Norton, 1998.

Davis, Kenneth C. *Don't Know Much About History*. New York: Avon Books, 1990.

Douglass, Frederick. *Narrative of the Life of Frederick Douglass, Written by Himself*. New York: Signet Classic 1997.

DuBois, W.E.B. *Black Reconstruction in America, 1860–1880*. New York: The Free Press, 1935.
_____. *The Souls of Black Folk*. Mineola, NY: Dover Publications, 1994.
Due, Patricia S., and Tananarive Due. *Freedom in the Family*. New York: Ballantine Publishing Group, 2003.
Dyson, Michael Eric. *I May Not Get There with You— The True Martin Luther King, Jr.* New York: Simon and Schuster, 2000.
Earle, Jonathan. *The Routledge Atlas of African-American History*. New York: Routledge, 2000.
Edds, Margaret. *Free at Last— What Really Happened When Civil Rights Came to Southern Politics*. Bethesda, Md.: Adler & Adler, 1987.
Estell, Kenneth, ed. *The African-American Almanac*. Detroit: Gale Research, Inc., 1994.
Foner, Eric. *The Story of American Freedom*. New York: W.W. Norton & Co., 1998.
Franklin, John Hope. *From Slavery to Freedom*, 3rd edition. New York: Alfred A. Knopf, 1967.
Garrow, David J. *Bearing the Cross: Martin Luther King, Jr., and the Southern Christian Leadership Conference*. New York: William Morrow, 1986.
Goldman, Roger, with David Gallen. *Thurgood Marshall, Justice for All*. New York: Carroll & Graf Publishers, 1992.
Holt, Len. *The Summer That Didn't End: The Story of the Mississippi Civil Rights Project*. New York: Da Capo Press, 1992.
Hornsby, Allen, Jr. *Chronology of African-American History*. Detroit: Gale Research Inc., 1991.
Hunter-Gault, Charlayne. *In My Place*. New York: Vintage Books, 1993.
Israel, Fred L. *The Federal Bureau of Investigation*. Broomall, PA: Chelsea House Publishers, 1986.
Jackson, Jesse. *Legal Lynching: Racism, Injustice and the Death Penalty*. New York: Marlowe & Co., 1996.
Johnson, Charles, and Bob Adelman. *King: The Photography of Martin Luther King, Jr.* New York: Viking Studio, 2000.
Johnson, Michael P. *Reading the American Past— Selected Historical Documents*. Vol. I. Boston: Bedford/St. Martin's, 1998.
Jones, Maxine D., and Kevin M. McCarthy. *African-Americans in Florida*. Sarasota, FL: Pineapple Press, 1993.
Kasher, Steven. *The Civil Rights Movement— A Photographic History, 1954–68*. New York: Abbeville Press, 2000.
King, Martin Luther, Jr. *The Strength to Love*. New York: Harper & Row, 1963.
_____. *Stride Toward Freedom*. New York: Harper & Brothers, 1958.
_____. *The Trumpet of Conscience*. New York: Harper & Row, 1967.
_____. *Where Do We Go from Here: Chaos or Community?* New York: Harper & Row, 1967.
_____. *Why We Can't Wait*. New York: Signet Classics, 1963, 1964.
King, Mary. *Freedom Song: A Personal Story of the 1960s Civil Rights Movement*. New York: Quill, 1987.
Klarmen, Michael J. *From Jim Crow to Civil Rights*. New York: Oxford University Press, 2004.
Kochman, Thomas. *Black and White: Styles in Conflict*. Chicago: University of Chicago Press, 1981.
Lewis, John, with Michael D'Orso. *Walking with the Wind*. San Diego: Harcourt Brace, 1999.
Loewen, James W. *Lies My Teacher Told Me*. New York: The New Press, 1995.
Magel, Frank N. *Great Events from History*. Vol. II, Human Rights Series. Hackensack, NJ: Salem Press, 1992.
Marable, Manning, and Leith Mullings, eds. *Let Nobody Turn Us Around: An African-American Anthology*. Lanham, MD: Rowman & Littlefield, 2000.
McPherson, James M., ed. *Blacks in America: Bibliographical Essays*. Garden City, NY: Doubleday, 1971.
Meltzer, Milton. *The Black Americans: A History in Their Own Words, 1619–1983*. New York: Harper Collins, 1987.

_____. *The Truth About the Ku Klux Klan*. New York: Franklin Watts, 1982.

Morris, Aldon D. *The Origins of the Civil Rights Movement: Black Communities Organizing for Change*. New York: Free Press, 1984.

Newman, Richard, and Marcia Sawyer. *Everybody Say Freedom*. New York: Penguin Group, 1996.

Oats, Stephen B. *Let the Trumpet Sound: The Life of Martin Luther King Jr*. New York: Harper-Collins, 1982.

Packard, Jerrold M. *American Nightmare: The History of Jim Crow*. New York: St. Martin's Press, 2002.

Pagett, Gregory B. *C.K. Steele and the Tallahassee Bus Boycott*. Masters thesis, Florida State University, College of Arts and Science, 1977.

Parks, Rosa, with Jim Haskins. *Rosa Parks: My Story*. New York: Puffin Books, 1992.

Patterson, Charles. *The Civil Rights Movement*. New York: Facts on File, 1995.

Powledge, Fred. *Free at Last? The Civil Rights Movement and the People Who Made It*. New York: Harper Perennial, 1991.

Rennert, Richard. *Civil Rights Leaders*. Chelsea House, 1993.

Rowen, Carl. *Breaking Barriers: A Memoir*. New York: Little, Brown, 1991.

Sargent, Frederic O. *The Desegregation of College Station: An Incident in the Black Revolution*. Charlotte, VT: Vervana Publishers, 1999.

Schlesinger, Arthur M., Jr. *The Almanac of American History*. Greenwich, CT: Barnes & Noble, 1993.

Sitkofff, Harvard. *The Struggle for Black Equality, 1954–1980*. Toronto: McGraw-Hill Ryerson, 1981.

Ungar, Sanford J. *FBI*. New York: Little, Brown, 1976.

Truth, Sojourner. *Narrative of Sojourner Truth*. Mineola, NY: Dover Publications, 1997.

Wade, Wyn Craig. *The Fiery Cross: The Ku Klux Klan in America*. New York: Oxford University Press, 1987.

Weisbrot, Robert. *Freedom Bound: A History of America's Civil Rights Movement*. New York: W.W. Norton, 1991.

Wicker, Tom. *Racial Integration in America: Tragic Failure*. New York: William Morrow, 1996.

Williams, Juan. *Eyes on the Prize: America's Civil Rights Years, 1954–1965*. New York: Penguin Books, 1987.

Wilmore, Gayraud S. *Black Religion and Black Radicalism: An Interpretation of the Religious History of African Americans*. Maryknoll, NY: Orbis Books, 1998.

Woodward, C. Vann. *The Strange Career of Jim Crow*. New York: Oxford University Press, 1966.

Young, Andrew. *An Easy Burden*. New York: HarperCollins, 1996.

Zinn, Howard. *A People's History of the United States*. New York: New Press, 1997.

Encyclopedias and Special References

Altman, Susan. *The Encyclopedia of African American Heritage*. New York: Facts on File, 1997.

American Jurisprudence. 2nd edition, State and Federal. Vol. 15, Charities to Civil Rights.

Congressional Quarterly's Guide to the Supreme Court. Washington, DC: CQ Press, 1979.

D'Emilio, John. *The Civil Rights Struggle: Leaders in Profile*. New York: Facts on File, 1979.

Hampton, Henry, and Stevee Fayer. *Voices of Freedom: An Oral History of the Civil Rights Movement from the 1950s Through the 1980s*. New York: Bantam Books, 1990.

Higgenbotham, Evelyn Brooks, ed. *The Harvard Guide to African-American History*. Cambridge, MA: Harvard University Press, 2001.

Hine, Darlene Clark, ed. *Black Women in United States History: Trailblazers and Torchbearers, 1941–1965*. Brooklyn, NY: Carlson Publishing, 1990.